Exploring Philosophy

Exploring Philosophy

The Philosophical Quest

SECOND EDITION

Brenda Almond

University of Hull

BLACKWELL
Oxford UK & Cambridge USA

First published 1995

Blackwell Publishers, the publishing imprint of
Basil Blackwell Ltd
108 Cowley Road
Oxford OX4 1JF
UK

Basil Blackwell Inc.
238 Main Street
Cambridge, Massachusetts 02142
USA

British Library Cataloguing in Publication Data
A CIP catalogue record for this book is available from the British Library.

Library of Congress Cataloging-in-Publication Data

Almond, Brenda.
Exploring philosophy : the philosophical quest / Brenda Almond. —
2nd ed.
p. cm.
Rev. ed of: The philosophy quest, 1988.
Includes bibliographical references and index.
ISBN 0-631-19485-1 (alk. paper)
1. Philosophy—Introductions. I. Almond, Brenda. Philosophy
quest. II. Title.
BD21.A38 1995
100—dc20 94-29551
CIP

Typeset in 11/13 pt Bembo by Best-set Typesetter Ltd., Hong Kong
Printed in Great Britain by T. J. Press (Padstow) Ltd, Padstow, Cornwall
This book is printed on acid-free paper

Contents

Preface

Philosophy is too large a subject to be trapped and pinned down within the covers of a book like this. All that is possible is to give an impression of what it involves. I have chosen to do this by describing a kind of pilgrim's progress, or journey of exploration through some of the paths and by-ways of philosophy. In this way I hope the whole subject will be seen, even if briefly and inadequately, through one person's eyes. But who, you may ask, is this person?

You will find the pronoun 'I' scattered quite freely throughout these pages. So you may, if you wish, take it that the person who is this 'I' is the author. But if so, then you should not assume that this is simply another instance of the authorial 'I' used to hand down received lore to would-be initiates. Better, though, if you regard the 'I' in these pages as a third person – neither you nor I – a Seeker engaged in a quest, asking questions which do not have accepted answers. This Seeker will move on from step to step, sometimes reaching conclusions, sometimes remaining in doubt. If you, reader, would care to stand beside the Seeker in this exploration, then you need not be constrained by either the conclusions or the doubts that emerge. Feel free to disagree. For the first principle of philosophy is simply this: form your own judgment.

A note, though, on practicalities: you may, if you wish, read the text as continuous, chapter by chapter, and follow the sequence of reflections set out there. In this way you will have made contact, by the end of the book, with many contemporary debates in philosophy.

Many large topics, though, are touched on in passing. To indicate these, there is a system of notes and references in connection with each chapter. Refer to the notes for information about the general theme of each chapter and about reading in specific topics.

There is, in addition, a *Reading Guide* on the chapter theme. The *Reading Guide* is a key to the academic literature on the subjects covered. The books listed there are first steps only in each field and in most cases, they themselves contain further bibliographies and detailed references which you may pursue according to interest, taste and time.

1

A Starting Point

Immanuel Kant

1

A Starting Point

You will not learn from me philosophy, but how to philosophize, not thoughts to repeat, but how to think.

Immanuel Kant

There cannot be a thought without a thinker. So since philosophy, for most people, represents thought at its most abstract, it is worth reflecting that people – not excluding philosophers – begin by thinking about themselves and their personal concerns before they move on, if they do at all, to profound reflection or broad speculation in the sciences, arts or philosophy. So let us – I, the writer, you the reader – try to conform to this natural order, and follow the path from the personal to the philosophical, the specific to the abstract.

This means that we need as a starting-point a person who cares. A person concerned about herself (or himself) and about the world; a person seeking answers to questions that don't have straightforward practical answers. Without this, philosophy can have no intrinsic appeal, although it might have some market-value in a world where most academic accomplishments have a use and a price. We might begin by asking what sorts of questions seem worth asking in this way? Answering this question could be a path towards an understanding of philosophy.

But as a preliminary ground-clearing operation it would be useful to begin by setting aside one popular idea of what philosophy is. This use of the term can probably best be recognised by the presence of the definite or indefinite article. Or by the fact that it can also be used in the plural. So people talk of *a* philosophy or alternative philosophies, meaning by this systems of answers, whole frameworks of thinking which settle once and for all a person's response to the situations or problems that come along in life. In this sense there can be not only philosophies of living but also particular professional philosophies – a philosophy of medicine, for example, or a philosophy of education. By contrast, the sense in which philosophy is the subject of this book is the sense in which the word is used without prefix – neither *a* philosophy, nor *the* philosophy – and the sense in which it does not have a plural. This is philosophy pure and simple, and understood like this, it describes not a system of beliefs but a method, an attitude or an approach. It deals in questions rather than in answers, problems rather than solutions. All the same, it would be a mistake to assume that the process of asking questions philosophically, even if it *begins* in doubt, must inevitably end that way.

But taking philosophy as a method rather than as a system of beliefs, there can still be a difference in approach which centres on this question of open-endedness or commitment. Recent philosophy in the English-speaking world, for example, has tended to follow in an empiricist tradition: the tradition, that is, that bases substantial knowledge on what can – or at least might in principle – be observed by sight, touch, hearing and the other senses. One distinction in particular that has been emphasized is that between facts – the kind of things that *can* be observed by the senses – and values, which cannot be. As a result, a style of doing philosophy has emerged which aims to leave moral pronouncements to others, preserving its own neutrality; at the same time, as far as other areas of enquiry are concerned, scepticism, which is the admission of defeat in the quest for knowledge, has become something of an occupational hazard for philosophers, although not all are equally concerned to avoid it.

But philosophy as a method need not be centred on this distinction, and indeed the original model of philosophy as a method was provided many centuries ago (in Athens of the fifth century BC) by the people whose activities and discussions prompted the coining of the term 'philosophy' in its original meaning of love of wisdom. In this original setting, the activity amounted, in the most general terms, to a willingness to pursue an argument to its conclusion, challenging it at every stage and seeing it as always open to refutation. This stance in itself involves a double commitment: first, commitment to the truth (the point of rejecting arguments which can be shown to be false is to arrive at some which may be reckoned to be true); and secondly, commitment to certain moral virtues implicit in such a method: honesty, openness and impartiality – terms which inescapably lead to some notion of moral right, justice or moral good. But, of course, a double commitment of this nature may well mean that sometimes conclusions are drawn as well as questions asked.

The questions, though, are quite distinctive. Once you have said that they lack straightforward practical answers, you have eliminated many questions that might otherwise have been considered candidates. And yet as human thought has developed over the centuries into its present highly specialized areas, many questions of this eliminable sort *have* been classified as philosophical. The first philosophers in the Western philosophical tradition did not make distinctions of this kind. They were omnivorous consumers of all that could satisfy their cosmic curiosity. They were concerned with questions about the nature of reality, about the 'stuff' or fabric of the universe, about the difference between seeming and reality; they were intrigued by paradox and fascinated by mathematics. Some of these are still matters for philosophy, but as practical ways of answering questions have emerged, many of these areas of questioning have been split off as sciences or bodies of knowledge in their own right, leaving philosophy with only the residue of unanswered questions. (The term 'natural philosophy' is still used in the titles of some ancient university chairs as a name for physics, and such studies as psychology and sociology have only recently – that is, within the last century – emerged as areas where systematic methods of solving problems make them sciences rather than areas of speculation.)

So this preliminary negative definition considerably narrows the field. Scientific, factual and historical question lie outside the present-day scope of philosophy. But that still leaves other questions that strike many people as questions of first importance. The double commitment mentioned suggests a way of categorizing these residual questions. They are questions about value, and questions about truth. For while a scientific question like 'What is the melting-point of gold?' does have, even if it has to be qualified, a straightforward way of arriving at an answer, the question 'How do I know that the resulting – or any other – scientific claim is true?' is very much more problematic, and is rightly seen as belonging to the province of philosophy, rather than to that of the science in question. More exactly, indeed, it would be right to describe it as a question in the philosophy of science. And while quantum physicists may reach agreed conclusions as to how to create nuclear fission, questions about the *use* of nuclear power or nuclear weapons are questions about value and areas for moral judgement. In either case, there may be conceptual questions – like, for example, What does 'gold' mean? – which will need to be settled first. But even a right understanding of the language will only tell us how our ancestors, who framed our language, construed the world, so the contribution from the analysis of language must be limited both on the question of truth and even more on the question of value.

Nevertheless, the starting-point for any list of questions which, lacking agreed methods of solution, are potentially questions for philosophy, might well include some which relate to meaning and language. But many other questions beginning 'How do I know that . . . ?' will feature as well. Apart from the problem of justifying scientific knowledge, and apart from questions that seek a moral direction for action, there are enquiries which *look* at first sight as if they *might* be settled by observation, but on reflection it seems that they can't. For example: what do I know of the feelings or reactions of a friend or associate? I know how *I* feel when hear some old jazz classic well played. No doubt it would be a mistake to infer that my friends feel the same. But when they see a fine sunset? Are confronted by some stressful challenge? Are slighted or treated with contempt? Are mugged, tortured or abused? Other people's responses to questions about

their feelings may be matters for psychology, or social anthropology. But justifying claims to know about the feelings themselves – and whether they exist at all other than as names given
to noises emerging from a black box – remains essentially an issue
for philosophy.

But seeing other people as people is not *merely* an exercise in
philosophical reasoning. It is also a matter of intuitive feeling,
empathy and awareness. Take, for example, a passage in Paul
Scott's *The Jewel in the Crown*, which illustrates strikingly how,
without this empathetic awareness, or this human intuition,
whole classes of people – in this particular case a whole race –
may simply not have attributed to them the feelings which are
extended to others:

It was at this period, after the visit to the pharmacy, [where Kumar, an
Indian educated at a British public school, has been systematically
ignored by the assistant and also by the other (white) customers] that the
notion of having become invisible to white people first entered his head,
although it took some time for the notion to be formulated quite in this
way. When he had become used to crossing the river from the bazaar to
the railway warehouse and used to the way English people seemed to
look right through him if their eyes chanced to meet his own, the
concept of invisibility fell readily enough into its place, but still more
time was needed for that concept to produce its natural corollary in his
mind: that his father had succeeded in making him nothing, nothing in
the black town, nothing in the cantonment, nothing even in England
because in England he was now no more than a memory, a familiar but
possibly unreal signature at the end of meaningless letters . . .'[1]

So the fact that people can fail to attribute to other people
feelings similar to their own and that this is not the sort of
mistake that pulls you up short like failing to notice a glass door
which is in your way – a self-correcting mistake – is not merely
an occasion for logical puzzlement. On the contrary, it has significant consequences for practice – consequences with an essentially
moral aspect. Other examples bear out this point. Where torture
is institutionalized, torturers are expected, in the interests of

efficiency, to refer to and think of their victims as numbers rather than names, and may be instructed to avoid looking at the face, particularly the eyes. Similarly, it is significant that firing-squads and executioners are usually presented with a blindfolded or hooded victim. It is quite possible, then, not to recognize the person in another human body.

So if there is knowledge about other people as centres of consciousness, this is not going to be the kind of knowledge that emerges as a result of reasoning through a tight deductive argument; neither is it likely to be the product of a further gathering of facts about what people say or do. Just as a scientific description of an experiment on a laboratory animal may simply record paroxysms, muscular spasms, and similar indications of extreme pain, without any actual reference to pain, in exactly the same way, other human-beings *could be* and sometimes *are* regarded in this dispassionate way. It seems that if a name is to be given to the kind of knowledge that may be involved in the case of either humans or animals, it might have to be described as intuitive knowledge.

This is not to put a large question mark over the claim, or to single out other people's, or animals', feelings as particularly dubious. For I may be able to make out no better case than this for recognizing my *own* feelings and selfhood – and yet this is hardly something I could question. I must accept my notion of myself as a starting-point for thought. This is, though, not a *bare* notion of myself at this moment in time but a notion of myself as a continuing being. And this suggests another range of reflections which I cannot immediately see how to answer. How am I to account for my notion of myself *as a continuing being* – my self-awareness? How can I justify it? At first, the factor I single out is my memory, which links the child I remember being with the person I now am.

But then I reflect that there would still be a continuous person, even if I lost my memory or became senile or confused. So I conclude, perhaps, that my self is simply a continuing body – a physical object in the world – whose history can be tracked back in space and time to the infant that emerged from its mother's body on a particular day in a particular place. But it is difficult to regard myself *only* in this light. This, after all, is first and foremost what my 'self' is to others. *I* seem to have a different kind of experience of 'self'. So is this experience or knowledge to be called 'intuitive' too?

But already, in discussing this last problem, a number of other questions have begun to crowd in – questions which must also be classified as philosophical if the test for this is not having straight forward practical answers: what, for example, *is* a 'physical object'? In classifying my body, or that of another person or animal, as a physical object, I may be implicitly making all kinds of claims I couldn't substantiate by either observation (looking, listening, touching, etc.), nor yet by simple argument (pure reasoning without factual input).

What sort of claims might these be? Calling something a physical object seems to involve the claim first of all that there is something constant there – something that does not simply re-appear each time I attend to it. Secondly, I suppose that I call this thing an object in the outside world, not just a figment of my imagination, because I want to assert that it is something that strikes other people in much the same way as it does me. Then, thirdly, it seems to be implied of this something that it is the kind of thing that, while it may reveal itself at one moment to just *one* of my senses – I may simply be looking at it just now, for example – it *could* be felt, smelled or listened to as well, as appropriate. In other words, what looks like a simple assertion about a fairly ordinary thing – tree, house, table – is actually an extremely complex and controversial claim involving reference to a great variety of present and future situations.

What is more, when I look further into my own beliefs, I see that I am, perhaps unconsciously, setting the object against a background of space. I single it out from some vague backcloth on which I can register position and shape. But do I have a notion of space? As children sometimes amuse themselves with indefinitely expanding addresses, ending up with their town, their country, the world and the universe, perhaps I experiment with setting, mentally, an object against an extending background of this sort: a leaf design with vase as background; vase with wall as background; wall as part of house; house against tree-sky landscape; tree-sky landscape encompassed finally by the boundaries of my vision, but located in a particular part of the earth-globe, itself set in a universe, set into . . . ? Even if I can fill *that* gap by reference to astrophysics, it seems that I must eventually end up with a gap I really cannot fill, but, what is more, with no very clear idea of what kind of difficulty this is.

Then, in talking about my self I referred to memory, and thus to time. So, first of all, and in general terms, how can I justify reliance on my memory? How is it that memory gives, if it does, access to the past? Can I afford to deny that it does this, or would that denial involve the breakdown of every other claim I make to knowledge? Both a continuing self and a continuing object are notions that involve a reference to time, and both involve at least a small span of memory recall. But what is the notion of time in which we locate talk about the self or about objects?

It may be that these are all in the end to be described as special kinds of knowledge. Or as presuppositions for thinking about anything at all. But certainly if there are any distinctively philosophical questions, they are these. It is not, though, just the questions themselves, but also the way they are approached that marks out philosophy from, say, poetry, mystical reflection, science or mathematics. Philosophy begins, it seems, when these questions, which a child or an unreflective person might think had easy answers begin to be seen as puzzles. St Augustine (354–430 AD), for example, prefaced his philosophical reflections on time with the words 'What then is time? I know well enough what it is, provided that nobody asks me; but if I am asked what it is and try to explain, I am baffled.'[2] In other words, seeing that there is a question may be a more accurate indication of distinctively philosophical concern than having an answer.

It so happens, however, that there is someone who is willing to listen to my questions and point me in the direction of the sort of answers I am seeking.

Interlude: The Story of Sophia

Sophia was already an old woman when I met her, although I had heard something of her story years before. Born in a troubled part of Central Europe, her life had been marked by tragedy, but she had not allowed this to deprive her of her happiness. In one of Europe's darkest phases, she had lost most members of her extensive and remarkable family and she herself had been imprisoned along with her husband and young son. Only she and her child survived, but she counted this her joy and her happiness – seeing it as the light set in relief by the dark – and when circumstances permitted, she continued the study of philosophy which had been her earliest interest.

Although she did not forget her heritage in the other languages of Europe, her reading was primarily in the analytic tradition. This happened because, following those experiences of her youth, she did not return to her birth-place, but passed most of her life in an ancient castle in Southern Ireland bequeathed her by a friend of her father. This friend had been a collector of all the published output of philosophy in the English language in the present century as well as, of course, standard historical works. This library was passed on, too, to Sophia and was a source of great pleasure and inspiration to her.

Cut off by physical infirmity from the troubles and wars of the twentieth century in this remote but beautiful place, Sophia has been troubled and saddened by what she reads at second-hand of man's inhumanity to man. But her own situation makes it impossible for her to play any part in the political, cultural or social life of her times, and she has made no attempt to contact any of the figures and personalities whose work has provided the interest and focus of her life.

In these later years of her life, however, she has shown herself willing to communicate with the younger members of her surviving family. A direct question on the subjects that interest her will always receive a direct answer, although I have noticed that, with failing eyesight and limited time left to her, Sophia never allows herself any of the usual social interchange of ordinary correspondence. But she knows and approves of my quest, and from time to time I shall write to her and record her replies. Here is what she wrote in answer to my first and most general question.

First Letter from Sophia

Dear Q,

As you might suppose, what philosophers do provides the best clue to what philosophy is. And so I would suggest that you begin by looking at one or two examples of the way in which philosophers have approached questions concerning truth, knowledge and justification. This should reveal something of the commitment involved in deciding to approach questions philosophically, or from the philosophical point of view. The first example I have for you is that of Socrates (b. 469 BC) who was put on trial in Athens in 399 BC and subsequently put to death. At his trial, Socrates made a reasoned defence of his life as a philosopher and this extract is part of that speech (called the Apology*). Socrates has been described as philosophy's first martyr, and this speech may be regarded as the earliest known statement of the way in which the occupation of philosophy is to be pursued. Plato (428–348 BC), who was present at the trial, made a written account of this speech, as he did of other conversations of the historical Socrates, and, having once established the dialogue form as a way of writing about philosophy, went on to employ it more creatively, using it later as a vehicle for his own rather than Socrates' ideas.*

Socrates suggests that his judges might say to him 'Tell us about your occupation; tell us what it is that you do' and he proceeds to

*give them this account of the background to his philosophical
activities and of the form that they took:*

I have gained this reputation, gentlemen, from nothing more or less
than a kind of wisdom. What kind of wisdom do I mean? Human
wisdom, I suppose. It seems that I really am wise in this limited
sense . . . Now, gentlemen, please do not interrupt me if I seem to
make an extravagant claim, for what I am going to tell you is not my
own opinion. I am going to refer you to an unimpeachable authority.
I shall call as witness to my wisdom, such as it is, the god at Delphi.

You know Chaerephon, of course . . . Well, one day he actually
went to Delphi and asked this question of the god – as I said before,
gentlemen, please do not interrupt – he asked whether there was anyone wiser than myself. The priestess replied that there was no one . . .

When I heard about the oracle's answer, I said to myself, What
does the god mean? Why does he not use plain language? I am only
too conscious that I have no claim to wisdom, great or small. So what
can he mean by asserting that I am the wisest man in the world? He
cannot be telling a lie; that would not be right for him.

After puzzling about it for some time, I set myself at last with
considerable reluctance to check the truth of it in the following way.
I went to interview a man with a high reputation for wisdom,
because I felt that here if anywhere I should succeed in disproving
the oracle and pointing out to my divine authority, You said that
I was the wisest of men, but here is a man who is wiser than I am.

Well, I gave a thorough examination to this person – I need not
mention his name, but it was one of our politicians that I was
studying when I had this experience – and in conversation with him
I formed the impression that although in many people's opinion, and
especially in his own, he appeared to be wise, in fact he was not.
Then when I began to try to show him that he only thought he was
wise and was not really so, my efforts were resented both by him and
by many of the other people present. However, I reflected as I walked
away, Well, I am certainly wiser than this man. It is only too likely
that neither of us has any knowledge to boast of, but he thinks that
he knows something which he does not know, whereas I am quite
conscious of my ignorance. At any rate it seems that I am wiser than
he is to this small extent, that I do not think that I know what I do
not know.

After this I went on to interview a man with an even greater reputation for wisdom, and I formed the same impression again, and here too I incurred the resentment of the man himself and a number of others.

The effect of these investigations of mine, gentlemen, has been to arouse against me a great deal of hostility, and hostility of a particularly bitter and persistent kind. But the truth of the matter, gentlemen, is pretty certainly this, that real wisdom is the property of God, and this oracle is his way of telling us that human wisdom has little or no value. It seems to me that he is not referring literally to Socrates, but has merely taken my name as an example, as if he would say to us, The wisest of you men is he who has realized, like Socrates, that in respect of wisdom he is really worthless.

But Socrates' view of wisdom was not as negative as this might sound, and towards the end of his speech he went on to say:

If you put me to death, you will not easily find anyone to take my place. It is literally true, even if it sounds rather comical, that God has specially appointed me to this city, as though it were a large thoroughbred horse which because of its great size is inclined to be lazy and needs the stimulation of some stinging fly. It seems to me that God has attached me to this city to perform the office of such a fly, and all day long I never cease to settle here, there, and everywhere, rousing, persuading, reproving every one of you. You will not easily find another like me, gentlemen, and if you take my advice you will spare my life. I suspect, however, that before long you will awake from your drowsing, and in your annoyance you will take Anytus' advice and finish me off with a single slap, and then go on sleeping till the end of your days, unless God in his care for you sends someone to take my place.[3]

As things turned out, the Athenians did take Anytus' advice and did finish off Socrates with a single slap, and indeed attempted not many years later to do the same for Aristotle. This could be taken as an early warning that philosophy – in the sense of stripping oneself and others of the comfortable old clothes constituted by the tired presuppositions with which one normally confronts life – can be a dangerous occupation. The double commitment already mentioned reveals itself very clearly in Socrates' speech: to truth, on

*the one hand; to virtue – doing what is right, and avoiding evil –
on the other. The second commitment comes out even more strongly
in another part of the speech, when Socrates says:*

You are mistaken . . . if you think that a man who is worth anything
ought to spend his time weighing up the prospects of life and death.
He has only one thing to consider in performing any action – that is,
whether he is acting rightly or wrongly, like a good man or a bad
one.

*I am sending you this extract from Socrates' speech because it so
strikingly illustrates that second commitment of true philosophers,
but I should like you also to see a passage from the French
philosopher René Descartes (1596–1650) because it is a fine
example of the first. It demonstrates Descartes' commitment to the
stripping away of presuppositions in even the most secure areas of
thinking:*

Some years ago I was struck by the large number of falsehoods that
I had accepted as true in my childhood, and by the highly doubtful
nature of the whole edifice that I had subsequently based on them.
I realized that it was necessary, once in the course of my life,
to demolish everything completely and start again right from the
foundations if I wanted to establish anything at all in the sciences that
was stable and likely to last . . .

But to accomplish this, it will not be necessary for me to show
that all my opinions are false, which is something I could perhaps
never manage. Reason now leads me to think that I should hold
back my assent from opinions which are not completely certain and
indubitable just as carefully as I do from those which are patently
false. So, for the purpose of rejecting all my opinions, it will be
enough if I find in each of them at least some reason for doubt. And
to do this I will not need to run through them all individually, which
would be an endless task. Once the foundations of a building are
undermined, anything built on them collapses of its own accord; so I
will go straight for the basic principles on which my former beliefs
rested.

Whatever I have up till now accepted as most true I have acquired
either from the senses or through the senses. But from time to time

I have found that the senses deceive, and it is prudent never to trust completely those who have deceived us even once . . .

What is more, since I sometimes believe that others go astray in cases where they think they have the most perfect knowledge, may I not similarly go wrong every time I add two and three or count the sides of a square, or in some even simpler matter, if that is imaginable? . . .

I have no answer to these arguments, but am finally compelled to admit that there is not one of my former beliefs about which a doubt may not properly be raised; and this is not a flippant or ill-considered conclusion, but is based on powerful and well thought-out reasons. So in future I must withhold my assent from these former beliefs just as carefully as I would from obvious falsehoods, if I want to discover any certainty . . .

I will suppose therefore that . . . some malicious demon of the utmost power and cunning has employed all his energies in order to deceive me. I shall think that the sky, the air, the earth, colours, shapes, sounds and all external things are merely the delusions of dreams which he has devised to ensnare my judgement. I shall consider myself as not having hands or eyes, or flesh, or blood or senses, but as falsely believing that I have all these things. I shall stubbornly and firmly persist in this meditation; and, even if it is not in my power to know any truth, I shall at least do what is in my power, that is, resolutely guard against assenting to any falsehoods, so that the deceiver, however powerful and cunning he may be, will be unable to impose on me in the slightest degree.[4]

What these two extracts reveal, then is a technique which is the distinctive hallmark of philosophy: a willingness to strip the mind bare of preconceptions, of received opinion, and to follow a path forward that is not laid down by any external authority, which imposes its own constraints, and which is not to be deviated from because the going is uncomfortable, or the results look unattractive, or make the person pursuing them unpopular.

It is not surprising that this commitment to truth, when harnessed to the kind of honesty or moral firmness that will not consider compromise, runs people up against the barriers – which may be legal and political – of other people's prejudices. There is, for example, the power of consensus, the tyranny of fashion and the prestige which attaches to 'hard' scientific knowledge, as compared with moral or philosophical reflection. These may operate as constraints on thinking quite as powerful as those – largely religious – which applied in the past. Then, many writers of philosophical works were obliged to pay lip-service to a belief in God which did not quite square with the rest of their beliefs. Descartes himself, for example, had carefully to make it clear that his sceptical thinking was merely an experiment conducted to see how he would reason if he did not have the benefit of faith. Religion today may still present a harsh face of dogma and enforcement hostile to the truly open pursuit of enquiry – this despite the fact that honesty and commitment to truth are compatible with an enlarged understanding of religion in at least some of its forms.

At the same time, major political systems which are entirely secular in their foundations may provide a setting which is as hostile to a pursuit which involves being able to think freely as that of any religious state. One result of this is that philosophy, more than any other academic discipline, may even in contemporary societies provide a focus for dissent within a closed political system and may, indeed, provide a rallying-point for people from diverse political settings. This happened in Czechoslovakia, for example, under communism, when police attempted to suppress unofficial gatherings of intellectuals committed to the study of philosophy.[5] This situation was not unique and indeed, in Poland, a 'flying university' was known even in the days of the Tsars.[6] More recently, in South America, gatherings of people committed to the study of philosophy met under another kind of repressive regime in an attempt to found an unofficial philosophy institute. These examples transcend local and temporal settings and frameworks and display philosophy as a highly general enterprise of the human mind, which everywhere and at all times struggles to free itself from the shackles imposed by closed systems of thought.

The questions you have put to me, then, are the questions of a concerned person, reflecting on your own life, the state of the world, and the kind of questions which lack obvious answers. This is enough to suggest to me that you are in fact already bound by that double commitment that I mentioned – the commitment to virtue and the commitment to truth – which marks the philosophical temperament. But this is only a point of departure. Write to me again as the questions begin to take shape in your mind and I will do what I can to guide you on your philosophical journey.

Yours,
Sophia

NOTES

1 Paul Scott, *The Jewel in the Crown* (St. Albans: Granada, 1973, p. 254). A similar theme occurs in Ralph Ellison's novel *The Invisible Man* (1952): 'I am an invisible man . . . I am a man of substance, of flesh and bone, fibre and liquids – and I might even be said to possess a mind. I am invisible, understand, simply because people refuse to see me.' The general question of how we may be justified in reasoning by analogy from our own case to the conclusion that others, too, have thoughts, feelings and sensations like our own has been a major interest of recent philosophy. For a discussion of the nature of mind and of mental attributes, see Chapter 7.

2 St. Augustine, *Confessions*, Book XI, sec. xiv. The difficulty in explaining time starts from the fact that all our measurements of time depend on cyclical events, such as movements of the hands of a clock, the rotaion of the sun, the alternation of day and night, the sequence of seasons. For temporal reference we select an arbitrary fixed point – the birth of a leader, for example, or some other unique or memorable event. Consequently, it may seem that time is a matter of the relationship of events, only to be defined relatively, and that the notion of absolute time is meaningless. But if we accept this, we risk losing touch with some important anchor-points in our understanding of our own experience: the idea of the movement or flow of time, for example, and the assumption that time has a direction, closing off the past and leaving the future open. To these problems may be added the difficulties involved in assuming either that time is made up of measurable moments, no matter how short in duration, or on the other hand that any 'moment' of time is infinitely divisible.

3 Plato, *Apology*, selected passages.
4 Descartes, *First Meditation*, selected passages.
5 See, in relation to this, Alan Montefiore's review of H. G. Skilling's *Charter 77 and Human Rights in Czechoslovakia*, in *Journal of Applied Philosophy* 1, 1984.
6 For an account of this, see N. Davies, *God's Playground*, vol. II, pp. 234–5.

READING GUIDE

There are many introductions to philosophy. Although it was first published in 1912, the best one to read first might still be Bertrand Russell's *Problems of Philosophy*. There are also:

M. Hollis, *An Invitation to Philosophy*
A. O'Hear, *What Philosophy Is*
A. Appiah, *Necessary Questions*

Having made a beginning, it would be worth moving on to read some reflective philosophical books which cover a broad perspective, for example, T. Nagel, *Mortal Questions*. For a view of philosophy with an aesthetic, literary and ethical emphasis, the reader might enjoy Iris Murdoch's *Metaphysics as a Guide to Morals*. Finallly, as an admittedly challenging suggestion, Wittgenstein's *Philosophical Investigations*, would, on its own, provide a stimulating way into philosophy for the adventurous.

For the history of philosophy, see Bertrand Russell, *History of Western Philosophy* or, for a shorter and selective account, R. Scruton, *A Short History of Modern Philosophy*. There is also F. C. Copleston's long and comprehensive *A History of Philosophy*, or D. J. O'Connor's *A Critical History of Western Philosophy*. For more recent developments, see J. Passmore, *A Hundred Years of Philosophy*, and its sequel, *Recent Philosophers*.

For reference, *A Companion to Philosophy*, edited by N. Bunnin and E. James, is one of a series of books which provide accounts by many authors of the various areas of philosophy. And another useful brief reference work is *The Concise Encyclopedia of Western Philosophy and Philosophers*, edited by J. O. Urmson and J. Rée.

But the best place to begin would not, after all, be with any of these, but by reading the dialogues of Plato relating to the trial and death of Socrates, in particular the *Apology*, *Crito* and *Phaedo*, and then reading Descartes' *First Meditation*.

2

Looking Inwards

*All the interests of my reason, speculative as well as practical, combine in
the three following questions:*
1. *What can I know?*
2. *What ought I to do?*
3. *What may I hope?*

Immanuel Kant, *Critique of Pure Reason*

After I had heard from Sophia, it struck me that the matters that
were preoccupying me could be summed up in three questions
put by the German philosopher Immanuel Kant (1724–1804).
And while much of what she said concerned the first of these
questions, it seemed to me that the second and third questions he
posed would almost certainly come first for a reflective person
determined not to operate unthinkingly on the sole basis of
received opinions. Indeed they might well be supplemented by
another, which is equally personal. This fourth question is difficult to formulate, but it is the question which might be answered
by following the instruction carved over the entrance to the
oracle at Delphi – the one consulted by Socrates' friend – 'Know
yourself.' Whatever that brief and enigmatic instruction was meant
to convey, it would surely evoke a response in many people. For
most people do have a primary interest in their own person and
concerns. And if they want to understand what lies outside
themselves – Kant's first question – still more gain some kind of
mastery or control over it, then it is reasonable to suppose that
they may have to begin by understanding themselves and gaining
some kind of control over their own lives.

The attempt at control necessarily begins, though, with personal decision-making which is the outcome of reflection on the question: what shall I do? This is a question that everyone must ask, explicitly or implicitly, because action is unavoidable, where speculation about what exists is not. The question is not, of course, a request for a prediction, but rather a weighing of competing possibilities for action. And so it may equally well be expanded to: what is the *right* thing to do? But that is a question open to an even wider variety of interpretations. For example, suppose that someone has made a promise on the strength of which someone else has made various irreversible and life-affecting decisions. The feelings of the person who made the promise change. 'What is the right thing to do?' here may mean 'what is the *convenient* thing to do?' – i.e. from the point of view of the person who made the promise. But alternatively, it might be a way of considering the convenience of the person to whom the promise was made. Again, asking what is the right thing to do might be a way of considering whether there is a *mutual* point of view which would be the best for both parties. Finally, asking what is the right thing to do might mean none of these, but something which ignores the question of convenience altogether. Used in this way, it coincides with Kant's second question 'What ought I to do?' And it seems to me that it is when someone wonders whether there *is* a viewpoint outside convenience – what might be called a moral point of view – that distinctively philosophical reflection about personal life begins.

Self-interest

But moralizing is a rather unpopular pursuit, and for this reason, if no other, it might seem at first sight worth trying to avoid judging situations or making decisions on the basis of morality. Better, perhaps, or at least more rational, to take expediency in some form or other as the deciding factor. In particular, I might

ask, what is wrong with self-interest as a guide to action? Indeed,
do I really have the capacity to act on any other basis? I know
from my own experience what it is to present a sham front to the
world – to do the kind or the charitable act for wholly selfish
reasons. Perhaps it is a form of self-deception to think I ever do
anything from any other motive. And if this could be true of
myself, what, I wonder, lies behind the mask of charity or
kindness that other people present? Perhaps again this naked
self-interest. Everyone is what he is as a result of a unique
combination of heredity, upbringing and social influences. Is
there any room for anything else? Anything one could call a
moral motive?

It was an implicit assumption of both moral philosophy and
religion in the past that if people were to be expected to act
rightly, then they would need to be persuaded that it would at
least not cut across their best interest. So Plato and Aristotle (384–
322 BC) hoped to show that morality, or virtue, would be for a
person's long-term good. If you could get away with murder,
Plato asked in *The Republic*, why shouldn't you?[1] (He answered his
own question by arguing that on a deeper more considered view
of the situation you couldn't 'get away' with murder – evil-doing
is a disease that destroys your own personality and so your happiness). Subsequently, Christian theologians were anxious to offer at
least a happy after-life as some compensation for the sacrifices
moral rectitude might demand in this one.

To some extent this seems a reasonable idea. Personal happiness
does not require a great deal of argument to commend it. But
already, both the Platonic and the Christian viewpoint seemed to
assume a notion of happiness which differs from the obvious.
Happiness, on both of those accounts was consistent with being
poor, ill, badly treated by other people, perhaps even killed. So
the sense in which I agree that happiness is an obvious goal is
clearly not the sense in which those positions support me. Of
course, if pursuing my own personal interest coincides with doing
right in a moral sense, there is no problem.[2] But if I take these
two views as guides, I can only suppose that doing right may

make extraordinary demands on me in the ordinary run of life, even if some final and ultimate compensation is being held out in this life or the next.

So I will suppose for the moment that the sense in which I might consider taking self-interest as my guide and yardstick is the obvious sense in which day-to-day individual decisions may be made on that basis, rather than some reinterpreted long-term sense which may not even apply until after my death. And here I notice some problems with the arguments of those who favour it. To begin with, if someone argues that I *ought* to consult only my own interest in deciding what to do on any particular occasion, then this suggests a belief that I have the option of doing otherwise. So the person who thinks external causes account for everything I do, and that I am pre-programmed to follow rational (or even irrational!) self-interest, can't be the same person who thinks self-interest the appropriate guide to action. This second position presupposes a choice. Once I notice this, I can look at the two questions separately:

1. Is there only self-interest?

This question itself has a double aspect:

(i) Must *I* act only from self-interest? Do I really have choices, including that of not being selfish? It seems a sufficient answer to this to say that I am strongly aware that I *have* sometimes been motivated by awareness of another person's need, or distress, etc. I *have*, metaphorically as well as actually, given presents (although some people give only nicely-calculated 'exchange gifts'). So much for myself. But I can also ask:

(ii) Must I assume exclusive self-interest in others? In trying to answer this, I reflect that I can see a very clear difference between, for example, Albert Schweitzer (who devoted much of his life to medical work in Africa); the Marquis de Sade (whose recommendations and reflections may have inspired some peculiarly brutal child-murders in Britain in the sixties); and between either of these and a playboy whose ostentatiously self-indulgent life-style I read about in the Sunday supplements. I can also appreciate the altruism of, for example, a pilot who remains with his plane, even though he might save his own life by ejecting earlier, in order to steer his plane away from a school playground or populated area. If he was aware that the result of that decision would be his own death, then, belief in an after-life apart, that action must be regarded as altruistic. So if philosophers, economists and people who work in advertising agencies try to persuade me that selfishness is universal, then I feel justified in dismissing the arguments which lead them to their conclusion – if they have arguments, and are not merely making unsupported assertions – in the face of examples like these.

This means that I will not feel compelled to accept that the end result of reflecting on my own life and of asking questions about the right thing to do must be an answer in terms of self-interest. I can see it might be possible to reinterpret self-interest so drastically that it could demand a good deal of what would usually be described as self-sacrifice of me, but that is another matter. I can also see that there could be a way of interpreting 'self-interest' so that *whatever* I in the end decide is in a trivial (tautological) sense, my own choice – my own decision, and therefore my 'interest'. But it seems doubtful if much would be gained by distinguishing between real and apparent altruism, real and apparent selfishness, in this way. The 'apparent' sort seems to have all the hallmarks of the real, and its practical consequences are indistinguishable. So in the obvious sense that interests me, the question of whether I, or others, *must* follow self-interest can be answered in the negative. I do have a choice. There remains the second question:

2. *Should* I take self-interest as my guide?

Once I have established that there are alternatives, this suggestion loses much of its appeal. There are, after all, to put it no higher, other people whose happiness matters to me. I am also impressed by the arguments of those who point out how elusive a quality personal happiness is – that the more you pursue it directly, the less likely you are to find it. And so, if I *can* select goals in life, why confine myself to this narrow one, particularly since it is bedevilled by this built-in paradox?

But there are not only problems in relation to myself and my own course of action. If I choose self-interest as my guide, what am I to recommend other people to do? A world in which *everyone* pursues his or her own personal interest and well-being does not sound an attractive one for *me* to live in, but I can hardly try to maintain consistency by recommending other people to pursue *my* good.

It seems, then, that the question 'What is the right thing to do?' does not have to be answered in terms of narrow self-interest. Maybe expediency *is* involved, but if so, it must be a wider expediency than this.[3]

The Common Interest

Supposing, then, that I say: the right thing to do is to aim at the best possible outcome in any situation. I mean by this that I should look at the consequences of alternative courses of action and then make my decisions on the basis of trying to produce the happiest, most satisfactory outcome, not just for myself, but for all who may be affected by them. Although at first sight an attractive suggestion, working out the application of this principle is not as straightforward as I initially expect. An individual action or decision is like a stone that I cast into a pond with an indefinitely extending ripple-effect. How limited a view should I take of consequences? Should I restrict my attention to those that happen in the next few hours? Or the next few days? Or should I have a much longer-term perspective than that? And *whose* involvement should I count? My own, of course. But beyond that? Do I stop with the immediate circle of those directly involved or should I look beyond those relatively narrow limits to the wider community? I can see that the answer I get to the question: what is the right thing to do? might well be different in these different cases. For example: I offer to drive someone home. *That* must be right in terms of mutual satisfaction. But perhaps there is an accident and the other person is injured. Now in the same terms – the happiness of those directly involved – it was, on the contrary, the *wrong* thing to do. But then, suppose that as a result of his lifelong disablement the other person promotes a cause – perhaps better social provision for the disabled – which provides inestimable improvements in the lives of many others. Do I now say that my original action was right after all? This case illustrates the difficulty of deciding where and with whom consequences stop. But it also reveals another important point – that there is a difference between judging an action on the basis of its *actual* consequences and judging it on its *intended* consequences. If I – very reasonably – decide that only the second can be my concern, then I have in fact moved from the idea of morality as promoting some outcome, and switched to the idea of morality as an inner attitude – a matter of motive rather than achievement. And if this is so, I cannot but ask whether this – aiming for the happiest outcome – is in fact the best and only motive available to me. Shouldn't I also consider questions of justice and entitlement – particularly those entitlements I may have created myself by making promises? And shouldn't I also give special weight to the interests or expectations of people specially close to me – people I am in a distinctive and unique way responsible for, such as spouse, companion, child, parent, friend? May I manipulate other people or withhold from them what is their due?

Then, I know that in practice, the word 'necessity' has been used to justify atrocity rather than to limit it, despite people's best intentions. (For example, the convention that was intended to limit the use of the more horrendous weapons of war, the Hague Convention, by introducing the term 'unnecessary suffering' opened the way to an interpretation which fell in practice on the question of military necessity rather than military restraint.) This makes me suspicious of any general argument for ends justifying means. So, finally, I ask whether what I hope to achieve will justify *anything*, no matter at what cost for others? If I believe, for example, that by planting a bomb in a cafe, supermarket or school playground I can bring about a revolutionary change that will be for everyone's long-term good, is my belief and my motivation a sufficient justification for the suffering I cause to the few individuals randomly affected by my act? Does *their* view of it matter? Where does my responsibility begin and end?

A problem with a view which focuses on consequences in this way is that actions can be valued only for their *causal* properties. This means that many otherwise appalling deeds become thinkable if they feature as links in a favoured causal chain. I see *myself*, too, only as an instrument, and the notion of 'knowing myself' and being responsible only for the manageable here and now that I can see clearly, becomes lost in a wider, more indefinite perspective. The view that promotes the goal of the common interest, when formulated as a full-blown theory, is known to moral philosophy, political theory and economics as utilitarianism. As a movement for legal, political and social reform in the early nineteenth century, it had much to recommend it, but as a guide to a personal ethic it has serious limitations. Jeremy Bentham (1748–1832) and John Stuart Mill (1806–1873), both of whom offered classic expositions and defences of the theory, were clear that it was not, in a sense, a theory that could be argued *for*. 'That which is to prove everything else,' said Bentham, referring to the principle of utility, 'cannot itself be proved.'[4] And Mill wrote: 'Questions of ultimate ends are not amenable to direct proof. Whatever can be proved to be good, must be so by being shown to be a means to something admitted to be good without proof.'[5] The question is, then, whether as an answer to 'What shall I do?', promoting happiness, or doing what is best for everyone concerned, is the best possible guide to action and personal life-style. Two features of the view that it is, are (a) that it makes right depend on results, and (b) that it takes it that pleasure or happiness is the only value. Both these assumptions seem sufficiently questionable for me to consider whether there might not be an alternative viewpoint, one reached, perhaps, by reversing both these assumptions.[6]

The Interest of Morality

I return to the case of the person who has made a promise on which another person has relied. If promoting the happiest outcome for all concerned were the only thing involved there, it would be a puzzling question as to why a promise should have been made in the first place. The two people could have agreed on a policy of promoting the happiest outcome without talking about promises, or committing themselves in advance to a course of action which might in the end *not* be for the best for everyone when the time came. It seems, in this case, that the nature of the action is as important as — perhaps more important than — its likely consequences. The very fact that a promise is involved, that the actions involved can be described as the keeping of or the breaking of a promise, seem relevant considerations to set against effects and results, and the keeping of trust seems an item of value as well as the happiness of the parties. In literature and life duty has frequently been set against inclination, and while it would be convenient if it could be shown that following the first would in the long run promote the second, it may be necessary to consider the daring suggestion — first made by Kant — that, whether this is so or not, morality understood as the viewpoint of duty, provides its own point and purpose: that there is, in other words, such a thing as a moral interest.

How, though, should I interpret the 'moral interest'? It is some answer to this to say that when it comes to other people's dealings with me, I know what it is to object to some course of action by saying 'but you promised' or 'it would not be fair' or 'that's unjust'. The problem with deciding on the right thing to do always in terms of the consequences was that that policy seemed to leave these other kinds of consideration out of account altogether. What is more, it seems that no description of the facts, either the ones that exist at present or the ones I may bring about by my actions, could possibly *determine* what my response should be. It appears, then, that what the 'moral interest' encompasses, and what I am seeking, may be some *principles* for action. Where should I look for them?

Both religion and cultural tradition are possible sources, but if I were likely to be content with either of these, I would not be raising these questions. Both represent the acceptance of authority. My search is for something that has an intrinsic appeal to me – something that compels my rational acceptance. And since some such initial commitment is needed for a person to accept a religious or traditional viewpoint in the first place, this requirement is in any case probably not one I could do without altogether, even if I did in the end favour one of these authority-based solutions. Is there, I wonder, a viewpoint from philosophy that avoids these difficulties? It is a question on which I should like to hear from my correspondent and adviser.

Second Letter from Sophia

• *Dear Q,*
You ask me whether there can be an independent standpoint. Well, you began your reflections by referring to the philosophy of Kant. Kant's own answer to the question you have posed was one defined simply by rationality – a reason-based morality reached by setting aside all purely personal or ephemeral wants and desires and all immediate inclination. The test of the rightness of a course of action would then become its universality or scope. 'I ought never to act,' Kant wrote, 'except in such a way that I can also will that my maxim should become a universal law.'[7]

Kant held that this principle could be applied so as to demonstrate the wrongness of, for example, lying or breaking promises, by a simple process of reasoning. A thought-experiment in which these become universal laws of action actually breaks down, he suggested, because by applying the 'universal law' test, it becomes clear that both lying and promise-breaking are parasitic on telling the truth and on keeping one's word – without this as the norm they are empty or meaningless concepts. Can you imagine a universal practice of telling lies or breaking promises whenever convenient? Kant's insight was not that this would be undesirable, but that it cannot even be carried through in imagination.

So, looked at from this point of view, a programme for action based on principles may be more rationally defensible than one based on maximizing happiness, or doing the best for everyone concerned in the context of a particular situation. But does this mean, you may ask, that there is a moral standpoint from which statements like 'this would be wrong' become true or false? Does it mean that moral principles are in some sense waiting to be discovered and that moral obligations are to be viewed as externally binding on human beings? If this were so, then the answer to 'What is the right thing to do?' could be found by consulting a brief but teachable set of principles like the Sunna or the Ten Commandments of the Old Testament. It would mean that there is a set of principles to which everyone has access through something that might be described as conscience, or an inner light.

There is much to be said for this point of view and a person of principle is certainly to be respected. But the reverse side of the coin of this firmness and steely predictability must be an inflexibility, a lack of human responsiveness and sympathy which is not so unreservedly admirable. There are other problems, too, with principles. To begin with, principles do not always point in the same direction. For example, you may be torn between the duty to keep a promise and the obligation to spare someone's feelings. Why should one, rather than the other, principle be given priority? And then, secondly, it is very clear that not everyone is agreed on any particular set of principles. There is a whole range of issues of principle which divide person from person – abortion, mercy-killing, capital punishment, and so on. So perhaps you will say that, as far as the first of these objections is concerned, conscience is unclear in its deliverances. And as for the second, you may conclude that it is

*hard to appeal to conscience at all, since it is difficult to see why its
deliverances should vary so drastically from person to person. If you
would like to think about these points, I will write to you again to
suggest an approach that might provide a solution for at least some
of your difficulties.*

Yours,
Sophia

Sophia's letter changed my perspective on some of the matters
I had been considering, but still I remained convinced that the
ethical question as I had defined it could be answered in some
clear-cut way. What, I wondered, was this alternative approach
that she had mentioned?

Third Letter from Sophia

Dear Q,
*I should not like you to think that principles have no part at all to
play in moral thinking.*[8] *Nevertheless, it might be useful if you were
to go beyond the idea of narrow rules and give some further thought
to what you called the 'fourth question' that occurred to you when
you read those three questions of Kant. You said then that the
injunction 'Know yourself' might hold an answer, and indeed there
are some who think that we should today return to those important
questions of character and training that were so central to Greek
ethical thought.*

*In particular, the question, How ought I to live?, some would
say, can best be answered by asking another: What sort of person do
I want to be? This involves thinking about the issue of virtue or
integrity: What makes a good person? Two separate questions are
involved here: the nature of the specific virtues or traits of character,
and the nature of virtue itself as a core quality. The cardinal virtues
recognized by the Greeks were the moral virtues of courage, justice*

and self-control together with an intellectual virtue, wisdom. In the thirteenth century, St Thomas Aquinas (1225–1274) in his Summa Theologica *brought Aristotelian ethics into conjunction with Christianity, by emphasizing, too, the theological virtues of faith, hope and love.*

Aristotle's conception of virtue was based on the idea of one single aim of a fully human life – a concept of happiness (eudaimonia), which is summed up in the notion of 'flourishing'. Anyone who tends plants or animals can grasp this idea by thinking about the conception they naturally have of a fully healthy and developed plant or animal of whatever kind is in question – a prime example of its type. So by analogy with what it is for a tree to flourish – or even a horse or a dog – we can understand what it might be to try to formulate the notion of flourishing in human terms.

Modern virtue theory includes many other topics you will find it fruitful to reflect upon.[9] How far is one responsible for – able to shape – one's character? What is the moral relevance of concepts like forgiveness, loyalty, shame, guilt, remorse? What is the link between character and manners, or between character and friendship? Thinking about this rich web of questions may lead you to deeper and more general questions about the meaning of life, hinting, as they do, at an answer in terms of thinking about one's life as a whole – the story or narrative of an individual life.

Because the virtue of wisdom is included, too, it may help you avoid the thought that either philosophy or morality is a matter of cleverness – mere technical skill; on the contrary, it is better to think of it as a matter of knowing how to live well, *and this can, on an individual level, even include making good decisions on such life-affecting matters as marriage or career. These decisions involve not just knowledge but moral judgement – judging, that is, what are the things in life that really matter. These considerations do not, however, really* compete *with a morality of principles. For someone who possesses the virtue of honesty or truthfulness is one who habitually, or, as we say, on principle, is honest and truthful. And someone who acts on the principles of honesty and truthfulness is rightly seen as being an honest person. There is no need, then, to seek to replace talk about duty and obligation, right and wrong, with talk about virtues because in the end there is no real conflict. There is a conflict, however, between either of these approaches and that notion of morality which would seek to settle questions about what we ought to do by appeal to consequences. There are also wider questions about justice and rights which you will need to consider separately, because they raise many new issues, beyond that reflection on the self which has been the source of your questioning so far.*

Yours,
Sophia

Reflecting on Sophia's words, I wondered whether morality might not, after all, be less complicated than some of the theories she has mentioned to me suggest, even though, in their different ways, they throw light on some of the darker corners of moral life. For while the promotion of good may be controversial, and the pursuit of duty may generate dilemmas, these do not exhaust the ways in which the moral interest may be represented. Recognizing that some things are bad, for example, may be less problematic than recognizing others as good; agreement on rights may be less elusive than agreement on principles. And if the idea of a cold and empty abstract morality of rules or principles lacks appeal, and the notion of 'ought' is fraught with difficulties, it may be possible to get more purchase on the notion of evil and on the idea of moral worth or value as the other side of that particular coin.

This is at least in part because it is easier to be sure of recognizing pain and suffering in another human-being than of identifying happiness. And the link between, on the one hand, causing pain and suffering and, on the other, displaying evil or wickedness, is far more clear-cut than that between causing happiness and being good.[10] This means that I can begin to see an answer to my own question about what I should do, which, as it happens, meets the 'Kantian' requirement that I can readily ex-

tend it as a demand that I make of other people too. This is an
answer initially defined in negative rather than positive terms.
Since I can see that the most undisputed evils and the grossest
forms of wickedness – for example, genocide, judicial murder,
torture and exploitation – are a result of some people's abuse of
others, I am ready to accept that I should recognize boundaries
within which other people may operate unhindered by my interference or molestation. I should recognize others, that is, as
people, and define their boundaries in moral terms. What name
can I give to this notion? The most obvious way to describe it
would be as the recognition of rights. Perhaps, as far as I am
concerned, recognizing others' rights will still give me a morality
of duties, but these will take their origin in the other person,
rather than in my own pursuit of virtue. Of course, on their own,
rights and reciprocal duties will not be enough to provide a
complete answer to my question, for the language of rights is
limited and negative; but it may be an essential part of the answer
to that broader question.

Rights

Traditionally, moral philosophy dealt in perfect and imperfect
duties. The language of rights reproduces this to some extent. A
complete or 'perfect' obligation may be involved when what is in
question is repaying a debt; a commitment of a more voluntary or
'imperfect' nature when it comes to doing a stranger a good turn
or contributing to a charitable cause. The first someone has a *right*
to demand of me; the second may evoke gratitude and appreci-
ation. The first I can demand of everyone else similarly placed;
the second I may admire in others, but cannot demand of them.

The language of rights, then, seems to express very well the
limitations on choice applying to my actions in relation to other
people. Certain choices would be an invasion of the right of
others to enjoy the degree of self-choosing autonomy that I need
for myself, in order both to ask and to answer my initial question

'what shall I do?' In particular, of course, a morality that encompasses rights will rule out the most flagrant abuses of other
people's personality – deprivation of freedom, torture, cruelty
both mental and physical. But it may be a relevant consideration
too, on a more personal, domestic or intimate scale. The general
question that I ask is: can I set limits to the ways in which I may
act towards other human beings? And it seems to me that I may
do this by reflecting, in the case of any particular issue, on the
area in which I myself claim freedom to act.

But if I decide to make respecting the rights of others a prime
moral consideration – although at the same time, of course,
attaching value to certain personal characteristics and perhaps,
too, to certain states of affairs (very often those where happiness
is a main component) – am I not laying myself open to a variety
of charges? Perhaps it will be said that the notion of rights is
baseless, that they come from nowhere, and have no justification.
Perhaps it will be said that they have validity but only in the
context of my own social setting, or even for me alone and not
for anyone else. Perhaps it will be said that, while specific and
defined goals can be evaluated in a hard-headed objective way, the
same cannot be said for assessing the value of types or classes of
action, or when considering rights as moral demands attaching to
human beings as human beings.

In the end perhaps I will have to think about the idea of rights
in a wider social and political context. For my purpose here, I can
justify my use of this notion by observing that these objections
are based on a presumption that some moral notions are better
founded than others. But why should rights be singled out for
scepticism in this way? Duty and obligation, for example, are
abstract moral notions, too, but do not seem to generate such
doubts. It was a 'hard-headed' philosopher of modern times, John
Mackie (1917–1981), who wrote: 'Moral entities – values or
standards or whatever they may be – belong within human
thinking and practice: they are either explicitly or implicitly
posited, adopted or laid down. And the positing of rights is no
more obscure or questionable than the positing of goals or obli-

gations.'[11] So rights – and values, too – do not have to *come from somewhere* to become valid; their validity is, at least in part, a function of their being recognized as such.

In the end, I will have to return to the question of moral knowledge when I have secured a picture of the problem of knowledge on a wider and more general scale. But on the issue of rights as a base for practical engagement and social interaction, I can make a beginning, if I wish to do so, by initiating their recognition in my own treatment of people, and my own appraisal of the way things are.

So what would be meant by saying that this would limit the validity of my judgements to me, or perhaps to my social class or group? I can only understand this suggestion as a personal declaration of my critic that he, or she, does not intend to join me in recognizing rights in this way. I need not accept the charge that my moral position is relative or essentially personal, since a charge like that could only be made from an external standpoint which is not available to human observers. We all (human-beings, that is) stand on an equal footing here. Of course, I am, I cannot but admit, the product of my own culture and tradition. But I have a mind, and a critical faculty, which I can apply as well as can my critics, to the moral standards I see around me – and in the end, the position I choose to take is just that – a choice of position. And it is therefore without apology or qualification that I may decide to take as central just that right identified by Mackie as 'the right of persons progressively to choose how they shall live'.[12]

Applications: Personal and Domestic

This conclusion comes close to another way in which Kant formulated his moral theory: it means treating persons as persons, as ends in themselves. Another way in which Kant put this point was that other people should be treated as equal lawmakers in a realm of ends. The first context in which I am likely to try out this or any other kind of principle of morality is the close family context – the familiar framework of intimate personal decisions.

Turning to this area, it is striking that many of the most difficult of these personal decisions – particularly those concerned with the beginning and end of life – are in fact posed in terms of rights. For example, decisions about whether, how and when to have children, and even what sort of children to have, are increasingly being brought by medical and technical advances from the realm of the haphazard and ungovernable into the realm of choice; in these circumstances, the right of a woman to choose how she will use her body, the right of an unborn child to sustenance and safe delivery, the right of a father to his progeny, and the right of any particular child to a certain quality of life, are all factors which compete for priority in judgements about what to do in complex personal situations.

But rights feature, too, in the wider setting of personal relationships, with marriage as perhaps the paradigm case of promising. Of course, in the context of marriage, appeal to rights may be an indication that the relationship is already crumbling. The *values* of loyalty, support and good faith are of more long-term interest here. But rights do feature, none the less, and children, for example, could be regarded as satellites of a marriage having their own rights to stability and security. Here the question is whether there is any way – if this is desirable – to combine flexibility and breadth of relationships with stability, and with regard for these other obligations. Is this an area where there is a choice, or is later choice excluded by an initial but binding decision? Clearly, whatever conclusions I come to, they must be made in a social context in which both differing ways of expressing sexuality, and sexual relationships outside marriage, are more widely accepted than in previous periods, and are reflected in a legal system which provides for easier divorce based on the fault of neither partner, as well as the removal of the ancient stigma of illegitimacy. This provides a setting in which old answers cannot be taken for granted, but where new answers must be supplied by me in the very process of living my life.

Not just my *own* answers, though. One way or another, both male and female are compelled first and as a priority to settle their attitudes to these questions of personal and domestic relations and agree on the nature of their mutual commitment. Nevertheless, many of these questions may not impinge as decisions, but remain as undefined ambivalences of attitude, shelved for future resolution. One problem, however, has special significance just because it cannot be shelved in this way. This is why, for those who face it, a situation in which abortion is being considered is one of the largest and most significant moral crises faced in life.[13] The legal *permissibility* of abortion is also a divisive and internationally significant political issue.

For the individual confronting the issue, it presents itself as a pressing dilemma because there is no third way. This follows from the fact that biologically, of course, non-action *is* action and results in general in the birth of a living child – perhaps the most significant positive and creative production of anybody's life. And not merely a feminine act of creativity; for pregnancy and childbirth are also the only way that a man, vicariously, can produce a child.

Here, then, is a moral decision which shows up the inadequacy of both a strictly utilitarian approach and also of an approach based on a cold and undeviating application of principles. Recognition of the fact that here the rights of a potential child may be in conflict with the rights of an actual woman does not, of course, provide an answer either – rather a further reason for hesitation. And whatever hard-headed reasons apply, there cannot be a guarantee that the decision taken will not be regretted. If a decision to abort later comes to be seen as wrong, then it is a more appalling wrong decision than any other that a woman – or indeed a man – may take. For the termination is the termination of the existence of one's own child, that which is biologically closest and most important to a person.

A wrong abortion decision, then, is not a trivial wrong decision. But, of course, circumstances may weigh; other values may be involved: the youth of the mother; conception following from criminal assault, incest or rape; health factors of both mother and child – all these are standardly recognized as special factors, and there is no reason to suppose that where the law stops is the place also where all moral latitude would cease. Degree of development of the foetus, too, is a not unreasonable factor to take into account, and different moral attitudes may well be appropriate at different stages on the 'slippery slope' of this particular argument.[14]

Here, then, in these deep waters of personal life, and similarly in other areas where death, disability and illness may intrude, philosophical reflection and more considered decision-making may have a place as an alternative to unthinking and uncritical action and reaction.

It may take the form of asking for example, whether, in my relations with other people, the pursuit of personal gratification, pure hedonism, can provide a policy for behaviour. For the reasons already given, it is clear it will not. Using other people merely as a means to personal gratification is not a moral or a philosophical possibility. But what a policy of promoting happiness on a wider scale would entail in relation, for example, to the institution of marriage and family-life, is so problematic that that, too, is hardly available as a solution to these pressing dilemmas of personal life.

The rigidity of a principle-based morality has already been noticed, and in relation to the particular institution of marriage, there is a special difficulty. Promises concerning personal relationships seem to involve a commitment to what is strictly outside the promisor's control. After all, there are certain kinds of feeling which make a marriage relationship impossible, at least in respect of the sexual and emotional satisfaction which make of marriage more than an empty shell.

On a personal level, then, there may be conflict between the ideals of exclusivity and variety; of loyalty to one person, and of richness of personal relationships; there may be tension, too, between the ideals of permanence or long-term affection and the facts of change and the seemingly inevitable transitoriness of love. Some limited answer is possible though, through the recognition of others as persons and the desire to respect their rights in the form of duties or obligations voluntarily accepted, with whatever

sacrifice that may entail. This partial answer may be comp-
lemented by the fact that I can also attach value to modes of
behaviour of my own that involve qualities such as kindness and
sensitive understanding. And finally, in my struggle for a coherent
moral perspective, I find an indisputable further value in states of
affairs free of misery and avoidable suffering for others.[15]

Applications: Ethics and the Workplace

But moral decision-making is not confined to the domestic
sphere. It may play an important role in the workplace where a
decision, for example, as to whether or not to join a union,
whether or not to participate in a strike, may impinge as moral
rather than merely practical questions. Or perhaps a problem of a
different sort arises, as I come into possession of information
about the practices of my employer, which poses a conflict of
loyalty for me between what I owe to my employer and what I
owe to the wider community.

What kind of moral questions are these? Once again, to describe the conflicts in terms of rights may clarify for me what is
involved. The power of the unions and the power of multinational
corporations affect the lives of individuals in ways that may create
personal moral dilemmas for the nonconformist. If I have a right
to join a union, do I also have a right *not* to join a union? Where
compulsory union membership obtains, then others – maybe not
I myself – may be prevented by their beliefs, perhaps only their
beliefs in freedom of association, from gaining their livelihood by
the skills in which they have been trained. On the face of it, there
exists a right to be protected. But freedoms can sometimes be
outweighed by other moral or political considerations. And other
workers may advance an argument from injustice. Why should
one person be allowed to profit from the work and sacrifice of
others? Why accept a share in the benefits achieved by union
bargaining whilst not contributing to the struggle? Although a
straightforward appeal to fairness, this is an argument with utili-

tarian overtones. It presupposes that the people working in an industry or business are better off because of unions. But a wider utilitarian argument is possible and may also be used. This is the argument that national prosperity depends on industrial efficiency; that strong unions are needed for industrial efficiency and that compulsory union membership is necessary for strong unions.

At least some of these factual claims may be true. But of course, the argument does not only turn on utility. People may have religious objections to union membership; they may also have moral objections in the sense that they believe people should not be forced by others to join an association against their will; and they may have political objections in the sense of wishing to retain a personal right to complain, for instance, about conditions of work; or to take a decision to strike or not to strike. In the latter case, a moral objection to striking may be involved, perhaps because the job in question is in medical services or in vital services where strikes cause suffering or danger to uninvolved other people; and it may be this that accounts for the reluctance to transfer that ultimate right to the strike decision, through union membership, to a representative. And finally, a union may itself adopt policies, or support political causes or parties, with which the individual member disagrees. So since these grounds of objection variously suggest circumstances in which a person may lose his or her job for religious, moral or political reasons, I may, as an individual considering these facts, be confronted with the need to take a moral stance immediately in relation to my own employment. The personal nature of these decisions is dramatically illustrated in the case of some strikes where bitter personal feelings are aroused. Sometimes such issues split families and friendships. A decision to cross or stand upon a picket-line is, or may be, an agonizing personal dilemma, a personal moral crossroad where the direction-signs are missing or obscured.[16] But, of course, dilemmas are no less acute on the other side – as a manager I might have to balance my company's efficiency against the personal needs of employees, perhaps being asked to

make difficult decisions as to whether and how to impose redundancy on fellow-workers.

These are matters, essentially, of the rights of individuals within
an organization. But a workplace dilemma can arise, too, where
the rights of people *outside* the organization or industry are
concerned. Perhaps I find out that safety procedures are being
deliberately flouted, that environmental hazards are being con-
cealed, or that potentially lethal corners are being cut in the
manufacture of a commodity. There are many possible examples:
the leakage of nuclear contamination; an escape of lethal dioxin;
a car-design in which a safety device is deliberately omitted as a
result of a cost-benefit calculation where payment of compensation in the few unfortunate cases is deemed cheaper and therefore preferable to standard provision of the device. As a scientist or
engineer working in the fields, I would be specially well-qualified
to recognize the lapse, if there is one, and might therefore
consider it my special responsibility to open up the issue.

Or, in public service, perhaps secrecy rules are applied to cover
the profiteering or inefficiency of politicians or public figures. If
I were such a politician, I might wonder whether my role carries
with it different responsibilities from those applying to individuals. Whatever the specific situation, if I am the only person in a
position to blow the whistle, to alert the unsuspecting public, I
am likely to find myself in a situation of personal moral conflict
– first of all one of loyalties – to the company or organization, to
colleagues, to the wider public. If the decision is made in favour
of the public, then the problem becomes no less a moral problem,
but one of a more familiar sort – a problem of weighing the
personal consequences, which may include a threat to career and
livelihood, and deciding whether or not to face them; a problem
of weakness or strength of will. But these calculations and considerations go beyond the personal. Whatever my decision,
whether in the work-place or the domestic setting, it is made in
a social and political context. A framework of law provides the
backdrop against which my moral perplexities are played out.[17]

So if I challenge the policy of a company or a branch of
government – if I set my individual morality against a prevailing

practice or received opinion – I can only do it because I have some wider judgement of the way things ought to be. My personal concern, in other words, becomes a wider, public concern. Morality merges into politics. My concern about myself becomes a concern about the rest of the world. And I can no longer, therefore, consider my own situation, my own answer to 'What shall I do?', outside this wider context.

NOTES

1   The reference is to the discussion in Book II of Plato's *Republic*, 359d–362d, which begins with the story of a shepherd, Gyges, who acquires a ring that can make him invisible. This gives him the option of doing wrong with impunity and thus raises the question: are the only sanctions against crime the ones society is able to impose, or can morality be justified *for the individual*?

2   Joseph Butler (1692–1752), who was Bishop of Bristol and later became Bishop of Durham, argued in his *Fifteen Sermons* (in particular Sermon 11) that, whatever might be the case with hot, or impetuous, self-love, 'cool' self-love and virtue coincide.

3   For a classic discussion of psychological hedonism, see G. Ryle, *Dilemmas*, chapter 4. Ryle exposes the fallacy of basing a theory of universal selfishness on the belief that if I want to have or to do something, then what I want is the *pleasure* of having or doing it. As Bishop Butler also pointed out, it is only by wanting things, bad or good, *for their own sake*, that I *can* derive pleasure from them.

   Nevertheless, in the past philosophers – notable Plato and Aristotle – did assume that if a course of action was to be recommended, it was necessary to show that it would be for a person's own good, or at least not in conflict with it. The starker theory of psychological hedonism, particularly as put forward by the British philosopher Thomas Hobbes (1588–1679) gives a narrower materialistic slant to such an assumption, linking it to a theory of basic and simple psychological drives that leaves no room for altruistic action or action stemming from a purely moral motive. Psychological hedonism subsequently became one of the pillars of Bentham's form of utilitarianism, expressed in the claim that human beings are motivated solely by the desire to avoid pain and seek pleasure. Its other pillar, not easily reconciled with this, is that they ought to pursue the greatest happiness of the greatest number of people. While Mill and Bentham concurred in this opinion, they held differing views as to the nature of happiness. Unlike Bentham, who took a quantitative view of pleasure, Mill believed that pleasures could be graded as 'higher' or 'lower', that human happiness and fulfilment is distinctively associated with the former, and that our obligation is to maximize the intellectual, cultural and spiritual pleasures rather than purely material ones.

4   J. Bentham, *Principles of Morals and Legislation*, ch. 1, sec. 11.

5   J. S. Mill, *Utilitarianism*, p. 4.

6   A useful modern discussion of the pros and cons of utilitarianism, is J. J. C. Smart and B. Williams, *Utilitarianism: for and against*. For a non-utilitarian account of ethics, see R. Gaita, *Good and Evil: an absolute conception*.

7   I. Kant, *Groundwork of the Metaphysic of Morals*, 402, in H. J. Paton, *The Moral Law*, p. 70. This was one of several formulations Kant offered of his famous 'categorical imperative'. Another formulation contained the injunction not to treat people solely as means but always to treat them as well as ends in themselves.

8   For a discussion of the need to have principles, but also to qualify them in particular circumstances, together with the problems this raises for moral education, see R. M. Hare, 'Principles', *Proceedings of the Aristotelian Society*, vol. 73 (1972–3), or see his more developed views in *Moral Thinking*.

9   Virtue theory takes ethics as being concerned with character. For the virtue theorist the key question is: what makes a good person? The cardinal virtues for the Greeks were wisdom, courage, justice and self-control. Later, the Christian virtues of faith, hope and charity were seen as part of a more complete account of virtue. A key article in the modern development of virtue theory is Elizabeth Anscombe's 'Modern Moral Philosophy' (1958) and Alasdair MacIntyre has pursued the argument in *After Virtue*, advocating a return to the Aristotelian tradition as being better able than liberal individualism to answer the common human desire for coherence and meaning in life. Philippa Foot's *Virtues and Vices* raises a range of more detailed questions both about particular virtues and about virtue in general.

10 Mary Midgley has discussed this in *Wickedness*. She argues there that

it is only by recognizing the human capacity for wickedness (as opposed to explaining it away under such labels as social conditioning or mental illness) that there will be any hope of developing a realistic and effective morality.

11   J. Mackie, 'Can there be a right-based moral theory?' in J. Waldron (ed.), *Theories of Rights*, p. 171.

12   Ibid., p. 175.

13   For a discussion of the centrality of the dilemma of choice in women's lives resulting from the possibility of effective birth-control and the availability of legal abortion, see Carol Gilligan's article, 'In a Different Voice: women's conceptions of self and morality'. She writes in relation to these situations: '[T]he relationships that have traditionally defined women's identities and framed their moral judgements no longer flow inevitably from their reproductive capacity but become matters of decision over which they have control' (p. 490). These findings and a full account of her position are presented in her book *In a Different Voice: psychology and women's development*.

14   There is a considerable philosophical literature on the subject of abortion. One particularly comprehensive study is that of R. Hursthouse, *Beginning Lives*. For discussion of both abortion and euthanasia from a legal as well as moral perspective, see R. Dworkin, *Law's Dominion*.

15   For fuller discussion of moral aspects of marriage and sexual relationships, see B. Almond and D. Hill (eds), *Applied Philosophy: morals and metaphysics in contemporary debate*, Section II. Involved are such questions as: how far should the state, for social and economic reasons, impose through law the institutional structure of family relationships based on marriage as an exclusive sexual relation? For further discussion of the nature of love and human relationships see R. Scruton, *Sexual Desire* and P. Gilbert, *Human Relationships*. See also M. Fisher, *Personal Love* and B. Almond, *Moral Concerns*, ch. 2.

16   R. M. Hare has written on the issue of compulsory union membership in 'A Kantian Utilitarian Approach', one of a collection of articles on these themes in *Moral Rights in the Workplace*, edited by Gertrude Ezorsky. Problematic issues in the area of employment and business practice are also discussed in T. Beauchamp and N. Bowie (eds), *Ethical Theory and Business* and in Joan Callahan (ed.), *Ethical Issues in Professional Life*.

17   On these issues, see Sissela Bok, *Lying* and also her later book
      Secrets. In the latter book, Bok examines the way in which inter-
      national tensions, both military and commercial, have combined
      with technological advances to generate moves towards secrecy that
      threaten open societies. In both books she argues for truth-telling
      and open information in the main areas of public and private life.

READING GUIDE

The subject of this chapter has been moral philosophy. There are many
good introductions to this subject, including:
   R. Gaita, *Good and Evil: an absolute conception*
   G. Graham, *Living the Good Life*
   J. Rachels, *The Elements of Moral Philosophy*, 2nd edn.
   W. Frankena, *Ethics*
   See also R. Norman, *The Moral Philosophers*, or A. MacIntyre, *A Short
      History of Ethics*
The pros and cons of utilitarianism as a moral theory are well
presented in: J. J. C. Smart and B. Williams, *Utilitarianism: for and against*.
   Important modern works of broader scope include:
   R. M. Hare, *Freedom and Reason*; and *Moral Thinking*
   J. Rawls, *A Theory of Justice*
   A. MacIntyre, *After Virtue*; and *Whose Justice? Which Rationality?*
   B. Williams, *Ethics and the Limits of Philosophy*
A primary resource is P. Singer (ed.), *A Companion to Ethics* which
contains a comprehensive range of articles by specialists on all aspects of
ethical theory.

CLASSICAL SOURCES

Plato: *Dialogues*, particularly *Republic*, *Meno*, *Protagoras* and *Gorgias*
Aristotle: *Nicomachean Ethics*
Epictetus: *Moral Discourses*
Kant: *Groundwork of the Metaphysic of Morals*
Hume: *Enquiry Concerning the Principles of Morals*
J. S. Mill: *Utilitarianism*

3

Looking Outwards

. . . although politics itself is a difficult art, no art is required to combine it with morality. For as soon as they come into conflict, morality can cut through the knot which politics cannot untie.
Kant, *Perpetual Peace* 380

Making my own decisions, reflecting on my own life, are not, then, things I can do in a vacuum. Instead, I am constantly brought up against the boundaries of legal restraints, social pressures and political and economic structures. I may not choose conformity, but even the nature of my nonconformity is set by this social context. In addition, there seem to be things I want that I cannot achieve for myself, not least the benefit that law brings by making other people's actions predictable and acceptable to me.

As I have seen, when I reflect even on those personal and intimate decisions which seem most in my hands – the domestic, the sexual, the parental – I am bound to approach these decisions with prior answers to another range of questions: for example, am I to regard myself and others as atoms, units, isolated individuals colliding with each other and then passing on to other collisions? Or do I accept that human-beings can fuse, pair, join together in groups and associations which themselves constitute new entities or collectivities?

In the case of the simplest of associations – that between a man and a woman – must I see this as providing the natural locus for child-raising – a process which can occupy the most active and productive years of adult life? If I am inclined to a positive answer here, then since what I have described is the basic social and economic institution of the family, my answer must have implications for my views on love and loyalty, hedonistic and short-term indulgence, sacrifice and self-denial. It will also require me to answer questions about the role of women and of men in society; about equality in employment; about social and financial provision for children, and about education. But more than this, I have to accept that my individual judgement may not always coincide with law and social expectation.

As for my work-place decisions, these even more conspicuously involved my reaction to, rather than action within, a political and legal framework. The great classical theorists of morality, Plato and Aristotle, were clear that individual morality opens up into a theory of citizenship. It is not surprising, then, that my own moral reflections, my preoccupation with the question of my strategy for living and my conception of morality, should require me also to ask: what is the right thing for my community to do? And since the organized community can support *its* answer to this question with sanctions of punishment and enforcement, law becomes the first focus of my expanding concern. I may ask: what is the relationship between law and morality? Does law reflect morality? Ought it to do so? Conversely, should morality be embodied or expressed in law? Should it at least conform to it?

The example of abortion gave a particular point to these questions. If I regarded it as an individual matter, then this was to assume that either decision – for or against – would be legally permissible. But, of course, laws – and this one in particular – vary from place to place. So I can also ask, what *should* be the position of the law on this and other issues? And if the law does not fit with my conception of how it ought to be, I may go on to ask: why should I obey the law as it is and as I find it? What obligation do I have to conform either to other people's expectations or to the requirements of the state?

Even if in general I wish to answer this in a positive way – if I am happy for the most part to accept conformity – I am bound to set moral limits to this willingness. I must condone, in other words, a certain amount of disorder even if I opt for law and order. There are those, I know, who would say that the law is to be obeyed simply because it is the law – but equating the 'might' of the law with the morally 'right' is simply incompatible with the honest and open search for truth that I have set as my goal.[1] It is incompatible, too, with the idea of reaching, for myself, a view as to what is right, and then taking responsibility for my own choices and decisions.

Law, Conscience and Toleration

One solution to these problems might be to try, at least in thought, to separate the areas of law and of morality. Perhaps, echoing a famous phrase in the Wolfenden Report of 1957, which made liberalizing recommendations regarding the law in England on homosexuality and prostitution, I decide that certain aspects of private life are just 'not the law's business'. Indeed, I would have to have a very intrusive view of law and social living if I were to deny this, since the denial would mean that every aspect of my life could be regarded as a potential candidate for regulation – even trivial and personal tastes and pursuits, private interests and preferences.

I cannot, then, take the law as beyond criticism. Others may wish to change the law and so may I. A conflict between law and morality will provide a good reason for such a change. A blatantly immoral law should not remain in force, I am prepared to claim, nor even an illiberal one, where a practice is involved that seems a private matter. But if I decide in this way that the law should square with morality, whose morality is in question? Some, for example Lord Devlin, the British judge who has written in defence of the enforcement of morals, would say that not only is there a common morality within a community, but that this is the only sound basis of law.[2] This may be true. Perhaps there *is* a common morality which I can recognize as the dominant one in my society, but if it cuts across my own, I am confronted with the problems I have already considered. So the answer to my question – whose morality? – is the paradoxical-sounding one that it can only be my own. In the end I must have the courage of my own convictions.

But for law to square with morality and for law to impose it are two different things, and laws that are in existence for no other reason than to enforce morality – whether mine or a 'community view' – raise as many questions as immoral ones. Should there be laws against gambling, for example? Or against pornography? Should there be censorship of films and videotapes? In short, *should* morality be enforced by law? The answer to this can only be that a limit must be set to any such endeavour not just by the recognition of individual rights, but also by judging how the application of such values as freedom, toleration, equality and respect for the individual personality may work out in the case of each particular issue. Nevertheless, many issues which appear at first sight to be personal – drug-abuse, for example, or the viewing of violent pornography – may impinge upon the wider community in ways which make them public rather than private matters, and therefore appropriate subjects for legislation.

The problem of distinguishing the proper spheres of law and morality is most acute where the most difficult cases – abortion, for example, or euthanasia – are concerned. But it is in any case unlikely that there will ever be a perfect match between my notion of how the law should be and the way it in fact is. In the meantime, I have to accept as a fact the framework of law which I find in place. And yet I cannot abdicate my own responsibility to decide whether, if, in some extreme situations, moral claims conflict with legal ones, to follow these and my conscience, or to do what is expected of me. And at a certain level, law itself supports me in this. Watergate, My Lai, and Nuremberg are all names from this century's past which provide a reminder that individuals have, after the event, been held, legally as well as morally, responsible for actions which were judged to offend against a higher morality even if, at the time, set in some kind of context of authority or legality.

This may be less anarchic in practice than it sounds in theory. Accepting that it might in certain circumstances be right to break the law is not an argument for a *policy* of selective obedience to the law. I can imagine three kinds of situations where the case for disobedience would be strong:

1. Where what is forbidden is an essential aspect of a person's nature and personality – for example, homosexuality where this is a criminal offence.
2. Where the law itself is morally objectionable – for example, sitting in the part of a bus reserved for another race, where the law enforces racial segregation.
3. Where disobedience to the law is incidental to something else someone wants, possibly for strong moral reasons to do – for example, participating in a demonstration at a military installation in the hope of preventing the deployment of missiles designed to deliver indiscriminate death at a distance.

There are, of course, other even more controversial cases where the issue of law-breaking might arise: for example, where protest itself has been made illegal; or where the authority of the lawmakers is disputed; or in circumstances, perhaps, where a separatist organization aims to institute a break-away government expressive of a particular culture, language and race.

Even the first three cases listed, though, seem to undermine my earliest presumptions about law, disorder and the place of conscience, if initially I was inclined to assume that I must work within rather than against social and legal constraints. There are many cases of civil disobedience which have, retrospectively, won the respect and admiration even of those against whom they were directed: Ghandi's passive resistance, which contributed ultimately to the independence of India; the burning of draft-cards in the United States, which expressed a widespread demand that US involvement in Vietnam be brought to an end; and, in the Southern states of America, the positive breaking of laws about racial segregation in the sixties which substantially altered the climate of thought for the next generation.

One thing these particular examples have in common, however, is that, if they involved violence to others, this was not as a matter of policy. Perhaps, then, I may endorse non-violent protest as an uncontroversial way in which my own moral perspective may be retained and expressed in a climate of law and opinion which runs counter to it? But there are two ways in which I may find this inadequate as a general solution to problems of law and disorder, protest and dissent.

First, such protest is not always successful. Lying down in front of tanks is effective only if there is a sufficient degree of humanity in those manning them, or those giving orders, for the tanks to roll to a stop. But not all political opponents count human life as valuable as this. And a hunger strike is effective only against people who would regard the death of a hunger-striker with concern, and whose system of government is open enough for public information about it to be released; but for many regimes human life is cheap and people may starve themselves to death in prison without fanfare. What is more, where political will is strong, peaceful protest will not always alter policies: it is true that the Vietnam War was brought to an end; not true, though, that Cruise missiles were excluded from Britain and other parts of Western Europe as a result of lay protests, nor that the deaths of hunger-strikers brought significant changes in British policy in Northern Ireland.

Secondly, even peaceful protest forces confrontation between protesters and the representatives of legal authority, often the civil police. Clearly, I must weigh the importance of the cause for which I make my protest against the damage I do to the fabric of law and order – a structure which I have already acknowledged provides the support and underpinning of my existence as a choosing, acting individual.

But if the issue *is* vital, and the end cannot be achieved by other means? Or if conformity to the law makes my life and existence intolerable by demanding, even where other people's interests are scarcely involved, that I suppress my deepest urges and abandon all hope of self-fulfilment? Even in these circumstances, the moral restraints I have recognized as affecting my own private life may make me unwilling to move from peaceful to violent protest, from placards to bombs, from political argument to terrorism. For these are activities I cannot engage in without transgressing the rights of others, too, to enjoy the conditions necessary for an unimpeded life. A passing stranger torn apart by a bomb, a traveller or embassy employee held hostage against the actions of governments – these are inevitably being deprived of the very things I claim against others for myself. So if such values as humanity or fellow-feeling do not restrain me, I must at least contemplate the stark plea of other people's rights.

Consideration of my own position, then, in respect of laws as they are and as I find them, suggests that my ultimate retention of a right to moral judgement leaves me with a limited right to frugally and discriminatingly exercised civil disobedience, so long as this stays short of gratuitous invasion of the rights of others to life, happiness and health.[3]

But when I consider my attitude to the actions and behaviour of others, then I find a different issue engaging my attention. This is the issue of toleration. In considering my own position, I have recognized my own prior interest in a secure framework of conformity to the law on the part of other people; if I find myself surrounded by dissent and nonconformity, I may be unable to pursue my own goals and aspirations without hindrance. As a minimum I may find the chosen life-styles of others offensive or alarming.

The kind of limits to protest which I have just defined for myself will, then, be what I will demand of others, whatever their degree of moral conviction, and no matter how important, in their own eyes, they take their cause to be. Where the dissent of others is concerned, two attitudes are possible: either I may decide that this is a case where the law should indeed be changed (for example, that homosexuality should be decriminalized) or I may believe that the case is not one for toleration, and thus that the law as it stands should be enforced.

But defining the limits of toleration is no easy matter. Two cases which press against these limits might be these:

1. The case of people who hold racist beliefs and wish to promote them;
2. The case of groups who believe in the subservience of women and so adopt educational strategies and religious or cultural practices which it is difficult or impossible for individual women to resist.

Are these cases for toleration, or cases for limiting by law what can rightly not be tolerated? The British philosopher John Stuart Mill, in his classic defence of toleration '*On Liberty*' [4] argued that a clear line could be drawn in answering such questions between the parts of a person's conduct that concern or affect only that person, and those which also affect others. Beliefs and opinions belong to the first category. Actions against members of a race or a whole sex belong to the second. But the problem with these two particular cases is to decide how far beliefs and opinions in such matters can be separated from actions. If laws relating to *actions* are called for by the recognition of rights, then perhaps laws against the expression of the *opinions* which give rise to the actions would be appropriate, too.

Here it seems that there is no alternative but to return to my own starting-point, the philosophical commitment to open discussion and freedom of thought. In doing this I see that acting and thinking are not totally separable and unrelated. Rather they shade into each other. There is, in fact, a continuum stretching from mere opinion, through the expression of opinion, proselytizing for an opinion, inciting to action, and finally to action itself. Drawing a line somewhere on this continuum will obviously not be easy, and where it *is* to be drawn may vary from case to case. But my presumption must be in favour of toleration where that end of the continuum is concerned that represents belief and discussion – only this is consistent both with my starting-point and with my chosen method of procedure. But my recognition of other people's rights, and of the need for those who may be otherwise defenceless to be protected by law and social institutions, will justify the outlawing of action and incitement to action which poses a threat to those rights.

At this point, however, I recognize that my judgements are becoming judgements, not about what I myself should do, but about what the law should be. And to reflect on what the law should be, to campaign perhaps that existing laws should be changed or new ones brought in, is to engage in a well-known and historic art: the art of politics. At this point, I have to recognize that my personal moral concern has broadened into political concern – that is, a concern that my country or government should reflect in broad outline the moral outlook I have arrived at as an individual.

Law, Morality and the Art of Politics

My reflections on protest, dissent and nonconformity suggested a difference in the way in which the authorities in any particular country might respond to them; indeed, in looking about the contemporary world, it would not be difficult to distinguish a spectrum of political practices simply according to the degree of responsiveness of governments to protest. Protest in a liberal democracy might therefore seem to raise different questions, differently answered, from protest under a totalitarian regime, or a regime which is itself illegal or self-imposed, the result of a military coup or of corruption and chicanery.

Seeing that my moral evaluation of governments may vary, I realize that I expect that governments, too, should operate within moral limits, that they should be regarded as being under the same kind of principles of restraint as individuals, particularly given their vastly greater powers and opportunities. So the kind

of reasons that operated against terrorism for the individual operate against the use of torture, summary execution, arbitrary imprisonment and the abuse of human rights by governments.

All this is to suggest that there is a relationship between the
individual and the state in which the power of the one must be
balanced by the claims of the other. I know that the nature of
this relationship, and the justification of the obedience exacted
of the individual to the demands of the state, have in the past
been the focus of some of the great classics of political philosophy
– Plato's *Republic*, Hobbes' *Leviathan* (1651), Locke's *Second Treatise
of Government* (1690), Rousseau's *Social Contract* (1762). What, I
wonder, could I learn from my correspondent about these ideas?

Fourth Letter from Sophia

Dear Q,

*One answer which was common to all the modern writers you
mentioned in your letter to me – Plato's views were rather different
– was that the obligation of individuals to obey must in some way
or other be shown to follow from their own agreement or consent:
the theory of the social contract. The idea of political power as
something which is simply imposed on people is no answer to the
question of whether they have a reciprocal obligation to obey. But a
variety of views are possible about the manner and nature of the
consent needed to secure such an obligation.*

*Plato had already presented, through one of the participants in
his dialogue on political justice (in* Republic, *Book II), a relatively
simple picture of people coming together to fulfil specialist functions
and to profit from exchange and barter. For Thomas Hobbes,
however, civil society was a matter of a once-and-for-all surrender of
one's political will to an absolute sovereign, limited only by the
freedom to resist an order for one's own death. For John Locke
(1632–1704), the agreement was a continuing tacit agreement,
signalled by a person's willingness to stay within the borders of his
country of birth. The conception of a social contract advanced by
Jean-Jacques Rousseau (1712–1778) came closer to the theory*

which underlies modern democratic voting systems: for him, what was involved was the generation of a consensus, the General Will, to which an individual might be deemed as contributing through a system of majority voting. The liberal democrat of today recognizes, of course, that the result of majority voting is not necessarily what each particular individual wants. But Rousseau held that the outcome of such a vote revealed what the individual really wanted, *as opposed to what he merely* thought *he wanted. In saying this, he is said to have pointed the way for subsequent totalitarian political systems for, according to such an account, dissent becomes error rather than legitimate difference of opinion. I will write to you again if you would like to know more about these more recent trends, as I suspect they may be important for many of the concerns you have been expressing.*

Yours,
Sophia

I did indeed think about what Sophia had told me and it seemed to me that she was right in suggesting that I would find it useful to know something about the focus of today's political debates. It was not long before I received a reply from her in answer to my query.

Fifth Letter from Sophia

Dear Q,
As I wrote to you in my last letter, political philosophy in the past has been centrally concerned with the issue of coercion: the individual person's obligation to obey, and the ruler's right to enforce compliance. Debate today still focuses on this tension between the individual and the political authority − the state − but the contrast is increasingly being seen in terms of a debate about the requirements of community and the place for individual liberty.

Anarchy, State and Utopia, by the contemporary American philosopher Robert Nozick (b. 1938), is representative of that view from the right that recommends minimal state interference in the life of the individual.[5] *Nozick argues there for the justification of what has been called a 'night-watchman' or minimal state — one limited to the narrow functions of protection for the individual against force, theft and fraud, and to the enforcement of contracts. In particular, he argues that the state should not use its coercive apparatus for welfare — that is, to get some citizens to help others — and also that the state should not act paternalistically: it should not prohibit activities people want to engage in simply for their own good. A basic element in Nozick's argument is the notion of entitlement as a principle of distribution. People who favour a welfare state, he argues, are regarding other people's assets, including their skills and talents, as belonging to a common pool, and they look for ways to distribute the benefits from these assets, as well as property more conventionally understood, on the basis of such principles as future utility, or equality. Alternatively, they might favour principles such as moral merit or usefulness to society. But Nozick's entitlement principle resembles none of these. It looks backward at how a right came into being rather than forward to how a good might be distributed. It is the reverse of Marx's dictum 'To each according to his needs' and might be described, by contrast, as 'To each his own'. It encompasses the controversial view that taxation is slavery, or at least forced labour.*

Such libertarian views, which are also associated with the work of Milton Friedman (b. 1912) and F. A. Hayek (1899–1992) — two economists whose ideas have been influential in promoting the tax-reducing, inflation-curbing policies of monetarist governments in America, Britain and elsewhere — start from a primary interest in the possession and management of property. But there is room for another form of libertarianism that is closer to classical liberalism. This is libertarianism tempered by the humanitarianism that Mill found consistent with his own defence of the individual. Better called, perhaps, simply liberalism, this kind of political view could even find a meeting-point with the humanistic left, which may itself be liberal in the sense of rejecting social and political curbs on individual action.

Representative of this latter position is the political philosophy put forward by Antonio Gramsci (1891–1937) and his followers. It is an undogmatic and humanistically-oriented form of Marxism, and it could be summed up in Gramsci's demand (made in 1917) for a revolution 'against Capital'. That is, against the belief that human action is insignificant, and against the idea that, in accordance with the historical, economic and social laws set out by Karl Marx (1818–1883) in Capital, *capitalism would collapse through its internal contradictions, to be succeeded by a classless communistic society. The humanistic view, which emphasizes Marx's debt to Hegel (1770–1831), is particularly associated with the work of the Frankfurt School.*[6]

Gramsci's rejection of historical determinism led him to advocate a 'philosophy of praxis' – he believed, that is, that philosophy should provide a way of interpreting the world that can be applied in practical activity – which accords with another famous dictum of Marx in his Theses on Feuerbach: *'So far philosophers have only interpreted the world: the point, however, is to change it.'*

Gramsci occupies an unusual position in relation to the extremes of right and left as they have been manifested in the present century. Living in Italy at a time when Mussolini and the Fascists were in power, he saw Fascism as the 'illegal aspect of capitalist violence' – the only way that capitalists could preserve their economic system after the First World War. At the same time, he regarded the Russian Revolution as practical evidence of human beings' capacity to take control of their own destinies – an essentially libertarian phenomenon. Gramsci's Marxism, then, propounded as it was in a series of notebooks written over years in a Fascist prison, is anti-totalitarian and his criticism of fascism is implicitly also a condemnation of Stalinism.[7]

More centrally located in mainstream academic philosophical debate is the liberal view represented by Isaiah Berlin's (b. 1909) 'Two concepts of Liberty'[8] *and by the widely influential book in the liberal tradition by the contemporary American philosopher John Rawls (b. 1921),* A Theory of Justice, *which represents a modern version of the social contract theory.*[9] *These last, in particular, suggest that what is common to various forms of philosophical liberalism is concern with a range of principles, beginning with those of personal liberty and toleration, but including also opposition to arbitrary government on the one hand, and rule by mere majority* diktat *on the other – in other words, commitment to the rule of law. Personal liberty here includes such specific freedoms as those of thought, speech, publication and religion. There is a natural association between advocating freedom and respecting equality. So liberalism may – as, for example, it does in Rawls's theory – also include a commitment to equality. Hence its sensitivity to the rights of minorities and of women and children. It is also characteristic of a liberal approach that it assumes politics to be a matter of trial and error – a pragmatic view of politics as piecemeal engineering rather than as Utopian reconstruction put forward by Karl Popper (b. 1902) in* The Poverty of Historicism.

Rawls's theory, while it fits within this tradition and approach, is worked out from first principles. Rawls derives rules for ordering social life from a thought-experiment in which members of a society decide on basic moral principles for organising their life from behind a 'veil of ignorance.' This protects them from knowledge of their own position in society, as well as of their own competences and propensities. These conditions – called by Rawls the 'original position' – are what are necessary to secure impartiality of judgement, if it is assumed that the participants in the agreement are both rational and self-interested. In Rawls's 'general conception' there is, subject to the priority of freedom, a presumption in favour of the equal distribution of social goods. An unequal distribution would be acceptable only if it were to improve the situation of the worst-off in society. This could be the case if, for example, great disparities of wealth or privilege were instrumental in raising the standard of living of a society beyond what it would be if equality were the rule.

Rawls's theory is a detailed working out of a philosophical argument which is not, in fact, incompatible with a free-enterprise system like that of modern America – provided, that is, that inequalities do as a matter of fact work in favour of the under-privileged.

Berlin's defence of liberalism is not dependent on any such factual assumptions. Delivered in Oxford in 1958, Berlin's 'Two Concepts of Liberty' sets out two conceptions of liberty, one negative, the other positive. The first answers the question 'What is the area within which a person should be left to do or be what he wants to do or be?' while the second, positive, sense answers the question 'Who, or what, is the source of control or interference?' The first view is consciously derived from Mill, and Berlin argues that it is Mill's individualistic conception of the human being that lies behind: '. . . every plea for civil liberties and individual rights, every protest against exploitation and humiliation, against the encroachment of public authority, or the mass hypnosis of custom or organised propaganda.' On the other hand, Berlin claims, the positive conception is at the heart of all those political theories of self-realization which operate through 'magical transformation' or 'sleight of hand' to turn domination into liberty. 'Enough manipulation with the definitions of man, and freedom can be made to mean whatever the manipulator wishes.' At the heart of Marxism and other totalitarian creeds, Berlin writes, is the view that knowledge liberates. We will cease to want what we see to be impossible or unattainable. But Berlin himself believes in a pluralism of values which, even if they are not necessarily all achievable together, and even if they turn out in the end to be a minority commitment, are nevertheless worth pursuing.

The current debate about community starts from a challenge to the individualism implicit in such views. Its focus is the idea that individuals can only be understood as members of a community; the personality of an individual is deeply embedded in its cultural and social context. This contrasts with the liberal conception of the individual as a being free to shape a life largely independently of social context and – at least in spirit – unconstrained by such identifying features as gender, class or race. Ethically, this view may be sympathetic to the Aristotelian ideal of developing the virtues, particularly civic virtues. In contrast to the liberal stance of toleration and detachment from passing judgement on others, it conceives of life-styles as a public not a private matter. According to this school of thought, the late twentieth century has seen too much *toleration of deviant and socially destructive individuals, as a result of which today's liberal societies are plagued by problems of family break-down, homelessness and crime.*[10]

If you have been in the habit of placing political views on a spectrum from left to right, you may find it hard to classify the new communitarianism. This doctrine of 'embeddedness' has echoes of what has been called the 'political correctness' of the left; but the political right, too, favours a morality of 'my station and its duties' over the universalism and potential moral neutralism of liberal doctrine.

In another respect, too, the familiar boundaries break down. The communitarian stance advances a notion of citizenship as em-powerment. In place of negative freedom it recommends positive freedom or autonomy which, paradoxically, can only be achieved by activity on the part of the state – in education, health, welfare, and in protection against unemployment. Liberalism, of course, is not opposed to these goals, but the emphasis and perspective of liberal-ism in its classical form is different. It hesitates to ask the state to supply what the individual could offer voluntarily and, in a more complex argument, it would see the nature of these goods as being subtly but importantly changed by the manner and source of their provision. I have not been able to do more here than sketch out for you in this way the shape of an argument as yet still incomplete – an argument that must be conducted not only in philosophical discussions, but on the stage of world events. But let me set out for you what might be called the four pillars of liberal thought – the doctrines which are challenged by some these assumptions. These are:

1. *commitment to reason (with concomitant ideals of free will, truth, and toleration);*
2. *commitment to the protection of individuals in pursuit of their legitimate ends;*
3. *belief in a universal morality to which the notion of rights is central, and;*

4. a belief in a common underlying human nature – essential
    ingredients of humanity which are at least to a degree inde-
    pendent of social context.

If you keep these points in mind, they will serve to remind you
that liberalism can be conceived of as a positive rather than a
negative doctrine. Interpreted postively, liberalism can be as strong as
any other political philosophy in opposing the violations of rights
inseparable from a disordered crime-ridden society; and in supporting the contracts people make with each other, whether explicitly or
implicitly, when they marry or found families; and in protecting
individuals on a more global and international basis from violations
of rights, whether by governments who use torture, imprisonment
and execution to stay in power, or by international business interests
pursuing profits without regard for ethical constraints or for longterm
environmental considerations.

But, you may say, while liberal theory can be defended in this
way, the communitarian rejection of liberal individualism may be
justified by practical considerations. For individuals are of dimin-
ishing importance when it comes to the macro-world of politics. To
begin with, they can have little effect on policy within the borders
of their own country; nor can they easily move away from the
jurisdiction of the country in which they are born, and then only to
that of another which might be equally objectionable to them. And
– perhaps the most important consideration of all – many important
issues are no longer within the jurisdiction even of single countries:
science and technology have, in a popular phrase, turned the world
into a global village in which the maladministration of one nation
is the practical problem of another. Faced with problems on this
scale, you may say, individuals have no alternative but to acknowl-
edge their helplessness.

You are right to point this out, and it is true that this feature
of the interdependence of nations is particularly striking where
some of the environmental issues that are preoccupying people and
governments today are concerned. Nevertheless, considerations such
as justice and rights play an important part here, too, and so I will

write to you on these subjects if this is to be the next step in your enquiry.

Yours,
Sophia

After receiving Sophia's letter, I continued reflecting on the points she had made. There are indeed many areas where the notion of justice seems to have an international, not merely local, application. Environmental problems are a particular illustration of this. I went on to reflect that when trees die in Scandinavia, this can be the result of industrial processes in other parts of Europe; that the waters of the globe receive the effluent – detergents, pesticides, oil and chemicals as well as sewage – of the industrialized world; and that incidents such as the chemical leakage at Bhopal in India, and the accident at the nuclear reactor in Chernobyl in Russia, were in different ways international, not merely national, disasters. I thought, too, how a single nation may, by its uncontrolled policies, hunt or fish a species to extinction. These problems can in general be summed up as problems of pollution and problems of depletion of resources, including energy-resources. I have often thought about these matters, of course, although in a practical rather than philosophical way. It would, I believe, be interesting to hear from Sophia how it is that matters of justice and rights – very general ethical conceptions – impinge on the many aspects of the debate about the environment and perhaps, too, as she has hinted, on the broader spectrum of international affairs. Her reply could provide some focus for my thoughts about justice, as well as for my thoughts about environmental problems.

Sixth Letter from Sophia

Dear Q,
'Environment' is a term that has many uses. It can refer to a city street in the Northern hemisphere, a village in some spar-

sely populated country, or to the air and water on which people in both these places depend. In the narrower sense we can – within, of course, personal and practical limitations – choose our environment. In the wider sense, we cannot. For the science of ecology has brought understanding of the intimate web of connections of humans, animals, plants, earth, water. It has increasingly led us to see ourselves as neither independent nor self-sufficient, but as systems within systems. Knowledge of the extent of these systems in either direction seems to be limited only by the present scope of our microscopes and telescopes.

There is, too, a developing historical perspective. We see our species, the various human groups, as having until a very recent point in the planet's history, lived in balance with other species and with planetary conditions. It is true that there were issues of conservation and preservation in the past. Conserving woodlands and stocks of fish or game has, from time immemorial, been a preoccupation of landowners. There was concern about over-cultivation of the land even in medieval times, and the rotation of crops was devised as a remedy for that. Since at least the seventeenth century, people have worried about the pollution and disease caused by the concentration of populations in large cities, and it is now nearly two centuries since Thomas Malthus (1766–1834) argued that if population and food-supply are not kept in balance by other means, then nature itself will do this through war and pestilence.[11] Nature has, of course, been extremely resilient in the past in coping with the worst that human beings could do. The problem, today is that the natural balance has been distorted by scientific and technological advance that has led to an unprecedented explosion of populations in some parts of the world, to the rapid depletion of irreplaceable resources including important species, and to a threat to the outer environment of the earth itself, its protective ozone layer. Moreover, the attempt to harness powers which are intrinsically beyond the control of humans within their limited life-span, has generated toxic (particularly nuclear) wastes which will remain with this generation and its successors further into the future than the records of humanity's past.

Justice, together with its central concept of rights, characteristically tries to set bounds to the ways in which people may behave, particularly in relation to each other. There are those who argue that the notion of justice can be extended to cover the ways in which they may behave, too, in relation to the rest of nature, particularly to the other species with which they share the earth, and also to the unknown world of the future. Justice is, after all, historically and philosophically connected with the idea of balance and harmony, and an overestimate of our own importance is, at best, an unbalanced assessment. But before considering these matters, it would be wise if you were to look more closely at the basic idea of justice and those related concepts such as equality and rights that have always featured in the discussions of political philosophers.

Yours,
Sophia

I awaited Sophia's next letter with interest, for justice and the application of justice to the problems confronting human beings must, I am convinced, be central and crucial matters of philosophical concern.

NOTES

1   For the debate about legal positivism, see H. L. A. Hart, *The Concept of Law*, chs. 8 and 9, and R. M. Dworkin, 'Is law a system of rules? in R. M. Dworkin (ed.), *The Philosophy of Law*, ch. 7. Jeremy Bentham, who rejected the notion of natural rights, is associated with the idea of law as command, which is distinctive of the legal positivist position. Legal positivism is the view that certain social facts (the will of the people, for example, or the commands of a ruler) determine what the law is. This is not, however, inconsistent with advocating reform of the law, and many positivists, including Bentham himself as well as his follower John Austin (1790–1859), have been legal reformers. Hans Kelsen (1881–1973)

reiterated the positivist view that law and morality are separate spheres.

2 P. Devlin, *The Enforcement of Morals*. Lord Devlin's lecture was a reaction to the Wolfenden Report which, in recommending the liberalization of laws concerning homosexuality and prostitution, initiated a continuing debate about morality, particularly sexual morality, and the law.

3 For discussion of the issue of civil disobedience, see R. M. Dworkin, *Taking Rights Seriously*, ch. 8. This was essentially the subject of the discussion in Plato's dialogue, *Crito*, in which Socrates resists his friends' attempts to persuade him to flout the laws of Athens by making his escape from prison and the death penalty that had been imposed on him.

4 J. S. Mill, *On Liberty* (first published 1859). An earlier classic statement of the case for toleration of opinion is contained in Locke's *Letters on Toleration* (1688 and following). The principle of religious toleration was defended by various religious leaders and philosophers in seventeenth- and eighteenth-century Europe, during times of religious upheaval and persecution. Many of these defenders of toleration subsequently ended their lives as victims of the religious oppression they opposed. One of the best-known advocates of toleration was Pierre Bayle (1647–1706). For an account of the history of ideas on toleration, see H. Kamen, *The Rise of Toleration*.

5 R. Nozick, *Anarchy, State and Utopia*. With publication of this book, Robert Nozick, a Harvard philosopher and younger colleague of John Rawls, offered a philosophical underpinning to a new libertarian trend in political thought.

6 Representatives of the Frankfurt School include M. Horkheimer (1895–1973), T. W. Adorno (1903–1969), H. Marcuse (1898–1979) and J. Habermas (b. 1929).

7 For this view, see A. Sassoon, *Gramsci's Politics*. Gramsci's own writings are best read in A. Gramsci, *Prison Notebooks*. For a classic criticism of Marxism and other totalitarian systems, see K. Popper, *The Poverty of Historicism*. The philosophical roots of totalitarianism are described in J. Talmon, *The Origins of Totalitarian Democracy* or see H. Arendt, *The Origins of Totalitarianism*.

8 I. Berlin, 'Two Concepts of Liberty', in *Four Essays on Liberty*. Berlin's short essay, first delivered as an inaugural lecture at the

University of Oxford in 1958, has had an influence disproportion-
ate to its length. It captures for contemporary readers something of
the high traditions and essence of liberalism.

9 J. Rawls, *A Theory of Justice*. Rawls's treatise on justice was acknowledged as a major and seminal contribution to a range of areas of
political and social theory almost as soon as it appeared in 1971. It
offers a rich field for reflection and discussion to philosophers of
law, economists, moral philosophers and social theorists.

10 The idea of community has featured in political philosophy from
Greek and Roman times, and is central to the writings of a number
of political philosophers including Edmund Burke (1729–1797),
Rousseau and Hegel. This rich vein of debate in political philoso-
phy has fed into contemporary politics and underpins the debate
concerning civic republicanism and liberal individualism. For a
useful collection of readings from a number of contemporary
authors who have contributed to the communitarian debate, see S.
Avineri and A. de-Shalit (eds), *Communitarianism and Individualism*.
For an account of some of these positions, see S. Mulhall and A.
Swift, *Liberals and Communitarians*. The London-based Institute for
Economic Affairs (IEA) has also produced a series of books and
pamphlets relevant to developing these philosophical ideas as political policies.

11 Thomas Malthus presented his theories in *An Essay on the Principle of
Population*, first published 1798.

READING GUIDE

This chapter is about political philosophy. A useful introduction to
themes in this area is W. Kymlicka's *Contemporary Political Philosophy: an
introduction*, or see A. Brown, *Modern Political Philosophy*. A comprehensive reference work is P. Pettit and R. Goodin (eds), *A Companion to
Political Philosophy*. A good way to begin reading contemporary work in
political philosophy would be by reading Isaiah Berlin's essay 'Two
Concepts of Liberty', in his *Four Essays on Liberty*. Other important
modern contributions are J. Rawls, *A Theory of Justice* and R. Nozick,
Anarchy, State and Utopia. It would be rewarding also to read two
contributions from different political perspectives written earlier in the

twentieth century, A. Gramsci's *Prison Notebooks* and F. A. Hayek's *The Road to Serfdom*.

For general discussion of several of the issues touched on in this chapter, see A. Arblaster, *The Rise and Decline of Western Liberalism*; S. Hampshire (ed.), *Public and Private Morality*; J. Raz, *The Morality of Freedom*; and H. L. A. Hart, *Law, Liberty and Morality*. A particularly useful collection of articles on rights is J. Waldron (ed.), *Theories of Rights*.

Advice on reading in environmental ethics is provided in chapter 4. A feminist perspective on traditional political philosophy is reflected in A. Jaggar, *Feminist Politics and Human Nature*. See also S. Okin, *Women in Western Political Thought*.

CLASSICAL SOURCES

Plato: *Dialogues*, particularly *Republic*, and *Laws*
Aristotle: *Politics*
Hobbes: *Leviathan*
Locke: *Two Treatises of Government*; and *Letters on Toleration*
Rousseau: *The Social Contract*; and *Discourse on the Origins of Inequality*
Burke: *Reflections on the Revolution in France*
Hegel: *The Philosophy of Right*
J. S. Mill: *On Liberty*; *Representative Government*
Marx and Engels: *The Communist Manifesto*

4

Applying Justice

If justice perishes, there is no further point in men living on earth.
I. Kant, *The Metaphysics of Morals*

Justice has, I know, been a favoured theme of philosophers from Plato to Rawls. As I have just learnt, Plato discussed a variety of possible views of justice before offering the substantial theory which forms the main subject of his dialogue, the *Republic*.[1] Looking more closely at these other views, I see that, through the mouth of Thrasymachus, in Book I, he set out and dismissed an idea which is current today in the works of Marx and his sociological successors, as well as of contemporary postmodernists such as Foucault: that justice equates with power – it is simply the interest of the stronger. Then, through Glaucon in Book II, as I have just heard from Sophia, Plato presented the case for viewing justice as nothing more than social convention – a compact, tacit or explicit, between rational egoists, who recognize that living in a community governed by laws to regulate behaviour offers the best way to achieve their own personal goals. But is that view of political obligation adequate to deal with the broad ethical concerns about which Sophia has written to me? Is there not some more substantial conception of justice and of rights available for the solution of problems like these?

Seventh Letter from Sophia

Dear Q,
You are right in thinking that the idea of justice as nothing more

than social convention continues to be influential. You are right, too, to suggest that it is not without problems. To begin with, such a view seems to confine justice within artificial boundaries of time and place. It seems to imply that the rights people enjoy apply only within a particular society and under a particular system of laws. However, it is possible to take a wider, indeed universal view, in which rights and justice are seen as transcending the barriers of particular times and places. In this sense, if you were to be put in prison, tortured or even killed, although you had done nothing to deserve any of this, then whoever did this would be unjustly violating your rights, even if local conditions, and particularly local laws, imposed no sanctions on him. Might, in other words, is not right.

The idea that there is another court of appeal, a higher or transcendent notion of justice, belongs to a tradition whose origins also lie in antiquity, that of natural law – a law or natural order which may be contrasted with laws of convention rooted in particular localities. The idea was eloquently expressed by Antigone in Sophocles' play, when she appealed to 'immutable and unwritten laws of Heaven' as a reason for disobeying a command which conflicted with what she regarded as her moral duty.[2] Aristotle set the distinction out more formally in this way:

There are two sorts of political justice, one natural and the other legal. The natural is that which has the same validity everywhere and does not depend upon acceptance; the legal is that which in the first place can take one form or another indifferently, but which, once laid down, is decisive.[3]

The idea of a natural or universal law that could be contrasted with the actual (positive) laws of states is, then, of long standing. It was an important element in Stoic thought and, reflected in Roman law and in the Christian tradition, was developed further in modern times. Locke declared that natural law is a test of the justice of positive law, and placed the rights to life, liberty and property beyond social negotiation. It was this conception of a sphere of personal inviolability that led in due course to the flowering of the contemporary notion of universal human rights. So an influential tradition leads from the Greek idea of natural law and justice to the present-day notion of universally shared rights. Within this conception, just as within the narrower framework of justice expressed in particular social or political systems, it is possible to see another important contrast. This is the distinction between formal *justice and* social *or* distributive *justice.*

Formal Justice

The first of these constitutes perhaps the commonest conception of justice. It is the notion of justice as reciprocity that is enshrined in legal systems; it is also the principle of formal equality which requires that like cases be treated alike. This implies first that justice should be administered according to rules rather than the shifting and arbitrary whims of despots or private individuals. Secondly, it means that there should be no discrimination between people on irrelevant grounds, but that all individual persons have, as far as their legal standing is concerned, equal status, and so should be treated with equal respect. These two aspects are captured in the two main formulations of Kant's Categorical Imperative: as the principle that one should be able to universalize the maxim of one's actions, and as the requirement to treat other people never solely *as means to other people's ends, but always to bear in mind that they are ends in themselves – of value and importance in their own right.*[4] *This belief in the right of everyone to equal concern and respect is at the root of contemporary theories of political liberalism. Metaphorically, it is the principle that justice must be blind – that discrimination is morally offensive, and that justice must not pay attention to such irrelevant differences between people as, for example, race, class, wealth or influence.*

Notions such as desert and entitlement play a role here. For what is due to people, whether positive or negative, punishment or reward, may be what they have deserved or earned in some way, or it may be what belongs to them through gift, inheritance, and so on. This idea is often expressed in the language of rights and it is

*widely held that claims of justice made on the basis of rights of this
sort are and should be enforceable by authorities established for that
purpose. The idea that justice may be imposed by force if necessary
is accepted from both ends of the political spectrum: it was seen as
essential to guarantee justice in this way both by Thomas Hobbes,
who advocated the rule of an absolute sovereign, and by John Stuart
Mill, who defended individual liberty. It is this that generates the
popular conception of justice – justice as embodied in a system
of publicly declared laws supported by sanctions or punishments.
And it is this that justifies, too, the social institutions – law-
courts, prisons, and a supporting bureaucracy – which are essential
to them.*

Yours,
Sophia

As I reflected on Sophia's account of formal justice, it occurred
to me that, valuable though it undoubtedly is, some would regard
this as quite a limited conception of justice, since it makes the
state a kind of umpire or referee, guarding citizens against interference in their liberties and protecting their contracts. But the
rights it protects are essentially negative ones – rights to non-
interference. Adam Smith evidently acknowledged this when he
wrote that 'Mere justice is . . . but a negative virtue and only
hinders us from hurting our neighbour.'[5] Is there not, I wonder,
some richer understanding of the notion, one that might require
me also to *help* my neighbour? Now I remember that Sophia
spoke of another conception of justice. Would this, I wonder,
provide an answer to my question?

Eighth Letter from Sophia

Dear Q,
*There is, as I wrote, another conception of justice. It is the idea of
distributive justice, which, because it is usually put forward as an*

economic or social conception, is sometimes called 'social justice'. This kind of justice is specifically concerned with the allocation of goods and benefits. Within the conception of formal *justice, the principle of reciprocity means that the punishment of offenders and the settlement of legal claims are to be dealt with on the principle of treating like cases alike, but within the area of* distributive *justice, it is accepted that people need not receive the same goods and benefits. Justice in this case means that benefits must simply be seen to be* fairly *received – hence it includes the idea of a just price, or a fair wage.*

The judgement as to whether a distribution of benefits is fair can be made from two different standpoints: first, distribution may be deemed fair because the process *or* procedure *for handing out social goods (whether this is done by governmental or by private agencies) is judged fair, or, second, because the resulting* outcome *is considered fair, whatever the process. In the first case, the question is, on what* principles *should the distribution take place? In the second case, Who, and how many, should have how much? What would a fair distribution look like? Would it encompass striking inequalities? These questions, too, have been widely discussed by philosophers in the past. It was in connection with this sense of justice that Hume said that in a situation of plenty, there would be no need for justice – it is a virtue only needed to provide principles for the distribution of resources that are scarce or in limited supply.*[6] *Justice in this sense, then, is linked with the notion of fairness or equity. Some possible ways in which goods and benefits might be distributed include:*

1. *An absolutely equal distribution;*
2. *Distribution according to need;*
3. *Distribution according to merit (in the sense of what a person deserves).*

It would also be possible to arrange distribution according to utilitarian principles – maximizing benefits, and minimizing cost. But this kind of goal might be consistent with a few people losing out altogether for the sake of the general welfare – a situation most

*would agree to be a departure from justice. From this point of view,
a principle which forms an important part of Rawls's account of
justice, which I mentioned to you earlier, may seem to offer a
criterion which has the advantage of combining a concern for
maximizing welfare with a greater regard for justice.[7] This is the
'difference principle', also called 'maximin' because it takes the
welfare of the least advantaged person as its yardstick. According to
this principle, inequalities are justified only if they work to the
advantage of all, in particular the most disadvantaged, under conditions of fair competition. Rawls's theory is important from many
points of view, legal, economic and ethical. It is important to notice,
though, that, like utilitarianism, it seeks to allocate social goods on
the basis of the most acceptable end-result, and there are some very
general objections to allocating goods on this kind of basis which
apply to most of the proposals for distribution I have listed here,
with the exception of the 'merit' principle. But let me return to
those other proposals.*

Equal Distribution

*As you will have noticed, perfect equality was a principle well
suited to the idea of formal or commutative justice. Judges are
expected, indeed requuied, to apply it in imposing punishments or
settling compensation claims; they should treat like cases alike. It is
also the justice governing contracts and exchange. Perfect equality, in
other words, is applicable in the area of law. Within the area of
distributive justice, however, where what is at issue is the distribution of material goods rather than of legal rights and privileges, it
is harder to justify. Left to themselves, people have a natural
tendency to become unequal, if only through specialization of
interests and pursuits, so that maintaining equality in goods, possessions, and way of life would require constant monitoring and
interference on the part of the state. While equality provides a
popular slogan, then, this may well be because it is so often
misinterpreted. In particular, it would be hard to defend a concept
of equality that denied that there are differences between people, still*

more between humans and other creatures. Nor is it easy to defend even the lesser claim that all should be treated alike. For this is to ignore differences in needs – a person who is sick needs different treatment from one who is well, an infant's educational needs are different from those of an adult, and so on. It is no doubt considerations such as these that have led to need itself being proposed as a criterion for just distribution.

Distribution According to Need

At first sight, then, need seems to offer a more plausible basis for the allocation of goods than blind equality. Need, however, can be a variable concept, unless it is limited to some strict and narrow conception of basic needs. This is not an impossible requirement. Vague talk about poverty or relative deprivation can usefully be replaced by reference to 'hard' measures such as infant mortality rates and life expectancy so as to identify certain societies or groups as needy. Given a sufficiently firm conception of absolute poverty, then, it is possible to make out a more secure ethical case for pursuing the aim of securing a basic minimum of food, shelter and the conditions essential for physical subsistence for all human beings, and for arguing that it is wrong, if human action can prevent it, that some should be left at a level of existence which is entirely governed by the threat of disease, malnutrition and early mortality. Above the level of basic needs, however, critics are right to argue that a judgement of justice must take account of background conditions and of the reasons for people's different situations. That is to say, someone who prefers leisure and an easy life is not necessarily entitled to live at the same level as others who have devoted their lives to hard work, nor is there any obligation on others to see that those who have neglected their talents enjoy the same standard of living as those who have lived more wisely and sacrificed short-term pleasures for longer term goals.

What both these proposals or criteria have in common, as I said earlier, is that they make justice a matter of outcome rather than process. But while it is true that vast inequalities may need explanation, it is unnecessary to assume that inequality is offensive in itself. If you can find out how some particular inequality arose, it is often the case that it can be justified. The third proposal which I mentioned is just the kind of explanation that might achieve this. For in specifying grounds for differential *rewards, it focuses on just* procedures *rather than just outcomes.*

Distribution According to Desert: the Idea of Proportionate Justice.

The criterion of merit or desert is summed up in Aristotle's notion of proportionate justice: the formula that it is as unjust to treat unequals equally as it is to treat equals unequally. In the area of distributive justice, since it makes what you get depend on what you have done or otherwise deserve, it is unlikely to produce actual or arithmetical equality as its outcome. Nor will it necessarily match up well with need. Some social philosophers find this unfair. One reason they advance for this is that merit and achievement result from skills and virtues that are a matter of genetic endowment. Since we cannot alter our character, our genetic endowment, they argue that it is unfair to make it the subject of reward or punishment. Rawls writes of a 'natural lottery' and says: 'There is no more reason to permit the distribution of income and wealth to be settled by the distribution of natural assets than by historical and social fortune . . . Even the willingness to make an effort, to try, and so to be deserving in the ordinary sense is itself dependent on happy family and social circumstances.' [8] *Although Rawls draws back from the brink of the implication that equality or justice requires the abolition of the family, his remarks are still surprising because of the view they imply of what it is to be a person. To argue in this way is really to suggest that we cannot make sense of the notion of moral responsibility unless there is some kind of person within a person − an inner controller of character, the product of neither heredity nor environment. The fact is, however, that persons are simply the persons that they are, as defined by character, abilities, disposition, potentialities and so on. This question of character, or personhood, is one you will no doubt wish to think about again. But even now, you can, I believe, see how such questions connect with the wide ethical and practical concerns you have been considering.*

Yours,
Sophia

Reading Sophia's account, I realize that these questions do indeed deserve wider reflection. Later, I must think further about this question of what it is to be a person, a human individual. Meanwhile, even while limiting my attention to the question of persons as subjects of justice and bearers of rights, there are a number of cases I can see are problematic. What, I wonder, does justice demand of me where people living in poverty in distant countries are concerned? How should the application of justice extend geographically? How far, too, should it extend on a time-scale which takes in the unlimited future? Must I regard myself as owing duties to those who are not yet born, to future generations? More problematically still, can I concern myself only with other *human* persons, whether present or future, or does justice apply, too, to my treatment of the other species with which I share the earth?

Justice and the Distant Poor

When I thought before of the environmental links between nations, it was clear to me that not all nations are on an equal footing in these matters. The wealth of the world is vastly un-equally owned; power and influence correspondingly dispro-portionate. Some people must live out their lives on the edge of starvation, or indeed die in massive droughts and famines; while others use enormous resources to replace worn hearts, lungs or other defective organs. In the West, the doctrine of the sanctity of life is applied to keeping alive those whose prognosis is tragic.

Elsewhere, young and middle-aged alike are swept out of existence by avoidable disease and malnutrition. A great gulf divides the developed and industrialised nations, largely from the northern hemisphere, from the underdeveloped and developing countries, largely of the southern hemisphere, where overpopulation, poverty and malnutrition are endemic problems and nations are subject to periodic droughts and cycles of natural disasters.

Are these matters of economics? Or of politics? It seems that only political will could apply economic solutions. That there is an obligation to seek for solutions is a matter of common agreement. Some contemporary philosophers, I know, have argued that an obligation to tackle these problems can be based on utilitarian ethical foundations – there is an overriding obligation to minimize pain and suffering. This is an effective argument, but one problem with the utilitarian position is that it can, of its nature, provide no upper limits to what it might be our duty to do. Nevertheless, the philosopher Peter Singer (b. 1946) has developed a strong moral argument to the effect that individuals in wealthy countries ought to use their income to reduce absolute poverty in poorer countries on the ground that they can, in general, do this without sacrificing anything of comparable moral significance, and that there is a duty to alleviate distress and suffering where this is the case.[9]

But can the notion of distributive justice be used to justify international redistribution from rich countries to poor? The American philosopher Garrett Hardin (b. 1915) has argued that it cannot, by means of a dramatic analogy.[10] The rich nations, he has suggested, may be compared to a lifeboat surrounded by desperate swimmers – the world's poor – trying to get on board. Hardin uses this analogy to ask practical as well as theoretic questions: what would happen if the numerous poor did climb aboard? Would the lifeboat sink? Applying such questions to the North/South issue, some argue for cutting aid and for the adoption of strong population policies extending even to compulsory measures. From a purely environmental point of view, however, such recommendations come uncomfortably from the rich countries whose citizens are each individually massive consumers of world resources and energy compared to villagers in, for example, Peru or Bangladesh.

In Hardin's analogy, the situation is painted in terms of stark alternatives: to help or not to help – to retain one's standard of living or to be completely overwhelmed. Singer, in contrast, proposes a compromise based on the ancient notion of the tithe. He proposes, that is, that the inhabitants of the richer nations should individually give up a generous proportion of their income, whilst not rendering themselves or their families destitute, or even excessively uncomfortable.[11] But in deciding the actual allocation of whatever aid is made available, it is still likely to be necessary to be selective. For this purpose, triage is sometimes proposed as an alternative principle of distribution. Triage involves identifying the cases where aid can be most useful and offering it there, rather than to cases which are so desperate that aid will be fully consumed, leaving the situation to return to what it was before. This, too, is a harsh programme to adopt in practice, since it involves ignoring the most needy and most tragic cases, helping some who are better-off, whilst knowingly leaving the worst-off to die. For this reason, it would hardly qualify as a principle of justice, even if there are situations in which it would be chosen on grounds of expediency or cost-effectiveness.

Implicit in Hardin's analogy is the idea that, whatever distribution strategies are adopted, it would not be possible for everyone to achieve the standard of life of The Western world, and Singer's compromise, too, implicitly recognizes this fact.

What, then, does justice require here? This is a question on which I would now welcome a letter from Sophia.

Ninth Letter from Sophia

Dear Q,
There are indeed philosophers who would argue against all redistributive theories and in favour of a minimal state which acknowledges and defends the rights of people to what they have

*legitimately acquired, whether by work, gift, inheritance or other-
wise. I have already written to you about one such view. This
conception of justice would confine us to asking the question: Are
others* entitled *to share what we have?*

*But I suggested to you earlier that the notion of distributive
justice may rightly take account of the equality of people's basic
needs. It may also look critically at the question of whether the rich
deserve what they have. But as critics have pointed out, inequality
as such is not objectionable. What is objectionable is poverty at a
level which makes the ordinary conditions of human life impossible.
Satisfying basic needs, then, can be taken as* in principle *a just
goal. Nevertheless, many will argue that in practice this goal may
be turned into an unattainable moving target by uncontrolled
population growth. There is currently much truth in this. But
unfortunately, the population objection must be balanced by some
more negative considerations. There are countries today which face a
real danger of depopulation by AIDS, whilst long-abolished ills
such as diptheria, cholera and tuberculosis are returning to parts of
Eastern Europe in the wake of social upheaval. Ordinary health
threats, too, apparently overcome in recent decades by the development of antibiotics, are returning in resistant strains to Western
Europe and the USA. At the same time, a proliferation of weapons
– nuclear, biological, chemical – is in the hands of unpredictable
rulers and irregular groups all over the world. In these circumstances,
Hardin's lifeboat may be less secure than it looks, and its occupants
may perhaps permit themselves the luxury of extending well-
considered aid, recognising that, after all, the hypothesis of perma-
nently increasing human numbers is the more optimistic of the
alternatives confronting humankind at the present time.*

Justice for Future Generations

But let us assume, since in a sense we must, *that these problems
will be solved, and that there will be a future for humanity not too
unlike its past for us to recognize it as requiring our ethical*

consideration. What, you asked me, does justice require of us in relation to future generations? The first thing to recognize here is that the principle of formal justice has an important part to play, in that it imposes on us a requirement of impartiality. For the idea that it is wrong for individuals to make an exception of themselves, can easily be extended to the principle that it would be wrong for one generation to privilege itself, leaving nothing for future generations. The understanding of injustice as taking too much, more than one's fair share, is a very fundamental notion. Also involved here is the ethical obligation of gratitude – gratitude to past generations which of necessity can only be repaid to future ones. Gratitude is due because – while recognizing that our ancestors were not all equally deserving of it – nevertheless, we owe our progress and our existence to previous generations; this is a debt which cannot be discharged backwards to our predecessors, only to the future and our successors.

The principles which could be said to apply here are, first of all, that we should seek not to close down options for future generations, for example, by making irreversible changes, such as eliminating important species of living creatures, or using up irreplaceable resources, and second, that we should seek to maximise the choices that are available to our successors by making a considered judgement as to what, if choices must be made, it is most important to preserve and protect. This might be, for example, the earth's protective ozone shield, clean air, or energy. The principles involved here may be summed up as (i) conservation of options, (ii) conservation of quality, and (iii) conservation of access. This last principle aims at balancing justice requirements between and within generations. It is based on the idea that it would not be right to protect the interests of future people at the expense of today's poor. This is a reminder that the web of causality is extremely complex, whether the issue is present or future people. Moreover, our apparent ability to set into motion chains of causation that, once initiated, cannot be halted, may well generate an altogether new kind of obligation to the future.

Justice for Non-human Animals
and Nature

*There are those who believe that all these considerations amount to
a need for us to remember our obligation to other human beings,
whether present or future, who will be affected by damage that we
do to the planet. But others would argue that this is too narrow a
view of the proper extent of ethical concern, which should at least
be expanded to cover other species with which we share the planet.
But can we speak of inter-species justice? Do animals have rights?
It would be absurd to suggest that animals are moral persons in the
same way as humans. If they were, then an animal would have the
same claim on us as a child. But few would hesitate to rescue a
drowning child before a drowning dog, and most would condemn
anyone who did the opposite. At the same time, however, it would
be wrong to count non-human animals as negligible. The English
philosopher, Robin Attfield, has proposed a compromise which
avoids this dilemma: this is to distinguish moral standing from
moral significance, and then to say that, while animals do have
moral standing, there can be degrees of moral significance which it
is right to recognise.*[12]

*An alternative solution is encompassed in the notion of steward-
ship. The idea that human responsibilities for animals and for the
natural world are responsibilities of stewardship has support from a
religious as well as a moral perspective. But where some religious
views would suggest that we should care about non-human animals
because they are for our use, others, as well as some non-religious
viewpoints, allow that this may be simply because they matter.
This leaves open, however, the contested questions of whether
practices such as vivisection, and the raising of animals for consumption are permissible. Some conservationists would allow for human
use and consumption of animals as part of the general pattern of
nature, in which species feeds upon species; Aldo Leopold's influential 'harmony with nature' form of conservationism, for example,*

took for granted the hunting, fishing and eating of animals. Others regard the eating of animals as on a par with cannibalism, and experimentation on animals as morally indistinguishable from the torture and exploitation of human beings. Others again argue both these points on a utilitarian basis. For them the issues turn, not on an intuitive ethical judgement, but on matters of fact: they may argue, for example, that only a complete change of human dietary and consumption patterns can preserve a viable world environment, and that scientific and medical knowledge can be advanced without experiments on living animals. To resolve these questions, though, you must turn to the scientists rather than the philosophers.

And so I will leave you to consider these matters. Whatever you conclude, however, I think you will agree that there is a sense in which something is indeed owed to the contemporary poor, to posterity, to other living creatures. There is, in other words, an idea of justice as moral reciprocity, that coincides with the Golden Rule – what is owed to others is nothing less than what you would wish for yourself in their position. But some would go beyond this to claim that justice may be involved in our relationship to the inanimate world around us, even indeed to the biosphere. Those who press for a new biocentred ethic argue that the liberal ideal of civil justice – justitia communis – is inadequate to yield the duties environmental issues require for their solution. Certainly it is necessary if you wish to continue to think about these duties in terms of justice and rights, to do so with an enlarged conception of the scope of 'community', so that it extends first to mankind as a whole, and then, in Aldo Leopold's words, to 'soils, waters, plants and animals, or, collectively: the land'.[13]

The environmental debate forces us, then, to focus on the interconnectedness of things. As far as other living creatures are concerned, this means awareness of the 'Great Chain of Being' that ties human interests firmly in with theirs – an earth which contained only humans and their artifacts would rapidly become a dead world. As far as the poor nations of the world are concerned, it means recognizing that the world has become an economic global village in which the rich live increasingly precariously balancing *appeals for aid against pressures for immigration, at the same time attempting to quell civil unrest beyond their frontiers, aware of its potential to destabilize not only those distant regions but their own, to affect their own lives through terrorism, or to lead to the use of horrific weapons of mass destruction.*

Yours,
Sophia

Sophia's letter led me to reflect further on my own role in relation to these large issues. Governments already exist and therefore *their* role and contribution can be, to some extent, taken for granted. But whatever form it takes – aid to drought-stricken areas, loans and technical assistance, or disarmament negotiations and peace-keeping activities – it must be accepted that all this will be within the limits of their structure: their need to be responsive to their electorates, to maximize the standard of living of their own nationals, to protect their own people; and to do all this subject to management, electoral and bureaucratic constraints.

Is there anything, then, that individuals can do outside the area of conventional politics? It is true that some rare individuals have indeed made a discernible impact on world events. They have done this sometimes through free-floating and independent organizations with a campaigning mission like Amnesty International, or Greenpeace. It has been individual activists, too, who have made a whole range of issues of principle previously taken for granted into live issues. Such organizations resemble, on the one hand, charities of a more well-established kind; on the other, pressure-groups or purely campaigning organizations.

Apart from these, two other groupings provide a means whereby an individual may, whether as volunteer or employee, make a personal contribution in some of these areas: these are, first, the major charities, now powerful and institutionalized, which are heavily involved in problems of poverty, hunger, crisis and emergency. And secondly, the international agencies set up under the United Nations to cover special needs and problems. I need not assume, then, the complete ineffectiveness of individual effort, particularly if channelled through such sources. But how far, I wonder, should I, personally, see solutions to such problems as in my own hands, and how far look to others or to a new international order?

Justice, War and Violence

This is a question that strikes me with particular force in relation to those topics mentioned by Sophia at the end of her letter, for these seem even further beyond the control of the individual than those which prompted my first reflections. How is justice to be applied in the context of war, conflict and political violence?

Tenth Letter from Sophia

* *Dear Q,*
  Overlying all other problems and dwarfing them in significance is the shadow and threat of war, together with the inextricably related issues of nuclear, chemical and biological weapons. You ask whether war can ever be justified? Well, there is a long tradition of theorizing about the 'just war'. Aggressive war has been outlawed by some international agreements but war in self-defence is usually recognized as morally justified. Nevertheless, many innocent people will die if a nation defends itself, including its own nationals, so that a case could be made for avoiding even a war of self-defence if causing the death of innocent people were taken as invariably and absolutely wrong.

  But in the past, the aim for which a war is fought has been seen as justifying it: to free slaves, for example, or to protect a small nation from an aggressive invader, or, more controversially, to free a population from a despotic tyranny. But war must be the bluntest of instruments for such purposes and contemporary conditions make the possibility of applying economic or diplomatic pressure, wherever it can be used effectively, an alternative and less painful weapon for use in this kind of cause.

Today's debates are often conducted, though, less in terms of war than of deterrence. So there is a question as to whether the morality of deterrence is different from the morality of war itself. This is a particularly potent question where nuclear weapons are concerned, where carrying out the threat would involve the slaughter and maiming of many innocent people: babies, children, old people, pregnant women, the sick in hospital, political dissidents and pacifists, as well as, through radiation, unborn future persons. Beyond this, the ultimate threat in a nuclear exchange is the doomsday threat of destroying the planet as an inhabitable environment for humans and other animals. Surely, you may say, since it would be wrong to do this – to launch such a conflict – it must be wrong even to threaten to do this.

Against this has to be set the fact that people (would-be aggressors, for example) are more inclined to do what they can do with impunity and to avoid what will have undesirable consequences for themselves. And secondly, that while everything may be lost if a threat has to be carried through, nevertheless if the danger is appalling enough, it may be worth the risk of using a dangerous threat to avert it. The spread of nuclear and biochemical weapons amongst those who may not make such rational assessments is nevertheless a matter for concern. Already, irresponsible people hold horrific weapons of war in their hands – and in this case, the measure of 'irresponsibility' is that one uses them. Undoubtedly, recent conflicts have seen the use or deployment of chemical and biological weapons, with major powers incapable of restraining their use. In the end, if the threat from such weapons is to be eliminated, it will best be done by the preservation of peace, but how can this be achieved?

Clearly no single government can guarantee such a goal. For the governments of the world exist in what Hobbes described as a 'state of nature'. And Hobbes depicted the existence of individuals, as long as they were in that condition, as a war 'of every man, against every man' and 'the life of man, solitary, poore, nasty, brutish and short'.[14] *If such a state is to be averted amongst the nations of the world and some equivalent of an international 'social contract' reached, then it seems that an international political entity must be the solution. In the present century, both the League of Nations and its successor, the United Nations, were set up with this aim, but neither could be said to have succeeded in meeting all the aspirations of the originators. Any bureaucratic organization, and not least an international one, is subject to perversion of purpose by the natural corruption of human beings − wheeler-dealing, fixing, a willingness to assert the morally absurd, the visibly false. No organization can be better than its officials, and people with a sense of moral purpose seldom progress in bureaucratic structures. If world-scale political action, then, no matter how desirable, is not able to provide an immediate solution to problems that cannot be deferred, the political questions you will have to consider are: what is to be done, and who should do it?*

Yours
Sophia

As I pondered Sophia's questions, I was struck by a distinctive aspect of the contemporary shape of politics. This is the way in which, while problems have broadened by becoming inter-nationalized, political action has narrowed, flowing into single issue groupings: animal welfare; feminism; ethnic rights; national liberation movements. It is true that there is a broad grouping of attitudes on these matters that coincides with the traditional party divisions of left and right, but this agreement on *image* covers a good deal of internal disagreement on *content*. In any case, since governments are based on parties, whether a single party or more, it is difficult for me as an individual to express a political wish, through conventional structures, for anything other than a pack-age-deal, parts of which will be bound to be unacceptable to me. There is, in other words, both a formal face of politics in which compromise on issues is a way of life, and a new, informal face of politics consisting of single issue groupings within which total commitment is the badge of membership.

Practical politics, then, whether in its old or its new form, seems to pose a difficulty for me as an individual who wishes to approach each issue in an open search for truth, rather than from an inflexible prior position, or in defence of vested interests. There is, too, a more general problem about determining truth in a political context, and here the thought that politicians, if not political parties, may have reason to conceal the true nature of issues takes on a special significance. I realize that, in assessing the issues and deciding on my own position, I am dependent on truth as it reaches me through media – the press, radio, television – which may be under the control, direct or indirect, of the very people whose position and views I am trying to assess.[15] If any single conviction has emerged from my reflections on my own position in relation to the world and to world issues, it is the conviction that I must be left free, particularly in the matter of my judgment. But if I am to be free in my judgement – if I am not to be manipulated by others – then I must have access to information and argument which is accurate, undistorted and fair. I must next consider, then, what these requirements amount to. Are there ways of recognizing bad arguments and misleading information, and, if so, can they be formulated?

NOTES

1   Plato, *The Republic.*
2   Sophocles, *Antigone* (trans. George Young), II, 452–60:

> ————— Nor did I deem
> Your ordinance of so much binding force
> As that a mortal man could overbear
> The unchangeable unwritten code of Heaven;
> This is not of today and yesterday,
> But lives forever having origin
> Whence no man knows.

3   Aristotle, *Ethics*, Book 5, 1134^{b}24.

4   Kant's categorical imperative, in its various formulations, is presented in I. Kant, *Groundwork of the Metaphysics of Morals*. The edition
edited by H. Paton is helpful in providing explanatory notes and
introduction.

5   Adam Smith, *The Theory of Moral Sentiments*, II (ii) 1, p. 199

6   D. Hume, *A Treatise of Human Nature*, Book III, pt. II, sec. II and
An Enquiry Concerning the Principles of Morals, sec. III, pt. I

7   The balance between welfare and justice is the subject of wide-
ranging debate in political philosophy. With the collapse of communism in many countries, political and economic preference has
turned to market principles and suspicion of state subsidy and state
support. Most countries, however, remain committed on moral
grounds to the protection of the vulnerable in society and to the
guarantee, if not the delivery, of services in health and education.
The issues are discussed in David Green's *Reinventing Civil Society*,
and by John Gray in *The Moral Foundations of Market Institutions*. See
also R. Goodin, *Protecting the Vulnerable* and M. Sandel, *Liberalism
and the Limits of Justice*.

8   J. Rawls, *A Theory of Justice*, pp. 73–4.

9   P. Singer, *Practical Ethics*, 2nd edn, pp. 230–1.

10   G. Hardin, 'Lifeboat Ethics: the case against helping the poor, in
J. Rachels (ed.), *Moral Problems*.

11   P. Singer, *Practical Ethics*, p. 246.

12   R. Attfield, *The Ethics of Environmental Concern*, 2nd edn.

13   A. Leopold, *A Sand County Almanac*.

14   Thomas Hobbes, *Leviathan*, ed. C. B. MacPherson, Part 1, ch. 13,
pp. 185–6.

15   For a collection of articles on ethics and journalism, see A. Belsey
and R. Chadwick (eds), *Ethical Issues in Journalism and the Media*.

READING GUIDE

Applied philosophy involves the exploration of philosophical and ethical
issues underlying controversial areas of public debate, including environmental and medical ethics, policy decisions in politics, education, law
and business. Philosophy has always sought to answer such perennial
questions as, How should we see the world and our place in it? What is

the good life for the individual? General introductions to this type of philosophy are:

P. Singer, *Practical Ethics*

B. Almond (ed.), *Introducing Applied Ethics*

Useful collections of articles on a variety of themes are:

J. Rachels *Moral Problems*, 3rd edn.; and R. Wasserstrom, *Today's Moral Problems*.

John Rawls's *A Theory of Justice* is a classic contemporary discussion of justice. See also A. Gutmann, *Liberal Equality*; M. Walzer, *Spheres of Justice: a defence of pluralism and equality*; and B. Ackerman, *Social Justice and the Liberal State*. For justice in relation to welfare, see also R. Goodin, *Protecting the Vulnerable* and M. Sandel, *Liberalism and the Limits of Justice*.

The idea of a universal conception of justice leading from the Greek notion of natural law to the modern conception of human rights is fully expounded in J. Finnis *Natural Law and Natural Rights*. See also L. W. Sumner, *The Moral Foundations of Rights* and R. Dworkin, *Taking Rights Seriously*.

For justice in relation to the environment, see D. Cooper and J. Palmer (eds), *Just Environment* and, in relation to the obligations of the rich nations to the poor, O. O'Neill, *Faces of Hunger* and R. Attfield and B. Wilkins (eds), *International Justice and the Third World*. Two useful collections of articles on environmental philosophy are D. Scherer and T. Atting (eds), *Ethics and the environment* and R. Elliot and A. Gare (eds), *Environmental Philosophy*. See also J. Passmore, *Man's Responsibility for Nature* and R. Attfield, *The Ethics of Environmental Concern*, 2nd edn.

On the subject of human relations to animals, see P. Singer, ed., *Animal Liberation*, T. Regan, *The Case for Animal Rights* and S. Clark, *The Moral Status of Animals*.

The theory of the just war is treated in M. Walzer, *Just and Unjust Wars* and in D. Lackey, *The Ethics of War and Peace*. On the specific issue of deterrence see S. Benn: 'Deterrence or appeasement? or, On Trying to be Rational About Nuclear War'.

CLASSICAL SOURCES

Plato, *The Republic*

Aristotle, *Ethics*; *Politics*

Grotius, *De jure belli ac pacis* (On the Law of War and Peace)
Hobbes, *Leviathan*
Hume, *Treatise of Human Nature*, Book III; *Enquiry concerning the Principles of Morals*
J. S. Mill, *On Liberty*
Adam Smith, *The Theory of Moral Sentiments*

5

Thinking about Reasoning

Can we isolate reason, and is it, so regarded, an independent source of concepts and judgements which spring from it alone?
I. Kant, *Critique of Pure Reason*, A305 B362

My existence as a thinking, deciding agent, then, and my ability to play a role as a moral or political influence or force, depend upon the accuracy of my beliefs. It is a commonplace that I cannot believe everything that I hear or that I read in the press, nor even that I apparently see on television. Most of what I see or hear in this way is illusion – I *pay* for fiction and make-believe. Can I trust those who tell me: this which you are seeing now is true? Or: what I am giving you now are the facts?

For political decisions such as those I have just been considering, I depend particularly on politicians and political activists for my information. But here I *know* that distortion, exaggeration, the emphasis on what it is in a person's interest to emphasise are the very stuff and form of politics. To confirm the facts in either of these cases may be more than I can attempt, given that I am simply a person, tied to a particular location at a particular time. Also, whatever the 'facts' are, there are, in a sense, too many of them, so that the selection of facts can itself mislead. But *some* claims that I hear I am able to judge without practical observation: these are the ones that involve the sort of sleight of hand mentioned by Berlin. Some of these I can already recognize

from experience. Words are sometimes used with double or shifting meanings, with equivocation on one side, and misunderstanding on the other. There is question-begging assertion, where what
is to be proved is assumed even before the argument begins.
There are hasty generalizations, false analogies, slanted arguments.
Essential aspects of an issue are neglected, cases advanced with
insufficient argument. The irrelevant, the inconsistent and indeed
the contradictory may all feature. In general, these may all result
in arguments which do not lead to the conclusion being asserted
or which end in contradictory claims. So can I find some general
principles to chart a course through these hazards? Are there rules
for clear thinking and right reasoning? Are there ways of avoiding
error, of recognising distortion or deliberate falsification?

I know, of course, that this has been a preoccupation of
philosophy from its beginning, and so I turn first of all to those
beginnings, where I find that the map of reasoning has already
been sketched out by others.

First Thoughts about Reasoning

From the time when the philosopher Heracleitus (who flourished
around 504/500 BC) said 'You cannot step twice into the same
river; for fresh waters are ever flowing in upon you', Greek
philosophers were impressed with the idea that hard knowledge is
possible only when the mind encounters something unchanging
and not subject to flux, to coming into existence and passing
out of existence. This effectively rules out the world the eye and
ear encounter, since this is characterized by its impermanence and
kaleidoscopic change. What remain, though, are certain formal
structures to be considered as possible objects of knowledge.
In particular, the worlds of numbers, of geometrical shapes and
theorems, and of logical relationships seem to have a constancy
and reliability which make it possible to build up a firm body
of knowledge where these are concerned. If there is truth to
be arrived at in these matters, then it is, in a sense, unchanging

truth. By contrast, if there is truth to be grasped in matters of fact – that a particular tree is in leaf, for example – this is a fleeting and ephemeral truth: it was not true previously, and there will certainly be another later time when it is not true. So whether my claim is true or not depends on where and when I make that claim.

But there seem to be other truths – those of geometry, for example – which are not restricted in this way. They seem to have an in-built formal or structural guarantee. These truths are necessary, where truths about matters of fact are merely contingent. Hence the appeal of form. (And I know that Plato envisaged, whether metaphorically or otherwise, a world of timeless Forms – pure, abstract concepts and relationships like, for example, beauty or equality – known independently of ordinary human experience – independently, that is, of what can be observed by the senses.[1]) So, setting aside what might be established by observation, the Greeks gave priority to what might be called *structural* truth and falsity. And certain striking and paradoxical cases of falsity seemed to provide a particularly fascinating starting-point. If following out the consequences of a statement could lead to contradictory conclusions, this was taken as showing that something must be wrong with it as a claim, although *what* was wrong was not necessarily equally clear. This illustrates the general point that it may be easier to see that something is wrong than to provide a satisfactory intellectual explanation as to why it is.

A good example of this is provided by what is probably the first known 'paradox.' The Cretan Epimenides was said to have uttered the statement:

'All Cretans are liars'

Now if what he said was true, given that he was a Cretan, it follows that he was lying. If he wasn't, then, of course, he was demonstrating the falsity of his own assertion by showing that Cretans could, after all, be truthful. In other words, when

Epimenides said 'All Cretans are liars', this statement was, if true, false; if false, true.

The paradox does not depend, though, on being uttered by a Cretan of ancient times. The same puzzle arises from considering, for instance:

'The sentence you are reading now is false.'

or simply:

'I am lying.'

Probably the most famous paradoxes of ancient times, though, were those devised by Zeno of Elea (born *c.* 490 BC) – paradoxes designed to shake people's complacency about their understanding of space, time, movement and mathematics. The best known of these is the paradox of Achilles and the tortoise. It consists in arguing:

In a race between the fastest runner, Achilles, and a tortoise, if the tortoise is given a start on Achilles, Achilles will never catch it up. This is because, before he can get to the place where the tortoise is, Achilles must first get to the place where the tortoise *was*. But by the time he gets *there*, the tortoise will have moved on at least a little. There is no (logical) end to this stipulation (even though in practice it doesn't seem to affect the outcome!) So Achilles can never catch the tortoise.[2]

This paradox, unlike that of Epimenides, does not produce two contradictory conclusions, but instead just one conclusion which contradicts experience; in other words, it does not square with what actually happens. But what the two cases have in common is that a perfectly convincing-looking argument leads to an unacceptable conclusion.

Trying to see what is objectionable about such paradoxes suggests that I assume, perhaps unconsciously, certain very basic rules of thought. If I am obliged to draw as conclusions both 'I am lying' and also 'I am not lying' I am in effect being forced to assert both A and not-A – to break, that is, the law of non-contradiction. And the implication that both may be true violates another similar law: the law of the excluded middle, which says: Either A or not-A. Attempting to entertain such contradictory ideas jars in a way which is immediately or intuitively repugnant.

I know that Greek thinkers looked for principles for drawing conclusions that would avoid both paradoxes and error, and that the ways in which they tried to formalize the structure of argument lasted largely unchallenged through mediaeval times right up to the late nineteenth century and the beginning of the twentieth. Reflecting on this, I ask myself whether I should not try to find out about contemporary moves in these fields of logic and reasoning, and so I turn once again to my informant.

Eleventh Letter from Sophia

Dear Q,

I received your letter about logic, but I am afraid I am not able to help in any detailed way, since you are asking about an enterprise of enormous proportions. But I can tell you a little about the way the subject has been approached of late, and it will be for you to pursue in other ways to the limits of your own interests and capacities.

So let me begin by saying that arguments are not always clearly presented. They may be embedded in complex verbiage; made inconspicuous by irrelevant additions: obscured by redundant considerations; distorted by rhetorical flourishes; tied confusingly to other arguments; stretched, compressed, hinted at, or lost in unnecessary detail. Premises may be suppressed; conclusions left unstated. Logic attempts to bring some kind of order into this jungle of possibilities by isolating the skeleton or bones of arguments. If you can acquire the habit of looking for this underlying structure, then perhaps you will be less susceptible to these various forms of either deliberate or unconscious obfuscation.

Typically, then, in an argument, evidence, reason or grounds in the form of PREMISSES *are presented as leading to a* CONCLUSION. *So the structure of every argument can be represented like this:*

premiss(es)

Therefore: conclusion

In practice, people may invert this order, or even not bother to mention every part of their argument explicitly. The essential point, though, is that inference does consist in drawing conclusions from premisses.

You will have noticed that arguments are sometimes described as sound, sometimes as correct, sometimes as valid and that these terms are often used interchangeably in ordinary conversation. In the context of formal logic, though, it is necessary to be more precise. You may say of some arguments, for example, that they establish the truth of their conclusions. But it is possible to look at the formal structure or shape of an argument quite apart from the question of truth or falsity. What purely formal rules can supply is standards of logical correctness or validity. A correct or valid argument justifies its conclusion, but to know whether it establishes it or not, it would be necessary to know independently that the premisses are actually true.

For example, the conclusion 'white elephants fly' follows from 'all elephants fly'. That is, the argument is formally correct or valid. But, of course, the starting-point is false. So it would be a mistake to assume that the conclusion has been proved, or established as true. Assessing the truth of the premiss of an argument is a different kind of undertaking, then, from deciding whether the inference — from premiss to conclusion — is correct. To check whether all elephants fly, it would be necessary to begin some factual investigations. But the inference is perfectly sound, and to check that, it is necessary to know something about correct and incorrect ways of arguing. The problem with the arguments of Epimenides and Zeno *that you mentioned is that they look perfectly correct; it is hard to see what, if anything, is wrong with the premisses, and yet the conclusions, in both cases, suggest that they cannot be sound.*

The contribution of logic is to suggest that there might – tricky cases like these apart – be patterns of argument which are always sound. That is to say, in these cases, if the premisses are true, then necessarily the conclusion is true as well. And equally reliably, an argument from true premisses to a false conclusion must be un-sound. At the same time, there are other patterns of argument where, even if the premisses are true, this does not guarantee the truth of the conclusion. Establishing the truth of the premisses, though, is in either case a completely different kind of enterprise. The Stoic logicians provided a compelling metaphor of the different degrees of assent one might give to the kind of factual assertion that often features as the premiss of an argument. Their comparison was with a more or less tightly-clenched hand or fist. Simply imagining something – like a flying elephant – would be like the hand spread out. But there is a spectrum of degrees of assent from there, through belief and understanding to the clear or firm knowledge that would be metaphorically represented by the firm grasp of hand surrounding fist. In the end the Stoics came to think that we might aspire only to probability on matters of fact, but the essential claim that they made was that, as far as reasoning was concerned, there were some argument 'shapes' that did give certainty.

Two main kinds of argument-forms were identified in classical times: those which take the form of syllogisms and were extensively categorized by Aristotle;[3] and those which centre on the 'if . . . then' relationship, and which were systematised by the Stoics.[4]

Aristotelian logic operates on statements which are, in a gram-matical sense, of subject-predicate form: in particular Aristotle ex-plored the relations between four kinds of statement: affirmative assertions, such as 'All fat people are greedy' and 'Some diseases are curable', and negative assertions, such as 'No cats are purple' and 'Some dogs are not trainable'. A typical argument constructed from these sorts of building-blocks would be:

All politicians are controversial figures
All controversial figures are the subject of media interest

_____

Therefore: *All politicians are the subject of media interest*

Since an indefinite number of arguments have the same form, irrespective even of what language they are expressed in, being able to pick out the form provides a means of checking their validity. And not all arguments of this type – called a syllogism – are valid. For example, it is not correct to reason:

No royal persons are controversial figures
Some controversial figures are seen on television

_____

Therefore: *no royal persons are seen on television.*

Why is this wrong? Well, even if we accept that some controversial figures are seen on television, this is perfectly consistent with some other people – who could, after all, be royals – appearing on television as well. In other words, none of our assumptions preclude royals appearing on television, as, of course, they do!

There are many possible varieties of arguments like these, and many possible categorical syllogisms, some valid, some invalid. But certain problems were implicit even within the structure of valid syllogisms. For example, in Aristotelian logic, it was assumed that the subject of an 'All A's are B's' statement did exist. But it is sometimes necessary to make statements of this form – which can be true statements – without assuming existence. That is so in the case of the First Law of Motion – a perfectly useful and true statement that does not involve an assumption of existence: 'All objects free from impressed forces persevere in a state of rest or in uniform motion in a straight line.'

To retain the possibility of making uncommitted statements like this, modern logic has abandoned the assumption that, if 'All A's are B's', then there do exist some A's which are B's. So, for example, 'All dogs are carnivorous' is to be understood as:

'For any x, if that x is a dog, then that x is carnivorous.'

For the inference to 'Some dogs are carnivorous' to follow, it would be necessary to add explicitly, as an extra premiss, that 'Dogs exist'. But this produces a gap between logic and ordinary language – a consequence which many modern logicians have preferred to accept. Ordinary language is in fact closer to classical than modern logic in its implications, for in ordinary language, if someone says 'All my investments are prospering', it would seem odd to discover that he or she has no investments. On the other hand 'All truly good people are free from envy' does not carry the message that there are any such people, so there clearly are ordinary language uses corresponding to the interpretation of 'All' in modern logic, even if these are comparatively rare.

This will give you some idea of the state of the subject in the early part of the twentieth century. It will be best if I write to you again about more recent developments.

Yours,
Sophia

I had scarcely had time to reflect on Sophia's account of traditional logic when her next letter arrived.

Twelfth Letter from Sophia

• Dear Q,
I said that I would write to you about modern logic. This is usually taken as beginning with the work of the mathematician and logician Gottlob Frege (1848–1925) and it was further developed by Bertrand Russell (1872–1970) There is a developed system of predicate logic which introduces the clarity and power of symbols into some of the areas I mentioned in my previous letter. However, unlike Aristotle, who was concerned with structure within sentences, modern logicians, like the ancient Stoics, have given a good

deal of time and attention to reasoning which takes whole sentences or propositions as the units for its operations.

This has been done by developing the notion of a logical system. I can best explain this by giving you an outline of a simple one. Its components are:

1. *Letters used to represent simple, affirmative sentences: usually p, q, r, s, etc., but sometimes p, p', p'', p''', etc. (If one thinks of programming a computer to do logic, or if, for more complex logical reasoning, an infinite stock of letters is required, then the advantage of the latter system is apparent. But the human mind is probably better able to cope with the former.)*

2. *Brackets to act as the punctuation-marks of complex sentences by indicating the scope of a sign. For example, 'p or q and r' is ambiguous: but brackets can differentiate '(p or q) and r' from 'p or (q and r)'. This is parallel to the way that in algebra '3 + 5 × 2' is ambiguous, but can be made unambiguous by brackets indicating either '(3 + 5) × 2' or '3 + (5 × 2)'.*

3. *Symbols for logical constants: these are terms which provide the structure or form of an argument. The constants which are used vary in different systems; since some can be reduced to others, it is in fact possible to work with only two, for example negation and disjunction. There are, then, different conventions. But a commonly used set of constants would be: 'and' (conjunction), 'or' (disjunction), 'not' (negation), 'if . . . then' (the conditional) and 'if and only if' (the bi-conditional), sometimes written 'iff'. To signify these, special symbols are used. One in common use represents these logical constants as: respectively:*

conjunction	•
disjunction	∨
negation	~
conditional	⊃
bi-conditional	≡

Although these correspond quite closely to the relationships indicated by the English language expressions used to explain them, the main reason for introducing them is that they can be made more specific and less ambiguous than ordinary language. There are, though, some important differences. The two most striking divergences are these:

(i) *'or', as indicated by the sign 'v' in 'p v q' is not exclusive: it is true if both alternatives are true, as well as if only one of them is. So in this notation 'Either he is innocent or he is a very good actor' does not mean, as it probably would in ordinary conversation, that he must be one or the other – he could be both.*

and (ii) *the conditional expressed by the hook '⊃' has an entirely distinctive meaning: this is that 'p⊃q' is false only when 'p' is true and 'q' false. In ordinary life 'If you sue me then I will become bankrupt' may be taken to imply a causal relationship, or at least some kind of dependence between the two parts of the compound sentence. But this is not the case where the conditional expressed by the hook is concerned. The causal aspect is omitted, leaving only the bare logical relationship.*

This kind of conditional is not, though, an invention of modern logic. In fact, it was first recognized by the Stoic logicians, whose interests centred on the different ways that 'if . . . then' can be used to form valid and invalid arguments. A classic example of this is the argument known as Modus Ponens. *For example:*

If he has sued her, she is bankrupt
He has sued her.

So she is bankrupt.

In the symbolism of modern logic, this becomes:

$$p \supset q$$
$$p$$
∴ q

The form displayed by these symbols is a valid form. That is, every argument which takes this form is valid. So this is a valid argument.

By contrast, if someone else where to reason:

> If he has sued her, then she is bankrupt
> She is bankrupt
> _____
>
> So he has sued her.

then the reasoning can be symbolically presented as

$$p \supset q$$
$$q$$
∴ p

and this is an invalid form. The argument is indeed invalid as one might see by reflecting that there are many other ways to become bankrupt. The appeal to this invalid form is a common error of reasoning – that is, a fallacy. Indeed, it is so common that it has a name. It is known as the Fallacy of Affirming the Consequent. (In an 'if . . . then' statement, the statement following 'if' is known as the antecedent; the statement following 'then' is known as the consequent.) This invalid statement is not to be confused with another valid form of argument called Modus Tollens:

> If he has sued her, she is bankrupt
> She is not bankrupt
> _____
>
> So he has not sued her

or

$$p \supset q$$
$$\sim q$$

∴ $\sim p$

There are, of course, many other valid forms of argument, and many other invalid ones. The conditional that is involved is recognizable as corresponding to some extent to the way in which 'If. . . then' is used in ordinary language. All the same, it is accepted as having two consequences which are so surprising, and so divorced from ordinary language, that they have been described as 'paradoxes' of material implication.

What these 'paradoxes' amount to is that, because of the meaning given to the sign '⊃', a false statement implies any statement whatsoever. Also, any true statement is implied by any statement whatsoever. This is because the only way in which 'p⊃q' can be falsified is by finding a situation in which 'p' is true and 'q' false. This can never happen (a) if 'p' is false, nor (b) if 'q' is true. Hence the so-called 'paradoxes'.

This results in other mismatches between logic and ordinary reasoning. For example, if in the above example 'p' is a contradiction or an absurdity, then it cannot be true. Therefore, anything at all follows from a contradiction or an absurdity, whereas in ordinary reasoning we are tempted to say that nothing follows from a contradiction or absurdity.

If some of these relationships appear surprising, they can be checked by a useful mechanical method, which consists in setting out truth tables which make it possible to read off the implications of various assumptions. The simplest truth table, with T standing for 'true' and F for 'false', could be set out like this:

$$p$$

T

F

Whatever 'p' and '~p' stand for they cannot both be true. So two possible combinations of a proposition and its denial can be set out in a truth table:

	p	$\sim p$
1.	T	F
2.	F	T

The complex assertion 'p.q' generates a more complicated truth table:

p	q	$p.q$
T	T	T
T	F	F
F	T	F
F	F	F

(This truth table is built up by first filling in the possibilities under p and under q, and then filling in the final column.)

The conditional can be expressed most clearly with a truth table:

p	q	$p \supset q$
T	T	T
T	F	F
F	T	T
F	F	T

Obviously, the more complicated arguments become, the longer and more complicated become the truth tables.

The paradoxes of material implication and the system of Truth Tables taken together display both the defects and the merits of logical systems. On the merit side, the advantages of formal systems consist in the fact that they do provide mechanical means, such as

Truth Tables, of testing for truth. The letters 'p', 'q', 'r', etc. are used as place-markers or tokens which can stand in for many different sentences, and the truth of a complex sentence is entirely a matter of the truth and falsity of its component sentences. This characteristic, known as truth-functionality, is a central advantage of formalizing arguments.

But there are also disadvantages, and these raise such new considerations that I shall write to you again about them when you have had time to reflect on these matters.

Yours,
Sophia

It was not long, however, before I received the promised letter.

Thirteenth Letter from Sophia

• *Dear Q,*
As I said in my last letter to you, a logical language is more precise and more rigorous than a natural language. But this advantage brings some corresponding disadvantages. In particular, the gap between logic and ordinary language presents a problem.

Certain kinds of assertions, for instance, do not fit into the pattern just described. These are, in particular, assertions about psychological states such as beliefs, desires or wishes. The use of verbs like 'believe' or 'want' (called 'modal' by some logicians) is a sign of contexts which are called 'intensional'. The terms 'intensional' and its opposite 'extensional' refer to the possibility of substitution without change of truth: for example, if Humphrey Bogart is the film star who played opposite Bergman in Casablanca, *then it seems I ought to be able to substitute the description 'the film star who played opposite Bergman in* Casablanca' *in any statement containing Humphrey Bogart as a term, without changing the truth or falsity of the statement. I can do this, for example, in the brief statement: 'If Humphrey Bogart*

*was a successful actor he must have been rich.' 'Humphrey Bogart',
then, is used extensionally in this context.*

*But there are contexts in which this kind of substitution will not
work. For example, supposing someone truthfully says: 'I believe
that Humphrey Bogart never played opposite Bergman.' Now the
fact is that Humphrey Bogart did play opposite Bergman in
Casablanca. But I certainly could not substitute for 'Humphrey
Bogart' the phrase 'the actor who played opposite Bergman in
Casablanca', since this would turn my statement into:*

> *'I believe that the actor who played opposite Bergman in
> Casablanca never played opposite Bergman.'*

*— something I definitely do not believe. Or supposing someone
says:*

> *'I wish that I had met Bogart.'*

*Again, if the speaker believes Bogart never played opposite
Bergman it would not be correct to assume he was asserting:*

> *'I wish that I had met the actor who played opposite
> Bergman in Casablanca.'*

*It seems then that a different type of logic is needed for evaluating
reasoning in intensional contexts like this. Something else is
needed, too, to account for certain other important non-truth-
functional contexts — those that involve reference to necessity and
possibility. For to say that the truth of a sentence is necessary or
possible is not the same as to say that it is true or false*

*Modal logic deals specifically with the problem of talking about
necessity and possibility. In addition, intuitionist and relevant logics
have been devised, which are based on abandoning those consequences of traditional propositional or predicate logic which do not
fit with the reasoning people intuitively take to be sound, or which
are irrelevant to the kind of arguments they sometimes wish to
conduct in the more flexible style of ordinary life. (So, for example,*

these logics may abandon the tenet that anything follows from a contradiction.) The intention is to preserve the rigour of a logical system without offending against the logical intuitions most people would claim.

It is true that all valid forms of argument prevent a move from the true to the false. They keep the careful reasoner on the path of truth, once that path has been entered. But some of these valid arguments suffer from irrelevance, redundancy, or circularity. So there is some reason for thinking we should be more selective in our acceptance of 'valid' argument forms. So-called 'relevant logics' attempt to do just that.

A central problem concerns 'If . . . then'. How is it possible to draw significant conclusions from unfulfilled conditionals? For example, people are prepared to debate seriously the rival claims of:

1. *'If Thatcher were Prime Minister now, Britain and America would have closer ties.'*

and

2. *'If Thatcher were Prime Minister now, Britain and America would be further apart.'*

Propositional logic, however, cannot take account of this kind of contrast. One recent method proposed for dealing with the troublesome conditionals without creating a logic of modality is to turn them, too, into the more tractable and amenable categoricals. This is achieved by the introduction of a language of possible worlds.

This is not entirely a new notion. The philosopher Gottfried Leibniz (1646–1716) envisaged an infinity of possible worlds conceived as ideas in God's mind, and he suggested that something was necessarily true if it was true in all possible worlds. He claimed that the actual world we live in is selected by God from the infinity of possibilities. Leibniz's interest in proposing this theory was primarily logical and metaphysical, but it was interpreted by the French writer Voltaire (1694–1778) as expressing a naïve religiously-based optimism. Voltaire's novel, Candide, *is a saga of human woes and misfortunes which features a philosopher, Dr*

Pangloss, whose doctrine consists simply in the belief that this is the best of all possible worlds – a belief which Voltaire cynically, but convincingly, throws into question.[5]

The idea of things or items which are not actual has been employed more recently by Alexius Meinong (1853–1920) who believed it necessary to accept that true and false statements could be made about items – for example, round squares or golden mountains – which do not exist. Otherwise, he argued, there is a problem in explaining what we talk about when we refer to non-existent entities. Even if we say 'golden mountains do not exist' or 'round squares cannot even be imagined' it seems that there must be something, in some sense, to which we refer, even if only to go on and deny its existence or its imaginability. So, it could be said, in some quite literal sense there really are these possibilities; and even, there really are these impossibilities.[6]

The contemporary debate is again conducted in terms of possible worlds: this time possible worlds are the names of states of affairs – possibilities or structures which might obtain; while actual worlds are realised states of affairs – actualised possibilities or structures which the world does contain. Thus possibility and necessity are represented like this:

> Something is necessarily true if it is true in all possible worlds.

> Something is possibly true if it is true in a possible world.

> Something is necessarily not true if there is no possible world in which it is true.

> Something is possibly not true if there is a possible world in which it is not true.

The contemporary American philosopher David Lewis (b. 1941), who is an exponent of a theory of possible worlds, believes that what makes this world the actual one is simply that this is the world we are in. In his view there are infinitely many *other worlds with other people in them which are actual for those people. Lewis's position is known as modal realism.[7] It is a position which seems a long way from common sense, but if it were to be rejected for this reason alone, then it would be equally necessary to reject most of modern physics for the same reason.*

The advantage of this type of theory is that it explains statements like 'Possibly there is a primeval creature in Loch Ness' or 'Possibly there is life on Venus', turning them into the kind of statements that can be handled by logic. It has the further advantage that it makes it possible to reason about unfulfilled conditionals. Take, for instance, 'If there were a world government, the people of the world would live in peace.' Conventional ways of dealing with the notion of possibility reduce it to consistency, but a great many assertions are consistent (i.e. not logically contradictory) which are nevertheless impossible. For example, there is no inconsistency in supposing that David Lewis might have known Leibniz and discussed the matter of possible worlds with him; but it is nevertheless impossible!

I will have to leave you to think about these things and to pursue the study of formal logic, if it appeals to you, in other ways and with other teachers. Meanwhile, there is one other important area of reasoning that I must write to you about if we are to complete our enquiries into these matters.

Yours,
Sophia

Sophia was as good as her word, and soon afterwards I received this final letter from her on the subject of reasoning.

Fourteenth Letter from Sophia

Dear Q,
As I indicated in my last letter, logic may be able, in one way or another, to handle reasoning concerned with the merely possible. And so it may also be able to deal with 'if . . . then'

sentences in which some stronger relation is asserted between p and q. Clearly, something more than a purely formal relationship is needed for science, which deals in probabilities, rather than in the straight deduction which is the hallmark of logical systems.

Another type of argument seems to be involved here, although its formal structure may look fairly similar. In ordinary life, it is much more common to find arguments such as the one implied in the following conversation:

> First speaker: *Matt is a farmer, so I expect he is a conservative.*
>
> Second speaker: *Why do you suppose that?*
>
> First speaker: *Because most farmers are conservatives – 90 per cent according to the latest opinion poll.*

Formally set out, this argument might be presented like this:

> *90 per cent of farmers are conservatives*
> *Matt is a farmer*
> _____
>
> *Therefore: probably Matt is a conservative.*

In spite of the similarity of form, arguments like these do differ from the deductive ones so far considered in important ways. In particular, if I argue:

> *All logicians are pedantic*
> *Susan is a logician*
> _____
>
> *Therefore: Susan is pedantic.*

My conclusion will not be in any way undermined if I add to my premisses. For example:

All logicians are pedantic
Susan is a logician and she is a mother.

In a deductive argument 'Susan is pedantic' does follow. But if I add to the premises in the present case, the result can be strikingly affected. For example:

Ninety per cent of farmers are conservatives.
Matt is a farmer and he is founder of the Farmers'
Revolutionary Front.

In this case, 'Probably Matt is a conservative' does not follow. It is highly unlikely that he is!

These pitfalls are more evident in the case of the inferences of Agatha Christie's sleuths, Poirot or Miss Marple; or in the assumptions behind opinion polls which take a limited sample of people and then go on to make predictions about who will win the next election.

Agatha Christie's sleuths are often engaged in reasoning within the compass of psychology – their deductions concern the motivation and actions of individual people. The opinion pollsters are concerned with the social sciences in a more general way – sociology, demography, social psychology all play a part here. But since people are more complex than things, and, what is more, the investigators are themselves part of what is being investigated, it may be easier to see what is involved in these kinds of reasoning by analogy with what goes on in the 'harder' areas of the physical sciences.

Scientific method has, in the past, been seen as a part of the science of logic. But in order to make it fit the pattern of logical – that is to say, deductive reasoning – it is necessary to add an extra premiss to the type of argument which seems to typify scientific reasoning. It seems that a premiss of a universal nature is needed to unite particular observations. For example, it is possible to infer that your own particular cat is a nocturnal creature if you know that all cats are nocturnal.

On the whole, it is tempting to think that science works by discovering such general laws – not always quite as obvious as that *one, of course! – and it can hardly be denied that the assumption that there are such laws has been fruitful. But these laws unfortunately have to assume what they set out to prove – i.e. the reference to 'all cats' is already a reference to your cat, so either the particular or the universal claim is a reference to what must be strictly unknowable. The British philosopher David Hume (1711–1776) put the problem in this way: 'It is impossible to guarantee, that an unknown instance of the property A will also exhibit the property B, if A and B are different properties.'[8]*

Kant resisted the scepticism implied by Hume, arguing that the truth of causal laws has to be taken as a presupposition of human thought.[9] And it does seem to be necessary to make some assumptions about the future which a) are not necessarily true and b) can in any case be no better than claims. Science itself does not suppose that the world will continue forever as it is now, and yet it seems that the assumption involved in scientific reasoning – called induction – is precisely this: that the future will resemble the past.

Bertrand Russell once suggested that this assumption is rather like that of a chicken in the farmyard, which has come to expect to have a handful of corn thrown to it each morning, is continually reinforced in this belief, but ultimately finds that one morning the farmer has come out to wring its neck.[10]

Nevertheless, science has shown itself of considerably more use to human beings than the chicken's hypothesis is to the chicken. This is why the term 'scientific' functions as a prestige-word when applied to reasoning. Science is the name given to any enquiry which takes as its object describing, explaining and predicting occurrences in the natural world. It is distinguished from unscientific attempts to do these things by the fact that it looks for warranted, or justified claims on which to base its conclusions. In particular, for an enquiry to be scientific it is necessary that it accept, as a standard, testing by empirical means. (An empirical test is a test carried out in terms of observation by the senses.) The form that scientific enquiry takes, then, is this:

*Problem → hypothesis → drawing conclusions from the
hypothesis → testing the conclusions against experience
→ interpreting the results.*

In the past, the final stage of a sequence like this would be
described as confirmation or refutation. It was thought, that is, that
scientific theories could be rigorously derived from experience, by
observation and experiment – a view popular since Sir Francis
Bacon (1561–1626), Galileo (1564–1642) and Sir Isaac
Newton (1642–1727) replaced the view, prevalent from Aristotle
to medieval times, that it was possible to sit down and work out
from first principles how things – like the movement of the planets
– ought to be, with the more fruitful idea of seeking by observation
to determine how things are. This is, of course, the method of
experiment. But unless it is possible to solve the problem of
induction by showing how the assumption that the future will
resemble the past is justified, it seems that confirmation is out of the
question.
    Some people, though, would say that confirmation is not necess-
ary. It may be equally useful for practical purposes to be able to
show conclusively that some hypotheses are wrong, even if it is
impossible to show that any are right. This solution to the problem
of induction has been proposed by Karl Popper (b. 1902). According
to Popper, human knowledge is a matter of conjectures and refutations rather than of established certainty, and scientific 'laws'
survive, rather like species in Darwin's theory of evolution, only
until they have been effectively refuted by some inconsistent
finding.[11]
    As far as probabilities are concerned, though, Popper's view is
firmer and more 'objectivist' than that of subsequent critics. The
probability of a dice falling in a particular way, for instance, is on
his view, a matter of an objective propensity of the dice. Others,
however, have insisted on interpreting the probability of a dice
falling in a certain way subjectively: that is, as a matter of our
willingness to bet on it falling that way. This kind of computation

has been developed to a high degree of mathematical sophistication, with analogies from games and gambling, but its effect is to make of science a closed rather than an open system. Pursuing the gambling analogy, in a race there are a finite number of horses. But science, as it is usually conceived, is open to considering indefinitely many different hypotheses.

But if Popper seems to have challenged the credentials of science as something resting on a firm inferential base – if he has shown that there cannot be such a thing as inductive logic – he still believes in a logic of inquiry. That is to say, he does not want to explain away the procedures of scientific inference by explaining scientific discovery in terms of the psychology of scientists, nor does he suggest that our ways of construing the world change by some inevitable historical process.

Subsequent reflection on the philosophy of science has been less optimistic and more relativistic in its approach. You will probably accept that it may be a mistake to think that any method exists by which scientific theories can be 'proved true'; perhaps you will doubt whether they can even be conclusively proved false. But all the same, it seems there is a concept of scientific method which serves to separate science from pseudo-science. Some theories are more deserving of attention than others. Few scientists would take seriously, for example, astrology, numerology or flat earth-ism. But all the same, some distinctly unscientific beliefs, no better grounded than these, can be very fiercely held – as are these, of course, by their supporters. It is not so unusual to find people rejecting Darwin's theory of evolution in spite of fossil and geological evidence because they want, for other reasons, to believe that the earth, together with human and animal life, was created in 4004 BC. These pseudo-scientists are no doubt best recognized by the fact that they refuse to accept the burden of proof.

Even if you dismiss these, though, along with the occult and the obscurantist, you may still wonder how to justify the day-to-day scientific and practical assumptions of ordinary life. Rather than concede that any belief or claim is as good as any other, you might prefer to scale down your claim and simply say that confirmation is increased, the more instances you are able to gather of some belief of yours being true. For example, the claim at issue might be about the tendency of metals to expand when heated. It seems plausible to argue that the more instances you can assemble, the greater the probability *of the universal claim. The problem is, though, that no matter how many observations you make, they are going to be finite in number, while the claim that is made by a scientific generalisation like 'All metals expand when heated' is potentially infinite in scope.*

This could be called the problem of the necessarily inadequate number of cases . . . But if you take another example, it might seem that scientific probability is not a matter of piling up instances at all. To test

'Acid turns litmus paper red'

it would be normal to experiment on only a limited number of occasions – the later ones only for demonstration purposes, or as a check, perhaps, that nothing went wrong the first time. The import-ant thing is the background of theory to the experiment. Or, as Hume remarked, a single experience of being burned by fire is normally sufficient to convince someone that fire burns.

Should the attempt at justification be abandoned, then, in the face of these difficulties? Could it, perhaps, be the case that science is not a rational activity at all? Philosophers of science, like Paul Feyerabend (b. 1924) are prepared to make this claim. According to Feyerabend, science, although it seems to have become our modern religion, has no better claim on our support than Voodoo.[12] *What-ever method is proposed in scientific enquiry, Feyerabend argues, there will always be circumstances in which that method is not the best one to follow. In other words, it will be necessary to violate any rule at some time in order to make scientific progress.*

A reply which avoids this degree of scepticism, whilst at the same time challenging many naive assumptions, is offered by Thomas Kuhn, in The Structure of Scientific Revolutions. *The central idea here is that of* paradigms *– theories accepted as 'normal* *science' at any one time.*[13] *In this book, Kuhn argues that the history of science is not a mere cumulative account of scientific knowledge, wrong theories being mere myths; on the contrary, wrong theories were as valid for their practitioners at the time as contemporary scientific theories are for us. Scientific revolutions are, Kuhn argues, the displacement of one perspective or paradigm by a new one. The 'discoveries' of science are simply fruitful research programmes.*

Theories which displace others to become the new paradigms are defined by two characteristics:

1. *They must be revolutionary enough to attract an enduring group away from received views; and*
2. *They must be open-ended enough to leave problems for the new group to resolve.*

Scientific work, then, within such a paradigm, consists of: (a) determining which facts are significant, (b) matching facts with theory, or (c) articulating and defining the theory. Paradigms are supplanted by new ones on the discovery of anomalies – instances where the facts fail to fit the theory. But a single falsification, of the kind emphasised by Popper, is not, Kuhn points out, sufficient to cause scientists to reject an existing paradigm – they reject it only when a new paradigm exists with which to compare both it and nature. Falsification on its own would discredit the scientist and not the theory.

Paradigm change within the sciences, according to Kuhn, is a process like political revolution: it occurs through a challenge from outside the accepted framework, and ultimately depends on either persuasion or force. The determining factor is simply the assent of the relevant community.

Instead of the traditional view in which sensory experience is conceived of as fixed and neutral, while theories are seen as man-made interpretations of given data – Kuhn suggests that what are called 'data' are in fact specially selected for attention because they fit in with the accepted paradigm.

Popper's shift to the notion of falsification rather than verification is seen by Kuhn as essentially within the traditional empiricist conception of science. For falsification of one theory is only confirmation of a competing one, and the fact is that science is selective in the data of which it takes account, whether there are confirming or falsifying instances. Paradigm-shift is something much more radical; it alters the parameters within which the problem is viewed.

You can probably accept, then that even defining the problem is a matter of creative innovation where the goal of achieving scientific knowledge is concerned. Steam had pushed the lids off pots for many years before James Watt recognized it as an interesting phenomenon and went on to see steam as a source of power. Formulating a hypothesis, then, is itself dependent on context and on a certain kind of background knowledge.

Your answer, then, to the question about reasoning that initially prompted my observations, must vary according to the type of reasoning that is in question. In particular, reasoning in practical affairs and in science employs different methods and standards from those involved in abstract or logical reasoning.

To see what this distinction amounts to, ask yourself: which of my beliefs would – or should – I continue holding even without any further justification? At first, having adopted a policy of taking everything as open to question, you may be inclined to answer, with some indignation, 'But none, of course.' However, as I have, I hope, persuaded you, some structures of reasoning do impose their own constraints. You do not, of course, have to be rational, but it is a condition of your rationality that you respect that distinctive phenomenon, logical truth. You may assert contradictions, and hear others assert them. But then you will have deserted the commitments with which you commenced your enquiry. So the answer 'None' will not do. But, then, neither, as I hope you have come to see, will the unqualified answer 'Only beliefs which are directly based on observation.'

The question, though, is how widely logical truth can be construed, and whether, in fact, there is substantial truth to be found beyond the limits of sense-observation. Philosophers within the empiricist tradition have guarded the borderline between logical and empirical truth jealously, and have taken a frugal view of the applications of logical truth.

For empiricists, logical truth must either be explained as essentially empty – tautologous – or else, as J. S. Mill suggested, as a kind of empirical generalisation.[14] In general terms, empiricism is the view that the senses are the only source of substantive human knowledge. It is the theory represented in particular by the British empiricist philosophers John Locke, George Berkeley (1685–1753) and David Hume. More recently, the tradition is represented by philosophers, including particularly the logical positivists, who discuss the issue in terms of meaning and intelligibility, claiming simply, that all bona fide ideas must be derived from experience.

Hume's famous formulation of the principle involved is couched in these terms:

If we take in our hand any volume; of divinity or school metaphysics, for instance; let us ask, Does it contain any abstract reasoning concerning quantity or number? No. Does it contain any experimental reasoning concerning matter of fact and existence? No. Commit it then to the flames; for it can contain nothing but sophistry and illusion.[15]

The task for empiricism is essentially a matter of explaining in terms of experience alone, all the knowledge we appear to have that cannot immediately be seen to derive from the senses: for example, knowledge of the self, of causation, of material objects, time, or other minds. The problem is that empiricism can very easily end up as scepticism (doubt that it is possible to know anything) or solipsism (the doctrine that all I can know about is states of myself). This problem is implicit in the tactic of basing knowledge on experience. For experience is a subjective, private concept, from which it is difficult, if not impossible, to move to an objective world – a world that is public and open to different observers.

As the extract from Descartes' Meditations, which I sent you earlier, showed, the rationalist preference is, by contrast, for pure *reason as the path to knowledge. It is based on the idea that it is possible to arrive at knowledge through pure thought.*

Empiricist ideas in the twentieth century were pressed strongly by the philosophers of the Vienna Circle – a group which formed round the philosopher Moritz Schlick (1882–1936) in Vienna from 1922 on. The group, which was science and logic oriented, was united in its condemnation of metaphysics and its acceptance of the verification principle. This was the principle that, at a minimum, ruled out a statement as meaningless if no empirical observation could conceivably be relevant to determining whether it was true or false. It could loosely be formulated as: 'a statement is meaningful only if there is a way in which it could – at least in principle – be verified or tested.' At the same time analytic statements (including those of logic and mathematics) were interpreted as tautologies, and ethical judgments were analyzed as not being statements at all, but expressions of emotion.

The ideas of the Vienna Circle were made widely known in Britain on the publication by A. J. Ayer of Language Truth and Logic *(1936), while the dispersal of members of the Vienna Circle to America and elsewhere as a result of the rise of Nazi power gave them yet wider circulation and influence.*[16]

These philosophical debates – and in particular the contrast between rationalism and empiricism, provide the backdrop for your present enquiry. But it is the preoccupation with empirical facts that is most relevant to your concerns. Clearly, for the sort of problems from which you started, it is empirical reasoning or judgement that you are most interested in. And it is judgement *in particular that must concern you next, since empirical reasoning, as I have indicated, must take as its premises, empirical judgements.*

Yours,
Sophia

These letters did indeed throw some light on my enquiry. At the outset. I had taken it that there were facts, and that these facts were important to my moral and political stance and to the way

I construed the world. Bad argument, as I have seen, can separate me from the facts, but it seems it cannot establish what those facts are. How, then, am I to arrive at knowledge? If I am to judge what other people tell me, then my picture of what is the case is inevitably going to be mediated by the language that they use. So, to place my judgement in some relation to the facts, I must form some view of the role of this intermediary – language – in interpreting events and describing what is the case.

NOTES

1   For Plato's Theory of Forms, see in particular the dialogues *Phaedo*, *Phaedrus*, *Republic*, and *Meno*. The Greek word for Form is *eidos* (our 'idea'), which, can mean form in the sense of shape or outline. Here it means something more like nature or essence. The Theory of Forms was both a logical theory about universal terms, including mathematical concepts, and also a metaphysical doctrine about the independent and objective existence of important moral qualities.

2   Not everyone would agree that Zeno's arguments *are* sound. They may include, for instance, suppressed premisses which are false. But the debate about Zeno, which continues to be a matter of interest and controversy to logicians and mathematicians, can be explored in a collection of articles by different authors, *Zeno's Paradoxes*, ed. Wesley C. Salmon.

   Such fragments as have survived of the works or sayings of early Greek (pre-Socratic) philosophers such as Heraclitus, Parmenides and Zeno are gathered in G. Kirk and J. Raven, *The Presocratic Philosophers*. See also J. Barnes, *Early Greek Philosophy*. Parmenides resisted Heraclitus' doctrine of flux with a theory that denied the reality of change and motion. It was to defend *his* position that Zeno propounded his paradoxes, designed to show that the assumptions of Parmenides' opponents were just as much in conflict with observable fact as were those of Parmenides himself.

3   Aristotle's logical system was set out in his *Organon*, which comprises the *Categories*, *On Interpretation*, *Prior and Posterior Analytics*, *Topics* and *On Sophistical Refutations*.

4 For an account of Stoic logic, see John M. Rist (ed.), *The Stoics*, ch. 1.

5 Voltaire, *Candide, ou l'optimisme*. Voltaire's satirical talents were displayed in his portrayal of Dr Pangloss, whose ramblings parodied the views of Leibniz. Although he rejected the view that suffering and evil contribute to the good of the whole, Voltaire nevertheless believed it was worth working for the betterment of human conditions. While the famous remark at the end of *Candide*, 'Il faut cultiver notre jardin', could be taken as recommending a retreat from the world, it could also be regarded as recommending a return to the tasks closes to hand.

Leibniz' *Monadology* is included in *Leibniz: Philosophical Writings*, ed. G. H. R. Parkinson.

6 There is considerable disagreement as to what Meinong claimed. There is currently, however, renewed interest in his ideas.

7 It is put forward in D. Lewis, *On the Plurality of Worlds*. 'Possible worlds' were mentioned by R. Carnap in his *Meaning and Necessity* in 1947, echoing Wittgenstein's reference to 'possible states of affairs' in the latter's *Tractatus Logico-philosophicus*.

8 Hume's views on induction and causal reasoning are set out in his *Treatise of Human Nature*, Book 1, Part 3. Kant said that Hume's radical scepticism had awoken him from his 'dogmatic slumbers' on this issue.

9 See I. Kant, *Critique of Pure Reason*, B 472–B 475. Kant sets out an antinomy concerning causality: on the one hand, it is possible to argue that 'causality in accordance with laws of nature is not the only causality'. On the other hand, however, there is a strong case for believing that 'everything in the world takes place solely in accordance with laws of nature'. This antinomy – two chains of reasoning leading to opposed conclusions – is resolved by applying the notion of the first type of causality to the world that is the object of our knowledge – a world which Kant sees as our construction – and leaving open the possibility that another type of causality applies to the world that lies *behind* the world of appearances, but which is beyond our knowledge.

10 B. Russell, *The Problems of Philosophy*, ch. 6

11 K. Popper, *The Logic of Scientific Discovery*. See also his *Conjectures and Refutations* and *Objective Knowledge*.

12 P. Feyerabend, *Against Method: a defence of anarchy*.

13   T. Kuhn, *The Structure of Scientific Revolutions*. Some of the debate
      that followed publication of this book can be found in, for
      example, I. Lakatos and A. Musgrave (eds), *Criticism and the Growth
      of Knowledge*, and in I. Hacking (ed.), *Scientific Revolutions*. Kuhn is
      a physicist turned historian and philosopher, whose influence on
      the philosophy of science has been considerable. His theory of
      paradigm change has been widely applied, particularly within the
      social sciences.

14   See J. S. Mill, *A System of Logic*, Book II, ch. 4. In Book III, chs
      8–10 of his classic study of eliminative induction, Mill went on to
      classify and categorize the methods of scientific investigation. The
      principles Mill set out for locating and identifying some causal
      factors and eliminating others form a useful guide to experimental
      enquiry.

15   D. Hume, *An Enquiry concerning Human Understanding*, Part III, sec.
      xii.

16   For an account of logical positivism and the history of the Vienna
      Circle, see A. J. Ayer's classical presentation in *Language, Truth and
      Logic* or the brief account in A. J. Ayer et al. *The Revolution in
      Philosophy*. See also O. Hanfling, *Logical Positivism*, and the collec-
      tion edited by Hanfling under the title *Essential Readings in Logical
      Positivism*.

READING GUIDE

The theme of this chapter was logic and scientific method. A. Flew in
Thinking about Thinking has trenchant comments on ordinary reasoning
and informal logic. E. J. Lemmon's *Beginning Logic* is an approachable
introduction to formal logic or see R. C. Jeffrey, *Formal Logic: its Scope
and Limits*, 2nd edn. *The Logic of Real Arguments* by A. Fisher represents
a less traditional approach associated with the critical thinking movement.

A useful introduction to modal logic is G. E. Hughes and M. J.
Cresswell, *An Introduction to Modal Logic*. On the subject of relevance
logic, see S. Read. *Relevant Logic* or R. Routley et al., *Relevant Logics and
their Rivals*, although it should be said that this is not a book for the
novice. The subject of counterfactuals is considered by David Lewis in

his book *Counterfactuals*, and the variety of logics is explained and discussed by Susan Haack in her *Philosophy of Logics*. See also her earlier book *Deviant Logic*. If the paradox of Achilles and the tortoise interests you, then see some of the extensive literature on this in Wesley C. Salmon's (ed.), *Zeno's Paradoxes*, or A. Grünbaum, *Modern Science and Zeno's Paradoxes*. See also ch. 2 of Salmon's *Space, Time and Motion*. An entertaining book on paradoxes is *What is the Name of this Book?* by A. Smullyan. See also W. V.O. Quine, *The Ways of Paradox* or R. M. Sainsbury, *Paradoxes*. But it is best not to assume that all paradoxes have satisfactory solutions. Mathematics and the philosophy of mathematics were thrown into disarray in the opening years of the twentieth century when problems arose with the notion of sets. Neither Russell's Theory of Types, nor subsequent attempts to escape the many paradoxes involving self-reference, provide totally satisfactory answers. For a very readable account from the point of view of philosophy of mathematics, see P. J. Davis and R. Hersh, *The Mathematical Experience*.

The fragmentary writings of the pre-Socratic philosophers are gathered in Kirk and Raven, *The PreSocratic Philosophers*, rev. edn., and in J. Barnes *Early Greek Philosophy*. See also J. Barnes' study *The Presocratic Philosophers*.

A classic discussion of induction and probability is N. Goodman, *Fact, Fiction and Forecast*, while Brian Skyrms provides a useful introduction to the subject in *Choice and Chance: an introduction to inductive logic*. Popper's views on the problem of induction were published in *The Logic of Scientific Discovery* and his more recent ideas are to be found in ch. 1 of *Objective Knowledge* and in *Conjectures and Refutations*. See also I. Lakatos and A. E. Musgrave (eds), *Criticism and the Growth of Knowledge*. On the philosophy of science in general, see A. F. Chalmers *What is this Thing called Science?* See also W. Newton-Smith, *The Rationality of Science* and I. Hacking, *Representing and Intervening*.

6

Talking about Things

Without sensibility no object would be given to us, without the understanding no object would be thought. Thoughts without content are empty, intuitions without concepts are blind . . . The understanding can intuit nothing, the senses can think nothing. Only through their union can knowledge arise.

Kant, *Critique of Pure Reason*

There is, then, the world of facts, of happenings and of things. But my own direct observations confine me to a minute corner of this rich world of objects and incidents. From this corner, do I see language, words, talk and reports as constituting a bridge or a barrier between myself and the universe that consists of everything there is or that occurs? And from this point of view, while it may be reports of what happens in China or Afghanistan that first strike me as problematic, I can see that similar doubts can apply to reports about what is happening nearer to home, or indeed anywhere outside the time-space I currently occupy.

So what other people may tell me is of first importance to me. But other people together with their reports, lie on the far side of this bridge or barrier of linguistic communication. (If I can cross it, it is a bridge; if it remains impenetrable, it is a barrier.) To accept the reports of other people, then, and so to enlarge immeasurably the data-base of my knowledge, I must understand what language is and how it functions. How do sounds that other people make, or marks on pieces of paper, visual shapes in print or ink, or vibrations deliberately set up on the air-waves, become invested with meaning? And how is communication between language users possible?

Language has been a dominating interest of recent philosophy, both in the English-speaking world and also in many countries of Western Europe, where reflection on the structure of the system of signs that constitutes language is of as much interest for psychology, anthropology and literary criticism as it is for philosophy. Broadly, in the English-speaking world philosophy has either concerned itself with the painstaking analysis of philosophically crucial terms commonly used in ordinary language – in particular, words like 'knowledge' or 'truth' – or it has been concerned with the construction of artificial logical languages, divorced from natural languages, and consciously freed from the untidiness and *ad hoc* qualities of ordinary speech.

But the questions I want to ask are not to be answered in either of these ways; for my questions are about language itself. My primary interest must be in language as report, together with the questions about meaning and reference that this involves, since it is through this that I can extend my knowledge of what there was, is, or might be. Lanugage as communication or as a tool for social interaction is wider than this, but to understand this, too, I must have some idea of where and how language and reality meet. But relevant to *this* question is an understanding of how the ability to use language comes about. So I may also ask, How are language skills acquired? And what is it to be a competent language-user?

The Acquisition of Language

I begin, then, from the assumption that my views about the purposes language serves, and about its relation to reality are conditioned by the way in which I think it comes about. Naïve theories of language-learning start with the child wanting to convey meaning by naming objects – 'Mama', 'spoon', and so on.

Children learn such words, it is sometimes assumed, because their elders point at the objects concerned, accompanying their pointing with the utterance of the object's name. This so-called 'ostensive definition' is opposed to verbal definition – definition, that is, in the way dictionaries do it, by an alternative turn of phrase – which, of course, is only possible where someone already has command of the language being learned.

These verbal pointings, though, can only work if a child has an intuitive grasp of the way that utterances, even as simple as these, are able to function as something more than mere grunts or babblings. A dog, by contrast, will never find a bone because a human finger is helpfully pointed in its direction, nor can it be tempted by a verbal promise of 'bone tomorrow'. Children seem to grasp easily how to add verbs to the limited vocabulary of nouns with which they may start; to form plurals; to add adjectives and so on. They then go on to use language not simply to manipulate other people, for the satisfaction of their needs, though this may be the originating impulse, but also to express ideas.

I might compare this prior grasp of the principles of language to the way in which a child might discover logical or mathematical facts or principles. Perhaps someone else *hands* them to the child ready-made, but then the child will only accept and understand what it is being told if it is already capable of assimilating the logical or mathematical points itself; alternatively, the child might invent or construct them itself – rather as the 12-year-old Blaise Pascal (1623–1661), French philosopher and mathematician, was said to have been found secretly working his way, unguided, through Euclid's mathematical discoveries. But then, this is 'construction' in a special sense: the child is not free to create these logical or mathematical structures just as it likes.[1] Similarly, in the case of language, there is striking originality and creativity about young children's language learning; at the same time, there is an equally striking uniformity or conformity in approach.

But all these are contentious claims, and it is issues like these that lie behind the debate about the origins of linguistic competence that centres on the work of the American philosopher and linguist, Noam Chomsky (b. 1928). Something of this background and of the views of the main protagonists in this debate, is already familiar to me; but nevertheless it is a contrast worth setting out.

Chomsky traces his philosophical ancestry to Descartes, to Leibniz and to seventeenth- and eighteenth-century grammarians who explored the notion of a universal grammar.[2] His primary debt, though, must be to Plato, whose Theory of Forms or Ideas was a theory about the universal terms – 'red', 'hot', 'equal', 'pretty', for example – that constitute a large part of talk about things. It was Plato who argued that we need, in some sense, a prior idea of equality in order to recognise as examples of equality, the approximate instances of equality that are all we are actually likely to meet with in experience.

This idea that we face the world with preconceptions and preformed dispositions appears in theories of language as the idea of a universal grammar. The contrast implied by reference to a *universal* grammar is with *particular* grammars – the grammars people are taught if they are learning a second or third language, or studying the syntax of their own. A universal grammar corresponds, rather, to the grammar they need to grasp in order to acquire their *first* language in infancy. There may be alternative ways of explaining any features that languages have in common. For example, it might be that in prehistory humans shared a common language. But since no one, whatever his level of intelligence, is unable to come to terms with his own first language, it seems that the common elements amongst the Babel of world languages might more plausibly be explained by the rationalist hypothesis that they consist of structures which the human mind is peculiarly fitted to grasp.

Chomsky's work is an exploration of this 'deep structure' of language underlying its surface structure, and he argues that its accessibility to human beings reflects the fact that it is in some sense innate in them. Unlike the old theories of innate ideas, Chomsky's is a scientific rather than a logical or metaphysical theory. The disposition he has in mind is one that is genetically or biologically predetermined. As he puts it, the characteristics of language he has discovered are, if true, empirical facts but they are *a priori* for the organism. His is a theory about language acquisition which conflicts with the empiricist view that what people know they must have learned or acquired entirely from their environment. It is no accident, then, that Chomsky has taken issue on this subject with the behaviourist psychologist, B. F. Skinner (b. 1904) as well as with other philosophers of language in the empiricist and positivist tradition.[3]

Skinner takes the view that the acquisition of language can be explained in terms of conditioning: that humans learn language through a process of stimulus, response, and reinforcement as these occur in a normal child's environment. These, he believes, set up linguistic habit structures: networks of association, fabrics of disposition to respond. Chomsky's view is that overt happenings like these, together with crude notions of stimulus and reinforcement, cannot provide a full account of how the ability to use language originates. He offers the example of an extraterrestrial observer who embarks on a scientific study of human beings – a Martian, for example, who knows both the English language and physics. The Martian, Chomsky suggests, would be unable to tell simply from what he could see, that while physics required generations of genius to develop, the mastery of English comes naturally to any child exposed to the language. As for terms like 'stimulus', 'response' and 'reinforcement', Chomsky argues that these are ambiguous and undefined when they are used in relation to human learning. They *may* be strictly defined, but in that case they will apply only within the laboratory and to simple organisms. Outside the laboratory they no longer function in a scientific and unambiguous way. It is not possible, then, on Chomsky's view, to extend the use of terms like these outside the laboratory, and certainly not to apply them to the complex enterprise of learning a natural language.

One feature of language which accounts for the difficulty of explaining it in these narrow and closed ways is that it is essentially open-ended. A small input is sufficient to give a child the capacity creatively to produce an indefinite number of completely original sentences, as well as to understand indefinitely many new sentences never encountered before. Hence the term 'generative' grammar. So Chomsky concludes that language is fitted to the human mind in a way that physics, for example, is not. In the case of language, he says, 'intrinsic principles of mental organisation permit the construction of rich systems of knowledge and belief on the basis of scattered evidence'.[4]

Many of the observations of Ludwig Wittgenstein (1889–1951) in his *Philosophical Investigations* can be interpreted as showing just how scattered the evidence is on which people base their linguistic reasoning. Take for example, the following passage:

. . . A writes series of numbers down; B watches him and tries to find a law for the sequence of numbers. If he succeeds he exclaims: 'Now I can go on!' – So this capacity, this understanding, is something that makes its appearance in a moment. So let us try and see what it is that makes its appearance here. – A has written down the numbers 1, 5, 11, 19, 29: at this point B says he knows how to go on. What happened here? Various things may have happened; for example, while A was slowly putting one number after another, B was occupied with trying various algebraic formulae on the numbers which had been written down . . .

Or again, B does not think of formulae. He watches A writing his numbers down with a certain feeling of tension, and all sorts of vague thoughts go through his head. Finally he asks himself: 'What is the series of differences?' He finds the series 4, 6, 8, 10 and says: Now I can go on.

Or he watches and says 'Yes, I know *that* series' – and continues it, just as he would have done if A had written down the series 1, 3, 5, 7, 9. – Or he says nothing at all and simply continues the series.[5]

These may seem enigmatic observations, but if one compares this to the case of a child learning language, it is clear that the ability to 'go on' in this case is even more puzzling than the ability to 'go on' in the arithmetic case. And yet the facility resembles the last two examples, rather than the first. It is this uncanny facility that Chomsky draws attention to, and it is this that an explanation in terms of stimulus and response misses.

Chomsky's solution, then, is to posit an innate capacity. Wittgenstein himself, however, offers a different explanation in the *Philosophical Investigations*. But his account of how language happens is also at the same time a theory of meaning, and in order to consider this and other theories of meaning, I must turn from the question of the origins of linguistic competence to more direct consideration of language itself.

The place to begin may well be with a distinction which originates with the Swiss linguist Ferdinand de Saussure (1857–1913). Saussure, who is the originator of the study known as semiotics, regarded language as a system of signs. The distinction he drew was between *langue* and *parole* – 'language' and 'speech'.[6] It is to *langue* as the underlying structure or sequence of rules involved in a language that both Chomsky's work and Wittgenstein's examples draw attention, and it is grasp of this that Chomsky describes as linguistic *competence*. At the same time, *parole* or 'speech' is what, without formulating rules, people, including young children, pursue in practice, and this Chomsky describes as linguistic *performance*.

Bearing in mind these distinctions, I see that my question initially must be at the level of performance or use. It is here that I must first seek to answer the question of meaning. Considerable light is thrown on this starting-point, when I observe that the learning of language is a distinctive human capacity – a point only confirmed by the occasional instance of an intelligent higher mammal achieving some rudimentary concept of naming and sentence formation. It is shaped, too, by my acceptance that grasping how to 'go on' as a language-user represents some kind of quasi-logical and intuitive leap. Given these two background assumptions, I am in a position to consider some of the accounts that have been offered of the relationship between speech and external reality. I am in a position, that is, to consider a question which I can provisionally pose as 'What do words and sentences mean?'

The Imagist Theory of Meaning

It would be natural to suppose that all words are used in a similar sort of way, and that this way is to *stand for* for something. This assumption lies behind the naïve view of a child's early language-learning, for example. The debate about language can indeed, historically, be looked at as a debate simply about what it *is* that words stand for. Early empiricist philosophers, in particular Locke and Berkeley, believed that words stood for ideas in the mind: an alternative view is that there is a one-to-one correlation between words and objects. So one answer to the question 'What does the word "moon" stand for?' is that it stands for the mental picture someone forms when thinking about the moon. Another is that it stands for the moon itself.

The first type of view was put by Locke when he spoke of 'signs of internal conceptions . . . ideas within his own mind, whereby they might be made known to others'.[7] Berkeley, on the other hand, having endorsed Locke's correlation between words and ideas, went on to point out that objects themselves become redundant. Locke had spoken of matter as 'something I know not what' but Berkeley argued that since we neither do nor *can* know it, everything we want to take into account is encompassed within the two regions of (a) words and (b) the ideas in our minds (and God's) for which these words stand.[8]

But even without taking this further step, there are problems about taking mental entities as the subject-matter of language. For example, ideas in the mind are essentially private to each person. How can they be compared? Locke himself wondered how it would be if perhaps 'the idea that a violet produced in one man's mind by his eyes were the same that a marigold produced in another man's?'[9]

A prosaic answer to this question, but one carrying some weight, is that both men have a common physiology, and that therefore a similar cause would produce a similar effect. Perhaps I never *can* know that what I see as purple is not seen by you in the way that I see orange. But why should I suppose this? Better to assume – because it is the simpler hypothesis – that our experience is comparable and also that our language in describing it refers to something beyond the purely mental.

The issue is essentially this: the idea of mental entities as the subject-matter of language suggests that meaning is a three-termed relationship:

THOUGHT   LANGUAGE   THE WORLD

Meaning in this format is something in the consciousness of a speaker, which he expresses through the symbolic medium of language. Language itself here appears as something which is completely transparent. But structuralists and deconstructionists have challenged this assumption. Jacques Derrida (b. 1930) is perhaps the most prominent of those who have stressed the obtrusive density of language, its use of metaphor and symbolism, particularly in literature.[10]

This is not the only reason though, why I might want to reject this account of language. To begin with, the theory of the triple relationship would mean, I notice, that a mention of the word 'moon' would involve:

1. a mental image or thought:
   the thought of the moon

2. what is said:
   'the moon'

3. an external correlate:
   the moon

I have already seen how an account like this might give rise to a temptation to dispense with the third element in this account. For Berkeley indeed took that step. I must now consider, though, whether another way of showing the triple theory to be wrong would be to show that the *first* element is eliminable. In other words, I must consider whether the relation between language and the world may not be, after all, in some sense direct. If so, then perhaps it is wrong to make a distinction between language and thought. Later, then, I must ask whether or not it makes sense to suppose that I engage in a *double* process, first thinking and then expressing my thought in language, rather than in a single process which has various manifestations. But first I must consider the other part of this possible trilogy of relationships: the relationship, that is between language and the world.

The Picture Theory of Meaning

If I focus on one particular use of language – that is, language as it is used to assert that something is the case – then I may become bewitched or entranced by a metaphor: the metaphor of language as a mirror of reality. I may believe that sentences provide a structural model, a picture, of the facts they describe. It is a theory of this sort, which he later came to reject as bewitchment, that Wittgenstein set out in his early work, the *Tractatus Logico-Philosophicus*.

There is a story that Wittgenstein took his image from a scale model of a car accident, assembled by the French police at their headquarters in Paris. The way in which the model cars and roads represented the crude fact of the accident seemed to Wittgenstein to provide a revealing metaphor of the relation between language and the world.[11] An alternative metaphor would be to say that language provides a map of the terrain of facts.

The theory itself, though, says nothing about how the human mind makes the connection between language and what it maps, and so the question of reference becomes a central concern. 'How does the word "car" represent a real car?' I might ask, looking at how the scale-model represents the car in the accident. I may feel I can answer this if, avoiding the complexities of the accident-scene, I limit myself to some simple spatial images: a rose, for example, lying next to a glove on a table. But what if I want to say there is *no* rose lying next to the glove? And no glove? And no table? What kind of picture of the facts would these be? Or if I want to make assertions about 'all' or 'some' roses? Or to indicate alternatives as in 'Either it is a rose or a carnation'?

It might be said that all these are difficulties flowing from the inexactitude of ordinary language. Hence in the *Tractatus* the relationship implied may not be one between ordinary language and ordinary objects, but between the logical elements of language and whatever it is in the world that these 'names' for 'objects' depict. An *ideal* language, it might be thought, should faithfully reflect the structure of the world. A *natural* language does not necessarily do this.

Whether in an ideal or natural language, though, the problem of reference is central to a 'picture' theory of meaning and the idea that objects can be named and pointed at – ostensive definition again – is a fundamental aspect of such a theory.

Meaning and Reference

A referential theory of meaning, then, seems to carry with it a certain view of language-learning. According to this way of explaining things, one might suppose that a child arrives in the world, and needs to come to terms with the surrounding language of its culture, rather in the way that a foreign anthropologist might arrive amongst a tribe speaking a totally unknown language. Foreign anthropologists, however, are assumed to know already what language *is*, and to be able to function efficiently in their own. They have simply to grasp that when the people of the tribe point to a bush and name it, this is a well-understood and unambiguous procedure. They have a name for a bush in their own language and have simply to carry out a straight exchange of names. But it is precisely this kind of assumption that the American philosopher W. V. Quine (b. 1908) and other recent writers on reference cast into doubt, both in the case of the anthropologist and that of the child.

First of all, certain assumptions have to be made about conventions (like pointing) and about expectations (the desire to communicate on some particular basis and for some particular purpose). As far as the first is concerned, it might seem that someone could point, for example, to a flower, and say 'flower' and be understood. But suppose he is really pointing to one of its petals – or its colour – or its shape – or even its smell?

It also has to be assumed that both parties to this exercise of communication construe the world in the same way – see it as broken down into individual animals, or plants, for instance, within a wider landscape, rather than as patterns of colour and shape, or as animal/plant *parts*, or animal/plant *groups*. The fact is though, that there *are* cultural differences between peoples, even if not as striking as this: snow, for example, seems a single concept to a European, while an Eskimo, for whom such distinctions are important, will have a number of different words for snow and a number of differing concepts covered by these words. An Australian aborigine may define many different kinds of blood relationship, while the modern European will take account, on the whole, of only a more limited range of parents, children, cousins and similarly close relatives.

So reference in itself is not unproblematic. But supposing one *could* point unambiguously at something. Supposing, that is, that naming is not quite such a hazardous procedure as these considerations suggest. In this case, the different question arises of what is the *content* embedded in this procedure. In particular, is it a certain description, no matter how brief? Or are names essentially devoid of descriptive content?

It was Frege who originated the modern debate on this question with his seminal distinction between meaning as Sense (in German, *Sinn*) and meaning as Reference (*Bedeutung*).[12] He pointed out that when people made the (empirical) discovery that the Morning Star was in fact also the Evening Star, they were noticing that the two different *phrases* – Morning Star and Evening Star – while their Sense was different, had the same Reference. The two phrases were in fact two different descriptions of an identical physical object. So, for Frege, as well as the sign, or name, 'Morning Star' and the Reference – the star itself – there is also the Sense of the sign: in this case, the star that appears in the morning.

But Frege's Sense (Sinn) was not a mental entity, like the 'ideas' of Locke and Berkeley. It was potentially something in the public domain, even though different people might use two different expressions to refer to the same object. Frege gave as an example of this a Doctor X who might be known to one man simply by his date and place of birth, by another simply as currently living in some particular place.

Proper names, then, seem at first sight to need both a Sense and a Reference. Frege's examples seemed to show that objects cannot simply be verbally pointed at. A word which expresses this notion of verbal pointing is 'denoting', and it was in a famous paper with the title 'On Denoting' (published in 1905)[13] that Bertrand Russell argued that a distinction should be made between the *grammatical* subject of a sentence and its *logical* subject, and that a definite description of the form 'the so-and-so' should be analysed so that the apparent subject becomes an element in the predicate. For example, 'The author of *Waverley* was S' should, Russell argued, be seen as involving three separate claims: (a) that at least one person wrote *Waverley*, (b) that at most one person wrote *Waverley*, and (c) that whoever wrote *Waverley* was S.

The point of this analysis was to reduce, rather than add to, what we claim to know. For, Russell believed, 'Every proposition which we can understand must be composed wholly of constituents with which we are acquainted.'[14] In the case of a proper name, like Julius Caesar, for example, we can talk about Julius Caesar but we do not *know* him in the sense of being directly acquainted with him; so, Russell believed, our reference must be to things we *are* acquainted with, in this case the elements of some description of Julius Caesar, not Caesar himself.

Russell's argument, then, virtually dispenses with naming, since it seems that in principle any content or meaning in an apparent subject-term can be transferred to the predicate by this analysis, leaving only an empty pointing-word as a logical subject. Later, Russell was prepared to say: 'The only words one does use as names in the logical sense are words like "this" or "that".'[15] As for the predicate terms, Russell saw these as pointing-words, too, in a different way. But in their case, he believed they pointed to universals of the kind Plato had postulated in his Theory of Forms.

Russell's elimination of the grammatical subject is continued in the work of the American philosopher, Quine, who has offered the idea of a language freed from referring expressions. Or, in Quine's words: 'Whatever we say with the help of names can be said in a language which shuns names altogether.'[16] In Quine's example, instead of saying 'Pegasus exists' and so referring to an imaginary horse, one might say 'Something Pegasizes.' Similarly, to be Socrates is to Socratize. Proper nouns become verbs; logical subjects become predicates.

The British philosopher Peter Strawson (b. 1919) has remarked on these suggestions that people would not be able to learn the Russell/Quine language unless they had mastered the ordinary language. And, indeed, it is tempting to suppose that there must be more to proper names than this.

But if there is more to proper names than this, it would have to be some kind of descriptive content. Arguments of Saul Kripke (b. 1940) however, demonstrate the difficulties involved in taking proper names to have any single or unique descriptive meaning or content. For example, William Shakespeare is widely known as the author of *Macbeth* and certain other plays. But it seems to make sense to say that Shakespeare himself might not have written these plays at all. They might, perhaps, have been written by Bacon. And Shakespeare himself might have spent his time in some quite different way. If this were so, it seems unlikely that anyone would insist that Bacon *was* Shakespeare on the grounds that 'Shakespeare' *must* be the name of the author of *Macbeth* and other plays.

In ordinary discussion, there may be *clusters* of descriptions associated with a proper name, and no single description may be essential for identification. Kripke, however, believes that a proper name can, conventionally, be bestowed on someone in some agreed way – in the case of people, this might well be a matter of parentage and birth. Once a proper name has a fixed reference like this, Kripke describes it as a 'rigid designator'. And once something can be designated rigidly, on Kripke's view, other true descriptions can be found by following through causal links and connections. A non-rigid designator, by contrast, is a description which various individuals *might* fit, although only one *does* as a matter of fact. For example, 'the Governor of the Bank of England in 1984' is a non-rigid designator.[17]

Why should there be this reluctance to accept that names amount to descriptions? I can answer this question by considering what I would have to say about language if names *were* nothing other than abbreviated descriptions – if, that is, there were *no* points where language touched reality. No matter how consistent it might be, a free-floating structure of linguistic practice would be simply that. A usable structure cannot be free-floating. It must have at least some anchor-points in the ground of reality. For these anchor-points, proper names and the objects to which they belong seem the obvious first place to look. The alternative is to say that my talk refers only to what is in my own mind – meanings 'in the head' – the 'psychologistic' view that Frege was first concerned to attack. A story to illustrate the problem was constructed by the American philosopher Hilary Putnam (b. 1926). His story of Twin Earth may be told thus:

'Twin Earth' is closely similar to our own – its inhabitants even speak English – except in one respect. This is that the liquid in the rivers, oceans and seas, which falls there as rain, and which Twin Earthers drink and find thirst-quenching, is not H_2O, but a different chemical compound XYZ. Twin Earthers, however, call it 'water'. Now if a spaceship from Earth were to visit Twin Earth the occupants might at first suppose that 'water' has the same meaning in both places. When they discover the chemical difference, though, they might report: 'On Twin Earth the word "water" means XYZ.'

But supposing that chemical analysis were for some reason impossible – supposing, perhaps, that the comparisons could have been undertaken in 1750 – then the difference would not be discovered, nor would the difference in meaning.

The moral to be drawn from this story is that if meanings are confined to what is in people's heads, it would have to be said that the Earthers and Twin Earthers had a common concept of water, since for most people in either world the mental image or concept of water is based on its surface characteristics, not its chemical structure. But in Putnam's view, at the time when he devised this story, this would be false, since they are talking about a quite different chemical substance. And by the criterion of chemical structure, the meaning of 'water' is *not* the same in both places.[18]

Putnam's story, then, is designed to support the view that meaning must be pinned down in some way to what is external – the world without rather than the world within. This is a so-called 'realist' view of meaning, to which an anti-realist might reply that the Earth explorers were warranted, or entitled, to describe what they found as water.

But Putnam argued that this is not either our commonsense or our scientific way of proceeding. What 'natural kind' a thing is, is a matter which present or future investigation might determine differently. The reference of 'water' is in some sense established independenly of the views of particular groups or individuals at particular times.

As far as water is concerned, Putnam's story seems unconvincing. Ice is frozen water; but is it still water after freezing or vaporizing? I do not know how to decide this. But a different example – an example of a different 'natural kind' – could have convinced me. Perhaps on Earth electrons are fundamental particles, while on Twin Earth whatever plays the electron-role is a composite of other particles. In a case like that, I think that I might follow Putnam and deny that there are any electrons on Twin Earth.[19]

I might prefer to do this rather than aboandon the idea of objective meanings. For suppose I *were* to abandon the idea that objective meanings can be found across social groups and cultures; suppose, that is, that I were to seek for an explanation of language entirely in terms of what words mean to the people who use them, in the context in which they employ them.

In Putnam's story, his two earths are not self-contained. His space-ship occupants make comparisons about language-use, although only one language, English, in involved, the example would work in the same way if the Twin-Earthers spoke French or German, or indeed, some completely unknown language of their own. But the very idea of translation between languages has been undermined in two very different ways. The logicians' attack is concerned with meaning and reference; while what might be called the 'social observers' attack' is conducted on a very wide front indeed. The 'wide front' would include Marxists, who relate language to social conditioning and class-consciousness, and social relativists – people, that is, who believe that standards of truth and morality are internal to a particular society – including those influenced by the findings of anthropology and linguistics. They would include, too, philosophical sceptics about meaning like Feyerabend who have have propounded an extreme version of the doctrine of 'incommensurability' between languages.[20]

Problems of Translation

The logician's attack is exemplified in the work of Quine. Quine describes two particular difficulties, the first the problem of translation either within or between languages, which he calls the lexicographer's problem; the second, a grammarian's problem essentially connected with the notion of what counts, in a language, as a significant sequence of sounds.

1. The lexicographers' problem is that, since they are unable to say what 'meaning' is, they deal only in the concept 'alike in meaning', i.e. synonymy. But the notion of synonymy itself, in Quine's view, defies analysis, except in terms of meaning, so the would-be lexicographer is trapped within a circle he cannot escape.

2. The grammarians' problem is this: faced with determining what it is to 'have meaning' they must deal in the concept of significance. They must try, that is, to determine what word-sequences are significant. The problem, though, is that the class of utterances studied by the grammarian is infinite. It is impossible as a matter of fact to describe all possible meaningful utterances. (And the converse difficulty, a sentence containing a nonsensical string of sounds can be intelligible if the nonsense is put in quotation marks: for example: 'Oompa-do-pa' is meaningless'.) This means that grammarians are not even free to discard any sequences of sounds, in order to approach their task of classification the other way round – that is, by saying what *cannot* be included rather than what can. And so, in Quine's view, the notion of grammar as straightforward description of what can be said in a language is mistaken. Quine's sceptical conclusions extend, then, to encompass a thesis of the *indeterminacy* of translation: this is that, in effect, no matter how much we might be able to find out about the behaviour of a group of people speaking an alien language, there is an indefinite number of ways of interpreting what they say. In other words, many systems of translation, internally consistent but incompatible with each other, would fit with that information.[21]

A yet more radical claim, though, is that languages can only be learned from 'inside' by a native speaker. This is the thesis of *incommensurability* – the thesis that one cannot measure what something means in one language against what it means in another; they just cannot be compared. It is a thesis closely connected with anthropological and cultural and social theories. For anthropologists, the problem of *Verstehen* has been familiar since the work of Wilhelm Dilthey (1833–1911) and Max Weber (1864–1920). A common example is that of the Azande and their belief in witchcraft. Anthropologists have argued that it is not possible to understand the Zande theories of witchcraft except by entering the Zande way of life and using their language.

A different, and equally famous, example of a radical restructuring of reality and language was offered by Benjamin Lee Whorf (1897–1941), on the basis of observations of the Hopi Indians in North America. While the claims made have been disputed, the Sapir-Whorf hypothesis, as it has been called, is important in showing what *might* be meant by such a claim, whether or not it is actually borne out in this case. Whorf's claim was that the Hopi Indians had no notion or intuition of time; that their language contained no words or constructions referring to past, present or future. Nevertheless, he claimed, their language was able to give a complete picture of their experience. At the same time, it conceals, he suggested, an alternative metaphysic, just as does our own view of static space and flowing time. Our own metaphysic is based on seeing the universe under the two great cosmic forms:

SPACE   and TIME

The Hopi metaphysic, by contrast, sees the world under the division:

MANIFESTED and UNMANIFEST

The manifested consists of everything that is or has been revealed to the senses, so it includes our present and past, while the unmanifest includes all we would call future as well as everything mental. Within the Hopi framework, expressions of space and time are avoided by using expressions of extension, operation and cyclic process.

Edward Sapir (1884–1939) summed up his own conclusions from such findings in these terms: 'The fact of the matter is that the "real world" is to a large extent unconsciously built up on the language habits of the group. No two languages are ever sufficiently similar to be considered as representing the same social reality. The worlds in which different societies live are distinct worlds, not merely the same world with different labels attached.'[22] Later, he wrote: 'Such categories as number, gender, case, tense, . . . are not so much discovered in experience as imposed upon it because of the tyrannical hold that linguistic form has upon our orientation in the world.'[23]

But can language really have such an effect? It is hard to imagine what it would be to be liberated from this tyranny – even more to be liberated from the tyranny of the 'hardest' of categories, that of logic. And yet, in *The Idea of a Social Science*, Peter Winch (b.1926) wrote: 'a knowledge of logical theory will not enable you to understand a piece of reasoning in an unknown language; you will have to learn that language.'[24] Winch himself was strongly influenced in his thinking by the later Wittgenstein. The theory of language that Wittgenstein advanced in *Philosophical Investigations* and in later works, has been summed up in the slogan 'meaning is use.'

Language-games and the 'Use' Theory of Meaning

The central idea of Wittgenstein's *Investigations* is that the question of what words *mean* is to be answered by seeing what they *do*. In this view, social context, intention and function are the keys that unlock language. To understand these, the unit of meaning must be, as Frege was the first to argue, whole sentences, not words taken in isolation.

Single words can themselves function as sentences, though, and indeed this happens in Wittgenstein's first simple model of what he calls a 'language-game'. In this model, two builders use a language consisting of the four words 'block', 'pillar', 'slab' and 'beam'. When the first builder calls out 'block' the second builder brings him a block which he has learned to bring just at that call. Understanding this language, for its two users, is to be able to engage in routines like these. Or, in this primitive language-game, as in more complex ones, the meaning of an utterance is its use.[25]

The minimum number of people, though, who might construct a language or, in Wittgenstein's terminology, play such a language-game, would be two. Empirically, occasional examples of, for example, a wolf–child – a human baby fostered by a wolf

– seem to bear this out. Language neither appears nor persists in conditions of prolonged solitude. It is not necessary, though, to base the philosophical argument on such disputable empirical grounds. Instead, I can ask, what would it be to create a private language – a language which only I can understand? I might think I could do this perhaps by keeping a secret diary. But how would I know that the secret mark I put down on Wednesday referred to the same sensation I had associated with that mark on Tuesday? What would it be to make a mistake? And if it is not possible to make a mistake, then the concept of getting it right cannot get any purchase. Of course, I can rely on memory, but as Wittgenstein says, this is like someone buying several copies of the morning paper to confirm that what he reads there is true.[26]

The 'use' model of language, then, is essentially social. Its implication is that there is no one answer to a question like 'What do words mean?' And in favour of this view, one may recall the many other diverse functions of language apart from naming: words can, for example, be used to express surprise, to make promises, to threaten, to describe actions, to flatter, to assent, to dissent and so on. So to see what any particular word means it could be argued that it is always necessary to embed it in an utterance, to become aware of the intention of the speaker – including his beliefs, wishes and desires – and to understand the role that the speaker's utterance plays in a particular social and cultural context.

To emphasize intention and communication in this way is to recognise the nature of language as an institution or, as the American philosopher John Searle (b. 1932) describes it, as a rule-governed form of behaviour. In the hands of ordinary language theorists like J. L. Austin (1911–1960) it is by finding out how a word or a sentence functions in a rich variety of contexts that illumination is to be found – the kind of illumination that a general formula cannot supply.

Does this mean, then, that understanding an isolated utterance is dependent on understanding an entire social context – the 'language-game' of which that word or sentence forms a part?

Contemporary followers of Wittgenstein have pursued this line of thought to the conclusion that even within an individual language there are self-contained 'forms of thought' – the languages or 'language-games' of religion, for example, or science or poetry, which do not intersect, cannot be translated into each other's terms, and have their own criteria of truth and falsity. This parallels the case of translation between different natural languages – if one were, for example, to come across some lost tribe speaking a hitherto unknown tongue – where the claim is that, since a culture is *expressed* in its language, learning the language could only be done from, as it were, the inside.

Is everything, then, relative? Does everything that is said depend for its meaning on who says it? Are words not capable of providing a common currency between human beings? Are there no common ideas which cross the boundaries of race, culture, social class, location in time and place? When I consider these questions, I am inclined to accept the importance of social context in explaining any particular person's language and orientation to the world. But I cannot *generalize* this notion without making it incoherent. A generalized and universal relativism in the end obliterates the distinction between what someone intends to say and what he actually does say. And even to interact for minimal purposes, this is a distinction it has to be possible to make. Without it language is reduced to the mere making of noises.

But insistence that there must in the end be, in some sense at least, a direct relation between language and the world is not incompatible with also recognising the connection between meaning and use. I cannot free myself from the notion that the possibility of using language successfully actually depends, in fact, on there being a correspondence between words and things, or between sentences and states of affairs. But at the same time, the question of how words come to be *understood* may be better answered by looking at the part they play in many kinds of social interaction. The alternative theory, though, continues to 'bewitch' with the thought that language must, after all, in some sense be a map if it is to be a guide. Or, as Putnam expresses this: 'Talk of use and talk of reference are parts of the total story.'[27] It is because I believe *this*, that I can also believe that my picture of reality can be deliberately distorted by the language of others who desire to mislead. Or, in brief, it is only because I believe in truth that I can also believe in lies.

NOTES

1   See J. Piaget, *Structuralism*, pp. 61–2. While some of Piaget's conclusions may be contentious, he established experimentally that children reject at one stage in their development logical or mathematical truths – for example, conservation of quantity – which will strike them as obvious at a later maturational stage. For Piaget's account of the development of children's logical and mathematical understanding, see J. Piaget, *The Language and Thought of the Child*.

2   For an account of this historical background, see N. Chomsky, *Cartesian Linguistics*. The most straightforward brief account of Chomsky's own views is Part 1 of *Problems of Knowledge and Freedom*. His considered philosophical position is set out in his *Language and Mind* and *Reflections on Language*. See also J. Lyons, *Chomsky*, and J. J. Katz, *The Philosophy of Language*.

3   See in particular Chomsky's review of B. F. Skinner's *Verbal Behavior*.

4   N. Chomsky, *Problems of Knowledge and Freedom*, p. 45.

5   L. Wittgenstein, *Philosophical Investigations*, para. 151.

6   There is a good exposition of Saussure's thought in J. Sturrock (ed.), *Structuralism and Since*. This includes also essays on Lévi-Strauss, Barthes, Foucault, Lacan and Derrida.

7   J. Locke, *Essay Concerning Human Understanding*, Book II, 1, 2.

8   Berkeley's theory of perception was put forward in his *Three Dialogues*. The two participants are Hylas, representing the materialist viewpoint, and Philonous, representing the idealist view which is Berkeley's own. This view was summed up in the phrase '*esse est percipi*' ('to be is to be perceived') – a brief way of saying that all our descriptions of objects involve reference to our own ways of perceiving or experiencing them.

9   Locke, *Essay Concerning Human Understanding*, Book II, 32, 15.

10 Derrida's work is discussed in J. Sturrock, *Structuralism and Since*, ch. 5. See, in particular J. Derrida, *Of Grammatology*. The phenomenologist Edmund Husserl (1859–1938) was an early influence on Derrida, whose *Speech and Phenomena* (1967) deals with Husserl's theory of signs. For an American perspective on Derrida, see R. Rorty, *Philosophy and the Mirror of Nature*.

11 L. Wittgenstein, *Tractatus Logico-Philosophicus*. For discussion of the *Tractatus* and the picture theory of meaning, see G. Pitcher (ed.), *Wittgenstein* and Rush Rhees, *Discussions of Wittgenstein*. For a full account of Wittgenstein's life and philosophical work, see Ray Monk, *Ludwig Wittgenstein: the duty of genius*.

12 G. Frege 'Sense and Reference' in *Philosophical Writings*.

13 B. Russell, 'On Denoting', *Mind*, 1905. It is interesting to compare the 'Waverley' example as presented in 'On Denoting' (1905) and in Russell's *Introduction to Mathematical Philosophy* (1919), p. 177. In one case the example used is 'The author of Waverley is Scotch'; in the other 'Scott is the author of Waverley'. Subsequent discussions have created another variation: 'The author of Waverley is Scott'. I have preferred an ambiguous abbreviation.

14 B. Russell, *The Problems of Philosophy*, p. 58. Chapter 5 sets out Russell's views on knowledge by acquaintance and knowledge by description.

15 B. Russell, *Logic and Knowledge* (ed. R. Marsh), p. 201.

16 W.v.O. Quine, *From a Logical Point of View*, p. 13.

17 For Kripke's views, see his *Naming and Necessity*, or his 'Identity and Necessity'.

18 H. Putnam, 'The meaning of "meaning"', in *Mind, Language and Reality, Philosophical Papers*, vol. 2. Putnam later abandoned the view that the meaning of 'water' (a 'natural kind' term) could be pinned down in this way, but not the idea that language must somewhere be anchored in reality. See in particular 'Reason and Realism' in *Meaning and the Moral Sciences*.

19 I am indebted to Peter Forrest for this example.

20 See P. Feyerabend, *Against Method*.

21 See W.v.O. Quine, *From a Logical Point of View*, ch. 3. See also his 'Mind and Verbal Dispositions' in S. Guttenplan (ed.), *Mind and Language*, p. 90. In *Word and Object*, Quine does not claim that all individual sentences are indeterminate in this way: he speaks of

'stimulus meaning' in the case of simple sentences expressing common sense-experiences, e.g. 'This is red'.

22   From E. Sapir, 'The status of linguistics as a science', *Language*, vol. 5, pp. 207–14 quoted in G. Sampson, *Schools of Linguistics*, p. 83.

23   E. Sapir 'Conceptual categories in primitive languages', *Science*, vol. 74, p. 578, quoted in Sampson, *Schools of Linguistics*, p. 83.

24   P. Winch, *The Idea of a Social Science*, p. 135.

25   L. Wittgenstein, *Philosophical Investigations*, para. 2.

26   See L. Wittgenstein, *Tractatus Logico-Philosophicus*, paras 243–363. In 'Can there be a private language?', A. J. Ayer challenges this position with an account of Robinson Crusoe on his desert-island. Crusoe *could*, he believes, name objects – both external objects like birds flying overhead, and also internal states like headaches or pains. When Man Friday turns up, Ayer argues, there will be no difficulty in principle in Crusoe conveying both kinds of meanings to him, although clearly it will be easier to make him undersand the first rather than the second. A. J. Ayer, *The Concept of a Person*, pp. 36–51.

27   H. Putnam, *Meaning and the Moral Sciences*, p. 100.

READING GUIDE

An excellent introduction to the philosophy of language is Ian Hacking's *Why Does Language Matter to Philosophy?* See also S. Blackburn, *Spreading the Word: groundings in the philosophy of language.* Two classic books on the philosophy of language are J. Austin, *How to do Things with Words* and J. Searle *Speech Acts*. See also G. Evans, *The Varieties of Reference*.

For Chomsky's position, see initially Part 1 of his *Problems of Knowledge and Freedom*; then, to set the debate in a historical context, his *Cartesian Linguistics*. For further discussion of the relationship between logical form and deep structure, see D. Davidson and G. Harman (eds), *Semantics of Natural Language*. Skinner's general position is to be found in his *Beyond Freedom and Dignity*.

Useful brief discussions of the work of Lévi-Strauss, Barthes, Foucault, Lacan and Derrida are to be found in J. Sturrock (ed.), *Structuralism and Since*. For an excellent and clear exploration of the implications of structuralism in various areas of human thought – biology, mathematics, language, literature – see J. Piaget, *Structuralism*.

For discussion of the problems encountered by the empiricist philosophers in connection with ideas, concepts and language, as well as their general philosophical theories, see J. Bennett, *Locke, Berkeley, Hume*.

G. Sampson in *Schools of Linguistics* offers a readable and comprehensive account of problems of meaning and translation, including the social anthropological issues mentioned here.

Kripke's views are presented in *Naming and Necessity*, and are commented on by Dummett in his *Frege: philosophy of language* and in his *Truth and other Enigmas*. See also D. Wiggins, *Sameness and Substance*.

On natural kinds, see the articles gathered in Schwartz (ed.), *Naming, Necessity and Natural Kinds*, particularly that by Quine.

7

Thinking about Minds

I find, then, that language starts from what is – what exists – and
is itself part of that external reality. The fact that it can distort that
reality is no more than a necessary aspect of its capacity, on
occasion, to reflect it. If I am satisfied that this is the nature of the
link between language and the world, then I am in a position to
turn my attention back from what is outside myself to what is
most essentially inner: thought itself. But I cannot separate consideration of thought from consideration of whatever it is that
thinks, reasons, reflects.

If it is this that I now want to consider, I can do it in two ways:
(a) by introspection – taking my own mental processes and states
as objects of scrutiny, or (b) by looking at the behaviour of others,
since that is all that other people reveal to me. 'Behaviour' here
can include *verbal* behaviour; 'others' can include non-humans,
both animals and artefacts: machines, computers, cybernetic systems.

Introspection sounds the more limited strategy since it does,
after all, confine me to a sample of one. But all the same, it is the
more immediately compelling. Once again, I find I am looking
inwards, but this time, perhaps, I can say that what I am looking

at is not 'myself,' but my Self. I may at first unreflectingly suppose that this Self is a kind of ghost that resides in my body, the source of thinking, feeling and awareness – what, if I doubt the reality of the soul, I would be inclined to call my mind.

Qualities of mind, in particular thought and reasoning, together with the language in which they are expressed, have long been taken as the defining features of the human being. 'Man,' said Aristotle, 'is a rational animal.' This is more significant than that he is a featherless biped, has hands, uses tools, important though all these characteristics may be.

But the role of introspection may be limited. If I subtract the *language* of thinking, which, as I have seen, is potentially in the public domain, is there anything left as thought? Can there be an unexpressed thought, or is thinking, perhaps, silent speech? I remember that up to mediaeval times silent reading was an unknown art, and yet it is one now taken for granted. Perhaps silent speech is a similar skill of civilization and sophistication, and perhaps there is nothing more to thinking than the reduction of what is essentially overt and social to something less easily perceived. In this case, the Self may be nothing more than a certain flow of perceptions, for as Russell put it: 'When we try to look into ourselves, we always seem to come upon some particular thought or feeling, and not upon the "I" which has the thought or feeling.'[1] This is to echo Hume who wrote in similar vein: 'When I enter most intimately into what I call *myself*, I always stumble upon some particular perception or other.'[2]

It is striking to notice here how the empiricist tradition, continued from Hume, through Russell to Quine and beyond, converges with the work of French structuralists like Michel Foucault (1926–1984) in eliminating the notion of the self as the source of consciousness, the arbiter of meaning, the unifying *thing* that thinks. Foucault's remark that 'It is not man who takes the place of God, but anonymous thinking, thinking without a subject'[3] sounds like an unconscious echo of Russell's statement in *The Analysis of Mind* that 'Instead of saying "I think" it would be better to say "it thinks in me" or better still "there is a thought in me".[4] And both these statements might be compared with the depersonalization of the *written* text – which is, after all, speech reified – that is a central feature of Derrida's philosophy of language. For Derrida something written or published becomes a thing in the outside world, divorced from its originator, who has no better claim than anyone else to say 'what the author really means'.

Perhaps, then, I should consider whether the self is a myth which I may, taking my cue either from structuralists or radical empiricists, eliminate by a better understanding of language. But whatever my ultimate conclusions, it seems clear that I must first attempt to answer some preliminary questions about the nature of *thought* if, as seems possible, it is thought that is the thread that can lead me to the elusive 'I'.

Thought and Language

I may start here with the American philosopher Donald Davidson's (b. 1917) dicta that 'only creatures with speech have thought' and that 'a creature cannot have thought unless it is an interpreter of the speech of another'.[5]

Lying behind these remarks is the idea, not that thought *reduces* to speech, but rather that language and thought can both be explained only by reference to the setting of beliefs and desires in which they arise. The possibility of belief, though, depends on the possibility of being right or wrong: getting something right is essentially connected with being able to make a mistake. And for this concept, which is in effect the concept of truth, a shared language is necessary. Belief, then, on Davidson's view, is not intelligible as a private attitude, only as an adjustment to the public norm provided by language.

Two views in particular would run counter to this. I might say, 'words can mean whatever I want them to mean'. Or I might say, 'words can mean whatever *we* – that is, members of my speech community – want them to mean.' Either of these positions can be described as an assertion of the indeterminacy of translation and the incommensurability of languages mentioned earlier. For both suggest that what one person or group means by a word, or whole system of words – indeed, a whole language – may not be able to be reliably grasped and translated into other people's words or languages. But talk of indeterminacy of translation, if it is taken on an individual level as in the first case, amounts to the claim that a 'private' language is possible, and I have already seen the difficulties involved in this. Indeed, it seems in the end to be an unintelligible position, as Alice's pointed question to Humpty Dumpty in Lewis Carroll's *Through the Looking Glass* suggests:

'When *I* use a word,' Humpty Dumpty said, in rather a scornful tone, 'it means just what I choose it to mean – neither more nor less.'

'The question is,' said Alice, 'whether you *can* make words mean so many different things.'

'The question is,' said Humpty Dumpty, 'which is to be master – that's all.'[6]

Although Humpty Dumpty has the last word, it is a word which serves simply to reinforce the irrationality of his position.

The second, though, is a more plausible claim. For example, if educated users of English agree in using 'inchoate' to mean muddled' or 'vague', then sooner or later this will be added to the dictionary meaning of 'budding' or 'incomplete'. That is an example of a tacit change, unplanned and uncoordinated; but concerted overt agreement is possible, too, as, for example, in the way the convention has been established of using 'gay' to mean 'homosexual'.

Within any particular language, then, there is a certain partial, but not total, room for manoeuvre. Davidson accepts that a theory of language has to be relativized to a specific language, but rejects a full-blooded 'indeterminacy' claim like Quine's. So Davidson is right to say that: 'Sentences are true and words refer, *relative to a language*.'[7] On the other hand, his own view ties meaning to truth and both of these to the speaker's situation and context. It does this by means of a *formula* derived from a theory of truth established by the logician Alfred Tarski (1902–1983). Tarski's formula, which was intended to apply only to formal or logical languages, was based on the idea that what, for example, makes the German sentence 'Schnee ist weiss' true is simply that snow is white. The language for whose sentences truth is being defined is called the object-language. His formula, then, says of *any* sentence in a language that:

S is true if and only if p.

So, for example:

'Snow is white' is true in English if and only if snow is white

and

'Schnee ist weiss' is true in German if and only if snow is white.

Tarski's so-called 'semantic theory of truth' is a powerful tool where logical systems are concerned, and in spite of its apparent triviality, it does explain how the concept of truth works.[8] Tarski's theory assumes an understanding of meaning; Davidson however, inverts the procedure so as to take for granted an understanding of truth.

For Davidson, the rule for understanding the meaning of a sentence is simply this: give the truth conditions. That is, say what must be the case if the sentence is to be true.

So Davidson's formula, described as the T-Convention, is:

(T)   S is T if and only if p.

Here, as in Tarski's formula, the sentence 'S' referred to says, with some qualifications, that p. 'T' replaces 'true'. Because this is meant to apply to natural language – language the way it is in fact used – it is necessary both to specify *which* language it relates to, and also to give details of context and setting. Observation then establishes in any language what the truth conditions are, so that in the end, by trial and error, it is possible to build up a system following the model of the T-convention. (The test that a sentence has been correctly understood will be that a native speaker of the language seems to assent to it.)[9]

But Davidson's claim that questions of truth and meaning cannot be taken in isolation from questions about the context in which an utterance is embedded is more extensive than this. The context of an utterance, for Davidson, includes details about the mental state – beliefs, desires, wishes and intentions – of the person who utters it. And these all feature in the explanation, not just of an utterance, but also of an action.

So, to explain a simple *action*, for example, that a man raised his arm, it is necessary to say (i) what he wanted (e.g. to attract the attention of a friend) and (ii) what he believed (e.g. that this *would* attract the attention of his friend). Just in the way, then, that I can only interpret someone else's *action* if I know the *reason* for it – i.e. if I can give a forward-looking (teleological) explanation rather than a backward-looking one – so my understanding of an *utterance* is incomplete unless I know something about the beliefs, desires and motives of the speaker. Of course, there is a public or objective meaning since once someone has grasped this, he or she can take advantage of various possibilities of dishonest assertion – joking, exaggerating, lying and so on – which trade on the 'autonomy' of meaning. Taken together, however, these considerations suggest that the truth and meaning which are implicit in the public world of language are inseparable from the 'private' world of belief, intention and desire: in a word, thought.

If this is correct, then thought and language interlock. At first sight this would seem to confine both to humans, since humans are undisputed users of language. But only at first sight. Instead of being restrictive, this stance could be enlarging. If I can attribute language to other living creatures, or if a computer can be programmed to engage in rational conversation, then the interdependence of language and thought may lead me instead to extend the attribution of thought, and therefore of mind, to them. But let me take these alternatives separately.

Dogs, Dolphins and Chimpanzees

Norman Malcolm (1911–1990) is not the only person to have owned a dog, nor the only one to have been impressed by his dog's mental capacities. But perhaps because he is a philosopher and a former friend and student of Wittgenstein, his dog's adventures are better known that most. Malcolm's dog is said to have barked up the wrong tree in pursuit of a squirrel. If a human were to make a comparable mistake, it would be natural to say 'H *believes* that such-and-such'. In other words, a *thought* would be inferred. So much I can accept. But is attributing 'a thought' to a creature the same thing as attributing 'thought' to it?

Perhaps, witnessing a laboratory experiment in which pigeons are trained to take food from a particular door, it might seem natural for an observer, ignoring the more limited claims of the experimenter, to say 'the pigeon thinks there is food behind this door'. But then, outside the laboratory all living creatures, down to the common earthworm, take strategic action in their quest for food, safety, shelter. Why not describe all this as the entertaining of non-linguistic thoughts? The answer can only be that if I were to do so, I should have lost sight of the real difference between thinking and being, acting and reacting. I might even be obliged to extend my notion of thinking to the search of a plant for sunlight or the roots of a tree for water.

So I may decide that what I should look for instead, if I am to attribute thought to animals, is evidence of an intention to communicate. No doubt this happens more than chauvinistic humans have in the past been prepared to grant. With either pity or contempt animals have been dismissed as 'dumb brutes.' But evidence of communication within species is increasingly impressive: dolphins have a communication system of their own which can without exaggeration be called a language; the frequency of notes in a bird-call has significance for other birds; there is a complex significance in the dance of bees; and many species have warning and mating cries that enable them to pass on simple information to other species members. Then as far as communication *across* species is concerned, dogs and cats appear to show understanding of human attempts to communicate subtle sentiments or even information. And chimpanzees brought up experimentally in a domestic situation have learned the elements of human speech, using tokens or deaf-and-dumb language to compensate for the lack of the physiological apparatus of speech. Individual chimpanzees have shown they can form and express a concept of self, and also, having learned how to convey true information, have used that capacity in order to lie.

Do these observations, then, show that the fact that animals cannot speak is simply a matter of the absence of such purely physiological requirements as larynx, lips and tongue? This would seem too great a claim given the difference in linguistic capacity between even the best-trained chimp and the worst-trained human child. All the same, the difference might be a difference of quantity rather than quality. I might agree with Quine here that what follows from the vastness of the language output of humans is not necessarily that there is a gulf between human and animal, but rather that the explanatory power of science is inevitably limited by the sheer complexity and volume of language.[10]

Nevertheless, if languages in any sophisticated sense are to be attributed to other living creatures, it has to be admitted that these languages would be truly incommensurable, beyond the way in which other human languages may be argued to be incommensurable. In relation to animal communication, the human is a Martian or extraterrestrial visitor, groping towards understanding.

In Wittgenstein's famous aphorism: 'If a lion could talk, we would not understand him.'[11]

Davidson's view, then, which formed my starting-point here, is better understood as the claim that only a creature with mastery of *human* speech can think. But can this limitation be justified? If animals can master *human* speech, then, I might ask, why not admit them to our speech-community with all that that implies? For even in the case of humans, this mastery of language must be thought of as potential rather than actual. The case of Helen Keller, who was born without speech, hearing or sight, shows that in the case of humans, ways can be found round purely physical limitations. But at the same time it shows, too, that there is a deeper capacity of understanding in a human being than in any other creature, which strongly recalls Chomsky's 'innateness' thesis. In the case of Helen Keller, there was a *content* to be conveyed by speech, which in the absence of speech could be conveyed by other systems of signs which themselves had to be established by mute and intuitive communication.

This explains, perhaps, why people are so reluctant to abandon the notion of the unexpressed thought, the words that, as novelists say, 'do not come easily' to the lips. Poetry, literature and art exist to give expression to what language in its more direct forms seems unable to convey. It seems, then, that I can distinguish thought from language in the sense that thought is what language seeks to capture or express.

But if language and thought are, after all, separable, there is no reason not to attribute limited capacities for thought and belief to other living creatures. It would be odd, then, not to attribute *intelligence* to creatures which both adopt problem-solving strategies and, moreover, may have their own language for communication within their species. 'Communication' after all, is not only a speech-related term. There can be mute communication between animals, and between animal and human, as well as between human and human. Can only creatures which have speech have thought, then? Where animals are concerned, it seems this is too rigid and immodest a claim on the part of humans. But what, then, of the case of machines?[12]

Artificial Intelligence: Computers and the Simulation of Mind

Thought and intelligence are, then, closely intertwined. Thought is, I may suppose, the capacity that intelligence displays. If some kind of intelligence can be created in a factory or laboratory I may look at the resulting artifact – computer, robot or device – and ask, does this machine think?

But is 'artificial intelligence' a contradiction in terms? If the machine, perhaps a highly sophisticated computer, 'thinks' in the way its inventor has enabled it to do, should I attribute this borrowed 'intelligence' to it? Should I attribute its inventor's powers of thought to it? If someone programmes the machine with objectives, should I then say that the machine has goals and purposes of its own?

In the early days of computer technology, it would have seemed obvious that these questions were to be answered in the negative. But as early as 1950 the British logician and mathematician A. M. Turing (1912–1954) was prepared to express the confident view that by the end of the century, people would have no difficulty in accepting that machines think, although by then both 'think' and 'machine' would no longer mean quite the same thing.[13] A new breed of super-computers seems to have brought us to the point Turing envisaged earlier than he anticipated.

In order to understand how these facts relate to the questions I am asking about language, thought, mind and reasoning I must know something of the goals of the originators of these machines. Clearly, there is a difference between what might be called the instrumentalist and the speculative reasons for attempting to create artificial intelligence – or even its more limited offspring, automated reasoning. The instrumentalist goal is the immediate practical problem-solving one that consists in devising machines specifically designed to fulfil a particular function – machines which may do the job, whatever it is, more adequately than a human-being because they are more sophisticated, faster and tireless. The speculative goal has practical implications, too: it is speculative only in the sense that it is the goal of discovering more about human mental processes by attempting to imitate them in computer programs. In the end, though, the two goals of problem-solving and simulation overlap: in devising a machine to solve problems I throw light on how the human mind approaches that problem; in succeeding in simulating mental processes I provide a blueprint for the invention of problem-solving machines.

I want to known, then, whether there are irreducible differences between minds and machines – whether 'artificial intelligence' is ineluctably artificial. But I must be sure I am comparing like with like. Perhaps instead of comparing, in crude terms, minds and machines, I should contrast the hardware the houses the computer processes with the embodied brain, the brain that is accessible to the neuro-physiologist and that houses, in some sense, human mental processes. And perhaps those processes themselves should be compared, not with the computer, but with its programs. If I make *these* distinctions, and *these* comparisons, then I may find the parallel more plausible and less offensive than I might initially have supposed. Both human and computer processes may have in common structure and function. And as a result, the difference in the 'stuff' which makes the process possible may come to seem less important.

Of course, the hardware makes a difference to *some* aspects of a self that I may regard as mental. Just because it lacks an organic body, a computer is proof against sexual urges, cravings for food and drink and a desire to rest. Lacking a body, too, there are problems a computer finds difficult that I would find easy simply because *my* embodiment enables me to handle and manipulate objects: spatial terms are readily within my grasp, so that instructions which would be elementary to me may be beyond the grasp of, for example, an industrial robot.

But I know that many of the ways in which I think myself distinctive and the machine inferior are ultimately imitable by machines. Programs may be written, for example, so as to leave some decisions open, to be taken by the computer at a later time, in the light of circumstances, or even to allow the computer scope to arrive, independently of human guidance, at new ways of *making* decisions. This means that a programmer cannot necessarily foresee everything that a computer will do. Nor is it the case that computers must work through all possibilities by the method of exhaustive search. Heuristic search theory provides general principles for making the exploration of possibilities systematic and so providing the kind of short-cuts in thinking that humans take for granted.

On the other hand, I can recognise some processes as peculiarly unsuited to computer-programming. While task-oriented programs fit with the computer's problem-solving skills, it is not clear by *what* kind of program I could arrange for a machine to experience pain, or emotions, or see an after-image. It seems that the computer's world is the world of the cognitive, rather than the world of the affective – the imitation of human knowing rather than the imitation of human feeling.

But the fact is that whatever the success or failure, the attempt at modelling creates a new situation: the new aspect is that where previous reflections on the nature of human thought were no more than free-ranging speculation, these simulation attempts provide a *test* of the accuracy or inaccuracy of the theory behind the program. If the theory about a thought-process or piece of reasoning is correct, the program is usable. If not, not. And amongst the features that *have* been established in this way are some which are particularly relevant to my own enquiry.

First is the discovery of the way in which actual perception is conditioned by setting and expectations. I know that where a machine is concerned, it is necessary to build in information about the 'frame' or setting within which any process is to take place – things which I can take for granted in human approaches to problem-solving. (In the human case, if I give someone a cake recipe, for example, I need not describe the kitchen and the oven.) Here, then, something must be explicitly *added* to a computer's information if it is to deal with a particular problem.

Conversely, in ordinary life, the mind is continually eliminating the irrelevant to hear what it wants to hear, see what it wants to see. A human picks out the sound of English sentences from a hubbub of noise, the shape of a familiar word from a careless scrawl. A machine is in the position of someone trying to pick out sentences in a crowded room where the speakers are using an unfamiliar foreign language. It needs to be told how to recognize patterns and how to eliminate the inessential. In general, what is usually taken for granted by humans has to be made explicit in computer programming.

Secondly, while the complexity of language and the difficulty of programming a machine to use language like a human being has become apparent, it seems significant that thought and reasoning can be translated into non-verbal, symbolic, and even pictorial or diagrammatic language. This strikes me more forcibly when I recall the problem that was faced by scientists who sent information into space in a search for other intelligence in the universe, and also that of others who left a buried capsule for our remote descendants to discover. In both cases, a common language could not be assumed, but the language of computers – numbers and diagrams – provided a realistic means of communication, a method of analogical representation. I know, too, that conversely, there are areas of science and mathematics where debate, argument and progress can no longer be interpreted in verbal terms, but can be expressed only in terms of symbolism and number.

Mind, Matter and Behaviour

I conclude, then, that in looking at thinking, I am looking beyond the purely verbal. I grasp this dimly when I envisage the possibility of intergalactic communication between intelligent beings; more concretely when for the sake of a computer program I attempt to express in diagrams or numbers what would more readily be expressed in words.

But is this, in the old terms of philosophical debate, a materialist view? Or does it protect the notion of the mental as something irreducible and untranslatable into materialist or mechanistic terms? One thing that the comparison has shown is that in a certain sense – or at least for the limited purposes I have in mind here – the matter-mind controversy is irrelevant. The constitution of the thing that thinks is not important if what I am interested in is the process itself.

But even this debate may be pre-empted if I find that the language of mental concepts is, after all, unnecessary for describing human experience. In *The Concept of Mind*, the Oxford linguistic philosopher Gilbert Ryle (1900–1976) offered a complete analysis and explanation of mental terms – terms such as 'know', 'believe', 'think', 'will' – in ways which referred only to overt behaviour, or at least to *dispositions* people might have to behave in certain ways.

Here I may compare the kind of behaviourism put forward by philosophers with that which some psychologists take as a background assumption. A philosophical or logical behaviourist like Ryle is trying to show how one might in principle dispense with mentalistic terms. It is part of his claim that there is no residue – nothing left unaccounted for. A psychological behaviourist, on the other hand, may merely be an agnostic about the mind. For methodological reasons, a psychologist may want to look only at what is measurable and observable. If there is a non-material mind, that is not his business. And in any laboratory experiments, the mentalistic stage in an explanation is, on a behaviourist view, simply redundant. For example, in the laboratory, the sequence:

deprivation of food → feeling hungry → eating

can be abbreviated without the loss of anything essential for research purposes to:

deprivation of food → eating

The psychological behaviourist may, however, draw stronger conclusions than this. B. F. Skinner, for instance, is clear about the implications for human thought: 'Human thought,' he writes, 'is human behaviour. The history of human thought is what people have said and done.'[14]

But perhaps I should distinguish the question of how I can tell what people have thought or what someone now is thinking from the questions (a) of what it is *that* someone has thought or is thinking, and (b) of *whether* thought or thinking is something that occurs in distinction from overt bodily movements. Perhaps, too, I should, as in the case of computer programs, distinguish those which are questions about cognition, from questions about other people's *feelings* – their pain, happiness, moods, level of consciousness.

In the first case, some kind of proposition always seems to be involved – a thought *that* something is the case. Or a hope that . . . , expectation that . . . , belief that . . . , wish that . . . In the second case, no 'that' clauses are involved. A person simply *is* happy, sad, or in pain.

In either case, though, the behaviourist perspective seems to offer a truth about *my access* to what is, as one says, 'in another person's mind'. But it is also a truth about other people's access to what is in mine. And I know how easily I can trick, mislead or conceal, but also, even if I do none of these things, how prone *they* are to misunderstanding.

Ryle's thesis is aimed at exploding the myth of mind as another kind of existent, located in the body like a pilot in a plane or a driver in a car. It is based on analysing mental terms *dispositionally*: that is to say, by analogy with concepts like 'fragility' or 'malleability'. Instead of interpreting these terms as ways of describing an abstract characteristic inherent in, say, glass or wax, it is possible to see sentences using the terms as translatable into sentences saying what would *happen* under specified circumstances. To say something is fragile is to say that it will easily shatter if dropped or struck with a heavy object. To say that it is malleable is to say that it can easily be moulded, given the right sort of conditions.

Similarly, in the case of mental characteristics to say, for example, that a girl knows how to ride a bicycle is not to attribute an abstract characteristic to her but to say that, given the right circumstances, she will successfully ride a bicycle. To say that a man wants something will be to say something about what he would do if offered it. To say someone hates someone is to talk about the aversive behaviour he or she is likely to adopt if that person is present. It seems it is *this* kind of analysis that the behaviourist is committed to, although no analysis like this can be entirely free from objection and the task of refinement may be indefinite, given the number of qualifications needed to guarantee the truth of any particular translation. (I might have to add, for instance, that the potential cyclist does not consider it undignified, that the person who wants something is not an ascetic or a masochist, that the hater has no reason for concealment, and so on.) Nevertheless, there is a certain truth in the behaviourist's point, well expressed by Norman Malcolm in this way: in the case of another person, he writes, 'I *see amusement in his face*, or *sullenness in his posture*. I am not compelled to infer these things from something else that I see.'[15]

I can see two main problems, though, with this position. One is that there are certain mental concepts it does *not* seem plausible to deal with in this way. How am I to account, for example, for reflective thought? Or the exercise of imagination? The other is the problem of transferring this, which is a good explanation of how I become aware of *other people*'s mental processes, to my own case. For the fact is that I do not attribute mental happenings to *myself* on the basis of behaviour. I do not have two concepts of pain, one for my own case, the other for the case of other people. It is true, though, that I verify 'I am in pain' differently from the way in which I verify 'He, or she, is in pain' or 'you are in pain'.

One solution to this problem might be to see 'I am in pain' not as a statement at all, but as the way in which other people have, on the basis of my behaviour in infancy, taught me to *express* my pain. Thus the problem of the asymmetry of meaning as between first person and second or third person uses of mental terms might be overcome by showing that they are, as Malcolm suggests, 'linked in meaning by virtue of being tied, in different ways, to the same behavioural criteria'.[16]

Nevertheless, there is a crudity about the behavioural analysis of mental terms that I would still wish to avoid, and since there is, in any case, so large a part of my mental life left unaccounted for, I have to consider whether the psychological position linked with this kind of philosophical analysis is itself plausible.

I note that even Skinner, although a leading exponent of behaviourism, denies his intention to eliminate the private world of the mind. He writes:

It would be foolish to deny the existence of that private world, but it is also foolish to assert that because it is private it is of a different nature from the world outside. The difference is not in the stuff of which the private world is composed, but in its accessibility.[17]

In other words, behaviourism, whether philosophical or psychological, encourages me to recreate the world in terms of public observable events. If I ignore my own introspective experience, though, it seems I may find myself obliged, as one writer put it, to 'feign anaesthesia'. Skinner's claim is that private experiences cannot be discussed in public interpersonal language without misunderstanding. The goal of self-awareness – the instruction over the door at Delphi, 'Know yourself' – is set aside as a handicap to psychological investigation.

But the message of the behaviourist programme, however agnostically presented, is essentially materialistic. The subject to which it is appropriate to attribute behaviour is a physical object: the body. Other forms of materialism, though, attach more importance to the brain and nervous system of the body than to the crude overt movements of the whole mammal, bird or other living-creature. Where views like these are concerned, it is the brain itself which thinks, feels, has sensations. But this approach is not necessarily hostile to behaviourism. Indeed, it may take the notion of *dispositions* to behave in certain ways as an intermediate step in telling a complete physicalist (i.e. materialist) story. For a disposition is more easily identified with a brain-state than is an actual bodily movement.[18]

From this point of view, then, the mentalistic terms of ordinary language are a heritage of 'folk psychology' – destined, like talk of witches or vital spirits to fall into disuse with the advent of sophisticated enlightenment, or else to continue in use, in the way we continue to talk of the sun rising and setting, with no longer any thought that this implies the pre-Copernican view of the planetary system. Whatever language we choose to use, advocates of this view say, the facts are better explained by neuroscience; and the resolution of problems about minds is in the end empirical, not linguistic. As I have seen, it was a fault of a cruder form of philosophical behaviourism that it made it seem otherwise. Neuroscience, on the other hand, instead of merely offering an alternative vocabulary, has revealed much about the brain's microstructure that can affect my understanding of mental states and conditions. I know, for example, that these can be manipulated and affected by deliberate or accidental damage to the brain. I know that drugs and alcohol or the process of senile decay can affect rational thought; that a vast array of chemicals can affect the emotions; and that consciousness itself is affected by anaesthetics that act on the brain and nervous system, or by the cruder eventuality of a blow to the skull.

Does this mean, then, that sensations are simply processes in the brain? When I talk about recalling the scent of blossom, am I really talking about a neural happening? Is that recall itself a brain process? The possibility of identification may make sense by analogy with certain other scientific identifications: for example, I may initially be willing to accept the identity of a cloud with a mass of particles in suspension, or of lightning with an electrical discharge.

Nevertheless, although there is a sense in which these *are* indisputably identities, there is *another* sense in which this is *not* what a cloud is to me, nor what a flash of lightning is to me. In this sense, what the recollection of the scent of blossom is to me is not something that would yield to physiological inspection by a scientist with the means to observe my brain processes.

Perhaps, then, I should say that these are two ways of seeing the same thing? After all, I can observe a cloud or a streak of lightning either with the naked eye, or with scientific measuring instruments. But in the case of human thought, is it 'the same thing?' And what would be the consequence of me thinking that it was? Would it, for example, simplify my approach to causal explanation where human beings are concerned? Or would I have destroyed distinctions which are necessary to my own self-concept — my own sense, that is, of myself as an agent, interacting with the world?[19]

Being a Person

The problem I am now confronting is this: if cybernetic systems — robots and computers — can imitate human processes, and if it is only the complexity of the human brain that makes it harder to forecast and explain the behaviour of a human being than that of any other living creature, then it might seem that the most distinctive and valuable parts of human existence have been evaporated by a harsh and antihumanistic science. Man is, after all, no more than a part of the nature he himself investigates. Or, as Derrida put it, these developments could be said to have a tendency 'to oust all metaphysical concepts — including the concepts of soul, of life, of value, of choice, of memory — which until recently served to separate the machine from man'.[20]

But is this necessarily so? At first, I may uncritically accept the mind–body dichotomy, seeing myself as essentially a mind which owns a body — after all, the notion of self-control *is* the notion of mind in control of body. But, then, I may notice that sometimes I have a notion of myself, my person, which lies outside both mind and body. I may decide to discipline my mind, as well as my body — to control my own thoughts and emotions.

This notion, though, is an odd one when I think about it. A person who is neither mind nor body – does this make sense? Better, perhaps, to say that a person is a unity which possesses both mental and the physical attributes. Might there not be a distinctive notion of a person as someone who both does things which are indisputably physical, like eating or walking, and also does things which are mental, like thinking and feeling? P. F. Strawson (b. 1919), in putting a view like this, writes of a person as the subject to which are attached both person-predicates (predicates which imply the possession of states of consciousness) and material-object-predicates, which do not. An experience, he maintains, can only be identified as *belonging to* someone, and the concept of a person must be taken as a primitive unanalysable concept.[21]

I can see that both this theory and the straight materialist position can solve problems I might otherwise find troubling in relation to causality. If, like Descartes, I want to maintain a duality of mind and body, the mental and the physical, then I must confront, as he did, the problem of interaction between the two. How can something which is non-material effect changes in a material body? For the latter, it seems that a full range of causal explanations is already available. Indeed, the problem might seem to be the embarrassment of causal explanations that are on offer. A neural physiologist may want to explain one neural process by reference to a preceding one; a psychologist, on the other hand, may look for an explanation in some immediate environmental stimulus. If the psychological tradition is Freudian, though, the explanation is more likely to be in terms of unconscious causes in early childhood; a sociologist, on the other hand, will offer collective rather than individual explanations in terms, perhaps, of social class; while a Marxist may appeal to inexorable laws of history.

In the end, a complicated series of reductions of one science to another – broadly, of sociology to psychology, of psychology to physiology and chemistry – may leave a materialist conception of human beings standing. Confident that this is so, the materialist may strongly reject the intrusion into this tidy universe of a nonreducible element: the mental. The distaste is well summed-up in the phrase applied to mental phenomena of this sort by J. J. C. Smart. They are 'nomological danglers', as are the psychophysical laws which would be necessary to explain them.[22]

This is a plausible use of Ockham's razor. (William of Ockham (Occam) (*c.* 1285–1349) was a fourteenth-century logician who enunciated a fruitful principle of frugality in reasoning: that one should not multiply entities needlessly.) However, the contrary view has difficulties, too, as Socrates showed when, in the *Phaedo* he argued that an explanation in terms of his body – its muscles, bones, flesh, skin – would totally fail to explain why it was that he was sitting in prison awaiting death, rather than hiding away in a hospitable foreign country. The reason Socrates himself gave for being there was *honour* – a different order of explanation altogether. It is different, first, in that it points forwards rather than backwards, and secondly, in that it posits a novel form of motivation – moral motivation.

So does the fact that human actions need to be explained in terms of what a person wants and is trying to achieve make the case of humans irreducibly different? Or can intentional human behaviour be explained and predicted in the same way that other phenomena are? Is man a subject for science, or a 'law unto himself'? The problem is that human acts are part of the natural order, but nevertheless it seems that they cannot be brought under deterministic laws. A person very often appears to have a choice as to what to do.

In addressing questions like these, Donald Davidson concludes that forward-looking explanations – explanations in terms of intention or reasons for acting, are not a different form of causal explanation from others. He reaches his conclusion which he describes as 'anomalous monism' by insisting that what we deal in are not mental states or processes but *events*. And in the case of events, it is easier to talk of an identity between the mental and the physical. Mental characteristics, he believes, may be supervenient on (i.e. arise out of and be dependent on) physical ones, though not reducible to them.

Davidson holds, then, that a psychological explanation is an explanation that someone acted in a certain way because he had certain desires and certain beliefs. But although this is a causal explanation, he thinks there are no strict laws relating the mental to the physical. They would require too much detail and it would be too complicated to settle that some particular action would be the outcome in any particular situation. Nevertheless, the events that we are relating in terms of psychological terms like 'believe', 'wish', 'hope' and so on, are, according to Davidson, also physical events, and as *physical* events subject to *physical* laws.

Do moves such as these towards a materialist perspective mean, then, that the apparently distinctive features of human beings are in the end to be subsumed under general causal explanations? And if so, must I lose my grasp on the mental which seems to be the seat of my commitment to reason and thought, as well as to the world of feeling, sensibility, emotion and the real power of the will? Would this mean, too, the loss of the notion of objective truth, which has allowed me so far to reject some ideas and directions as false, and to follow others fruitfully?

Pondering these questions, I am struck by an interesting, though frequently unremarked, feature of the identity thesis – the thesis, that is, that identifies mind with matter. This is that, like any authentic assertion of identity, it may be read in reverse. But if I invert the reduction

MIND – DISPOSITION TO BEHAVE – PHYSICO-CHEMICAL STATE

then the significance of the identification – the message that it apparently carries – seems to change. I find, then, that some physico-chemical states, those associated with living beings, and *possibly* with some artifacts of human making, are, at the level of the organism or object, to be identified first with behaviour, but in the end, in virtue of their structure and the functions that they serve, with mind.

In other words, to reduce the mental to the physical is also to elevate the physical to the mental. At the same time it is, it must be admitted, very much to enlarge the scope of the mental. Nevertheless, such a reconstruction means that I can now, finally, set aside as idle the argument about the 'stuff' of things. And I can now ask what, within *this* framework, does distinguish the human person?

Rationality, Freedom and Will

Three things in particular seem to me important: these are rationality, will and creativity. Animals, too, show motivation which is not directed simply to the satisfaction of bodily needs. They, too, demonstrate curiosity (in humans the spring of intellectual enquiry), a desire to explore and to have new experiences. But although these characteristics are present in rudimentary form in other creatures, the difference in degree between humans and the rest of nature is so great as to be in effect a difference in kind.

Perhaps it is because of this effective difference, though, that humans are also capable of love, self-sacrifice, spite, revenge, the impulse to be creative and – as the example of Socrates showed – to guide their own conduct by moral considerations.

It is this, in particular, which seems to fit most awkwardly with the materialist hypothesis. For moral agency and moral responsibility, it seems that freedom to choose – not to be bound by a network of extraneous causes – is essential. Freedom seems, I might say, incompatible with a close mesh of causality. But having glimpsed some of the layers of apparently conflicting causal explanation, the threat of the causal nexus impinges less immediately. And the fact that the 'mental' is no longer outside this network, but integrated within it removes the sting.

For the freedom that I need may be only the freedom that lies within my own hands – the freedom to 'be myself'. Perhaps freedom in the case of any living creature means simply that the causes of its behaviour lie within rather than wholly outside that creature. (But this provides the cut-off point where machines

would have to be refused a place in 'our' universe – their existence and functioning is a product of wholly external causes.)

For myself, I know that what I am is dependent on innate or
genetic factors combined with present and past environmental
influences. Nevertheless, I know that these two elements – or
indeed the first alone – make the pattern of my being unique.
Nature *always* breaks the mould after creating an individual. (*I*
cannot be, I might reason, less distinctive than my fingerprints or
voiceprint.)

Given this consideration, a metaphysical hypothesis about the
'stuff' of the universe or of human-beings cannot deprive me of
the freedom which is manifested in rationality, will and creativity.
'Both the invention of the wheel', I might say, 'and the acceptance of moral guidelines for living are evidence against crude
determinism.'

But if my own freedom and rationality are consistent with a
cohesive and causally explicable universe in which mind and
matter merge – a universe from which mind has not been ex-
pelled, but in which matter is not, as Berkeley put it 'stupid, inert
and unthinking' – then I am drawn irresistibly to recall the
starting reflections of philosophy in which appearances were rejected, and the search was instigated for an underlying structure
and reality: mind, soul, God or nature.

NOTES

1   B. Russell, *The Problems of Philosophy*, p. 50.
2   D. Hume, *A Treatise of Human Nature*, Book I, 6.
3   M. Foucault, *The Order of Things*. Foucault was distinguished as a
    critic of Western intellectual traditions. He is perhaps best known
    for his studies of madness and of sexuality.
4   B. Russell, *The Analysis of Mind*, p. 18.
5   D. Davidson, 'Thought and Talk' in S. Guttenplan (ed.), *Mind and
    Language*, pp. 19 and 9.

6   Lewis Carroll, *Through the Looking Glass, and What Alice Found There*, p. 269. Lewis Carroll was also the logician Charles Dodgson, and in that capacity he wrote in his *Symbolic Logic*: 'The writers, and editors, of the Logical text-books which run in the ordinary grooves . . . take, on this subject, what seems to me to be a more humble position than is necessary. They speak of the Copula of a Proposition "with bated breath"; almost as if it were a living, conscious Entity, capable of declaring for itself what it chose to mean, and that we, poor human creatures, had nothing to do but to ascertain *what* was its sovereign will and pleasure, and submit to it.

    In opposition to this view, I maintain that any writer of a book is fully authorised in attaching any meaning he likes to any word or phrase he intends to use' (p. 165, quoted on pp. 267–8 of *The Annotated Alice*).

7   D. Davidson, 'The Inscrutability of Reference' in *Enquiries into Truth and Interpretation*, p. 239 (my italics).

8   Tarski's theory was presented in a famous article entitled 'The Semantic Conception of Truth'. The paradox of the Liar, mentioned in chapter 4, is a semantic paradox. Semantic paradoxes have been explained as arising from the attempt to talk about a system from within that system. Such paradoxes have in common the fact that they combine a claim about truth with self-reference. Tarski's theory offered a way out of this and other semantic paradoxes, in part by distinguishing sentences from names of sentences. See the account of Tarski in W.v.O. Quine, *Philosophy of Logic*.

9   For this theory, see in particular D. Davidson, 'Truth and Meaning' in *Enquiries into Truth and Interpretation*, pp. 23 ff.

10   See W.v.O. Quine, 'Mind and Verbal Dispositions' in S. Guttenplan (ed.), *Mind and Language*, pp. 83–95.

11   L. Wittgenstein, *Philosophical Investigations*, II xi, p. 233.

12   This is not a new controversy. Descartes believed that animals, lacking souls, were mere machines – bêtes machines – and that intelligent speech and action distinguish human beings from them. Julien Offray de la Mettrie (1709–51) agreed with Descartes that animals are machines, but argued in his book *L'Homme Machine* (Man a Machine) that humans are not essentially different. They are machines, too, and it would be possible to manufacture a mechanical talking man.

13 See A. Turing, 'Computing Machinery and Intelligence' in Alan Ross Anderson (ed.), *Minds and Machines*.

Alan Mathison Turing (1912–1954) was an English mathematician, a cryptographer during his war service, whose interest in symbolic logic led him to the theory of computing machines. The name 'Turing machine' is given to the concept of a machine which is completely self-contained in its procedures once it has been given unambiguous instructions.

In a paper published in 1936, before electronic computers existed, under the title 'On Computable Numbers', Turing set out the nature and theoretical limitations of computing machines, although by the time he wrote 'Computing Machinery and Intelligence' (1950), he was prepared to argue that machines were in principle capable of fully imitating human intelligence.

14 B. F. Skinner, *About Behaviorism*, p. 117.

B. F. Skinner (1904–1990) was a behavioural psychologist who sought to establish conditioning as the explanation for human and animal behaviour, and who regarded it as an appropriate tool for political and social control. His novel *Walden Two* describes a society built on such principles; its distinctive feature is the way in which human beings are treated as manipulable by punishment and reward.

15 N. Malcolm, *Problems of Mind*, p. 101.

16 Ibid., p. 91.

17 B. F. Skinner, *Beyond Freedom and Dignity*, p. 101.

18 Quine, for example, holds that a behaviourist explanation is ultimately an explanation in terms of neural events.

19 For a classic defence of the Mind-Body Identity theory, see U. T. Place, 'Is Consciousness a Brain Process'.

20 J. Derrida, *Of Grammatology*, p. 9.

21 See P. F. Strawson, 'Persons' in V. C. Chappell (ed.), or his *Individuals: an essay in descriptive metaphysics*. P. F. Strawson (b. 1919) is a British philosopher in the analytic tradition who has been influential in promoting a return to metaphysics in a Kantian spirit.

22 J. J. C. Smart uses this term in his article 'Sensations and Brain Processes'. Smart takes it from H. Feigl who, in his paper 'The "Mental" and the "Physical"', uses the terms for the laws themselves.

READING GUIDE

A clear and interesting general introduction to the theme of this chapter, the philosophy of mind, is P. M. Churchland's *Matter and Consciousness*. *Mind and Language*, ed. S. Guttenplan, is a useful collection of essays on these topics. For Davidson's views on philosophical psychology, see his *Essays on Actions and Events*.

The classic statement of philosophical behaviourism is G. Ryle's *The Concept of Mind*, while a committed defence of psychological behaviourism is to be found in B. F. Skinner's *About Behaviorism* and *Beyond Freedom and Dignity*. See also his science-fiction novel *Walden Two*.

For discussion of many of the topics touched on in this chapter including cognitive psychology, artificial intelligence, and notions of freedom and responsibility, see D. Dennett, *Brainstorms* and his later book *Consciousness Explained*. While collections of articles do not always provide the best way into a philosophical topic, in an area like philosophy of mind which is bound to be affected by developments in the empirical and scientific explanation of both brain processes and artificial intelligence, good collections can be extremely useful. To be recommended are W. G. Lycan (ed.), *Mind and Cognition* and N. Block (ed.), *Readings in Philosophy of Psychology*. The smaller classic collection edited by V. C. Chappell, *The Philosophy of Mind* is also useful.

On the subject of folk psychology, see S. P. Stich, *From Folk Psychology to Cognitive Science* and the useful collection of articles edited by J. D. Greenwood, *The Future of Folk Psychology: intentionality and cognitive science*, which includes contributions by Fodor, Churchland, Dennett, Blackburn and Margolis amongst others. See in particular ch. 4. 'Connectionism, eliminativism and the future of folk psychology' by W. Ramsey, S. Stich and J. Gavon.

Specifically on artificial intelligence, the reader might enjoy R. Penrose, *The Emperor's New Mind: concerning computers, minds and the laws of physics*.

On the question of analogies with animals, see the article by T. Nagel, 'What is it like to be a bat?', while a good starting-point for consideration of the question of what it is to be a person would be B. Williams' essay 'The Makropolous case' in his *The Problems of the Self*. Other important though difficult books on this subject are P. F. Strawson's *Individuals: an essay in descriptive metaphysics* and D.

Parfit's *Reasons and Persons*. Not to be neglected, either, is *The Mind's I: Fantasies of Self and Soul* by Douglas R. Hofstadter and D. C. Dennett, an original and wide-ranging book which brings together, with commentary, extracts from sources which might otherwise be difficult to track down.

Free will is an ancient and much discussed philosophical problem. I have not attempted to expound the differences between determinists, compatibilists and libertarians in this chapter, but available literature is extensive. One clear and readable account of the issues is D. J. O'Connor's *Free Will*, or see P. van Inwagen, *An Essay on Free Will*, while there is a useful selection of readings edited by Gary Watson under the title *Free Will*.

8

Seeing Further

Weary therefore of dogmatism that teaches us nothing and equally of scepticism that promises us nothing at all, not even to rest in permitted ignorance; challenged by the importance of the knowledge that we need and made suspicious by long experience with regard to all the knowledge that we believe we possess, or that offers itself to us under the title of pure reason – we only have one critical question left, by answering which we can regulate our future conduct: is metaphysics possible at all?
Immanuel Kant, *Prolegomena*

The understanding I have reached, then, is that one of the great gulfs people have believed existed – that between mind and matter – is no more than a superficial crack on the surface of reality. As far as this is concerned, there is only one thing in the universe, not two. I leave it to physicists to define it further, and I know already, from what I have heard about the chemical basis of matter, that the results of their explorations will be subtle, surprising, and far removed from the mechanistic materialism of nineteenth century science. Indeed, the speculations of the pre-Socratic philosophers seem closer to twentieth-century truth on these matters than the received opinion of intervening centuries.

The Greeks, I know, thought of the universe as consisting of endless transformations of material. Nothing, they believed, can come out of nothing; nor is it possible that anything that actually exists could cease to exist for, as they said: 'it will always continue to be, wherever one may keep putting it.' Hence the attraction for them of religions like the Orphic one. Perhaps it is here, too, that

Western philosophy in its origins touches the wisdom and lore of the East. According to the Orphic doctrines, as in some Eastern religions, all existence is cyclical – a wheel of birth and death, with rebirth in other forms, as animals or other human beings – for those who apparently pass out of existence. The pre-Socratic philosophers, then, saw a need to account for the appearance of change, for change *is* essentially coming into being and passing away.

We think of this phenomenon as change rather than as cessation and commencement because when we refer to change we refer to a single aspect of some continuing existent ceasing or coming into being – change made visible by a background which remains constant. So when a leaf changes from green to brown, only the colour and texture change – the basic structure of the leaf remains as it was. It is a small step from that observation to the idea that when the leaf itself seems to decay and pass out of existence, there is simply a restribution in the atmosphere of the minute parts of matter which came together to create the leaf.

It is in this sense that philosophers like Parmenides believed that change is illusory and that behind the appearance of change, there is a constant and undifferentiated underlying reality. While Heracleitus, widely seen as the opponent of Parmenides both in antiquity and today, was making, not a different point, but essentially the same point with his doctrine of flux. Heracleitus' famous remark that it is impossible to step into the same river twice suggests that what strikes us as a continuing object is a matter of a certain relationship of parts which themselves have no permanence and which it is impossible to pin down.[1] Permanence itself is in fact constituted by the fleeting and impermanent.

It is interesting to notice how Greek atomists like Epicurus (341–271 BC) turned these ideas into theories which seem remarkably like the theories of modern science. (They appeared in poetic form in the work of the Roman writer Lucretius (95–55 BC) who set them out in his long poem *The Nature of the Universe, De Rerum Natura*.)[2] The Epicurean theory answered the question of how the universe was constituted in terms of atoms continually in motion and constantly re-grouping to form new but ephemeral entities. It was a materialism that left little scope for religion: it aimed to banish the fear of death by showing that death was indeed the end of life, and held that the gods or god, if existing at all, remained aloof and uninvolved in the affairs of humans.

Would these same consequences, I wonder, accompany a twentieth century view of a basically homogeneous universe which is nevertheless a maelstrom of movement and change? Should I, if I believe the apparent variety of the world is reducible to chemical combinations and reactions, dismiss the idea of God, despite the part this idea has played in human life? And if I have no notion of mind as separate, can I have no concept, either, of the soul? If mental and physical merge, what am I to say of the spiritual? What are the consequences of *this* for those aspirations to immortality that I and other human beings sometimes feel? And, finally, though perhaps most immediately important, what attitude should I have to the animal realities of pain, suffering and death?

As I reflect on these questions, I see that they can hardly be answered piecemeal or one by one. Both questions and answers present themselves only as part of a closely woven tapestry. I know that in the history of philosophy answers to *these* questions have most strikingly been offered in great metaphysical *systems* – whole, rather than partial, explanations, which include a total reinterpretation of the crude facts of experience.

Finding one of these systems acceptable as an answer to my questions may be less a matter of intellectual judgement than of intuitive grasp. As the French philosopher Etienne Bonnot de Condillac (1715–80) wrote: 'As for suppositions, the imagination makes them with so much pleasure and so easily. It is from such foundations that one creates and governs the universe., all this costs no more than a dream, and philosophers dream easily.' Echoing Voltaire, he added, '. . . One ignores details, the things under one's eyes; one takes flight into unknown lands, and one constructs systems.'[3] But even at the beginning of my enquiry, I noticed that some kind of intuitive awareness was essential for

answering questions that I listed then. Here, again, though, I feel
I need a mentor and a guide. And so I turn once more to Sophia
and in answer to my letter she writes to me in these terms:

Fifteenth Letter from Sophia

• *Dear Q,*
  *I think at this stage in your quest you may be interested to hear of
  a tale told by Plato in the* Republic.[4] *It is a metaphor which you
  may find fits your experience.*

  *In Plato's story, a group of prisoners lie shackled in an under-
  ground cave. A kind of primitive cinema screen is placed in front of
  them on which the shadows of objects are discernible. They cannot
  see the objects themselves, which are behind the screen. The prisoners amuse themselves and keep themselves occupied by guessing
  what the objects are of which they see the shadows projected on the
  screen. Some of them, in fact, become very proficient at this. But
  one of their number manages to break free of his shackles and,
  seeing a distant chink of light, manages with much hardship and
  effort to break out of the cave into the world of daylight and
  sunshine. There he sees for the first time the real objects, of which
  only the shadows were visible below, and he is struck by their
  beauty and luminosity.*

  *I suspect this may be the kind of experience of illumination you
  have written to ask me about. But I should add, if you are affected
  by this story, that in Plato's account, the prisoner who escaped and
  had this experience felt it his duty in the end to return to the cave
  and tell his fellow prisoners what he had seen. But, of course, when
  he got back, no-one would believe him — particularly as the bright
  light of the sun had dazzled his eyes, so that for a time he became
  rather stupid at the shadow-guessing game they all continued to
  play.*

  *Perhaps, if you think about this, you may be a little wary of
  continuing your quest. I hope not. But, all the same, you may ask,
  'What kind of experience is this glimpse of the sun? Is it some-*

*thing in line with the kind of discoveries I have made up to now
– just a further more advanced stage of enquiry? Or is it different
in kind from the modest advances in knowledge I have so far
made?' Well, Q, my dear young friend, there is a description in a
letter said to have been written by Plato of the kind of experience
it might be:*

> *It is not something that can be put into words like other branches of
> learning; only after long partnership in a common life devoted to this very
> thing does truth flash upon the soul, like a flame kindled by a leaping
> spark, and once it is born there it nourishes itself thereafter.*[5]

*This certainly sounds more like what you, Q, initially described
in your letter to me as intuition. It could even be called mystic
insight. Mysticism is not so foreign to twentieth-century philosophy
as you might think. Compare, for example, Wittgenstein's saying:
'There is indeed the inexpressible.' And his enigmatic concluding
remarks in the Tractatus: 'My propositions serve as elucidations
in the following way; anyone who understands me eventually
recognises them as nonsensical, when he has used them – as steps
– to climb up beyond them. (He must, so to speak, throw away the
ladder after he has climbed up it.)'*[6]

*I think perhaps you are ready for this kind of illumination. So
I can only suggest you look at some of the great systems of
metaphysics offered by philosophers such as Leibniz, Spinoza and
Kant, I should like to be your guide in these matters, but have to
tell you that age and health seem likely to prevent me. Do not
worry about me, but if I am able, I shall write to you over the next
few days with a few suggestions, telling you of directions which I
myself have found most helpful in these matters.*

Yours,
Sophia

Sophia kept her promise and I heard from her twice more, once
on the Stoic system, and once on Spinoza, before I heard that she

had died. I would have grieved for her, but then I understood why, evidently with some prescience, she had also sent me, folded inside her letter to me, this passage from Epictetus:

Was it then misfortune and unhappiness that the gods intended for us when they endowed us with reason? Did they want us to be miserable and spend our lives grieving? Imagine how it would be if everyone were immortal and nobody ever went away, but we all stayed tied to roots like plants. Should we really sit down and cry whenever one of our friends leaves us, and again, if he comes back, dance about and clap, like children?

Surely it is high time that we grew up and reminded ourselves of what we heard from the philosophers – if indeed we did not see that they were offering us a remedy for our pain when they told us that this universe is one city, and the substance of which it is constructed single, that it conforms to a regular pattern and the time must inevitably come for one thing to give place to another; that some things remain static while others change. The world is full of our friends, first of all gods, and next after them men, united as they all are in one family by natural ties. Some must remain together, but others must go their separate ways. We should enjoy their company while we have it, but not be sad at parting.[7]

Epictetus (*c.* 50–*c.* 138) was himself a Stoic. As a freed slave inhumane and barbarian times, he needed to find a philosophical instance or perspective which would be valid independently of external circumstances. He found this in the Stoic system. Sophia had obviously found his perspective illuminating, for she wrote to me in these terms:

Sixteenth Letter from Sophia

• *Dear Q,*
The Stoic system flourished in changing forms for many centuries in antiquity, and indeed you may be interested to know that I have heard rumours of attempts to revive it in a form adapted to the

present day.[8] However that may be, in its original Greek form, when it was associated particularly with the philosopher Chrysippus (280–206 BC), it involved an ascetic way of life. When later it became a philosophy for Roman emperors, some of that asceticism was muted, although it still embodied an ethic of strong self-control. In its later form, it flourished in the first and second centuries AD and it is that form which was moulded by Epictetus, Seneca (c. 4 BC–AD 65) – he was Nero's minister – and the emperor Marcus Aurelius (AD 121–80).

You will remember that I mentioned Stoic logic briefly when I wrote to you on that subject. Probably, though, it is Stoic ethics rather than Stoic theories about logic or again about scientific or physical reality that you will think of immediately as Stoicism. As far as that is concerned, it centres on two things: inwardly it involves self-control and tranquillity – outwardly social usefulness, not just on a narrow or parochial front, but on the stage of the world, on which all human beings meet as equals. This ethical system is based on the belief that God makes everything what it is and maintains the basic harmony of the universe. 'God' means the ultimate cause and fabric of everything that exists – something that can also be called the Logos or reason of the world – order, destiny or the law of nature. The idea of order, I might say, is fundamental.

So, in the Stoic system, the universe does not run one way in time, as we tend to think. Time is just an aspect of things. Instead, it follows through a never-ending series of cycles. Each cycle (the word was periodos – the Greek for a circular route: the 'road around') begins with creative fire, and ends, too, with fire. Like time, space is also only an aspect of things. Because they believed this, the Stoics held that the universe was a sphere bounded by a spaceless void (on the principle 'no space without body'). Of the things within our universe, the Stoics saw a gradation of ways of existing: least animate would be rocks . . . then plants . . . then animals, which possess some rudimentary psyche or soul . . . and finally, rational beings. These, possessing reason, have a spark of the creative divinity of which they are part.

The Stoics would have answered your question about God affirmatively, though their assent might not mean what you take it to mean. But they did think that because most humans do believe in some way in God, it would be a denial of reason not to accept this – indeed, they believed that using reason is to believe in God. They even advanced various proofs of the existence of God, which the ancient Sceptics, like modern ones, set themselves to attack. One of these proofs was based on the beauty and functionality of the universe – what today would be called an argument from design. But their opponents, the Sceptics, stressed the dark side of life – the disasters that afflict the world from time to time. They preferred to believe that the universe simply happened, just as it is – that there is no grand design, or Grand Designer.

The Stoic answer to this problem of pain and human suffering was that the dark is needed to give form to the light, as in a painting: the whole, though, is perfect and harmonious.

If these arguments have a modern flavour, put it down to the fact that these are perennial problems for human beings, and that where problems of this sort are concerned, people have never achieved the kind of shared conviction or consensus that they have arrived at in some other areas of speculation. Nor has anything parallel to scientific method emerged for settling such questions, or even for deciding who is to count as an authority on such matters.

As for the Stoics, it seems that it was the belief in the harmony of the universe that made possible the way of life that they advocated: one of the harmoniousness with the universe. They saw virtue as the ethical route to that harmony of spirit – and virtue included intelligence, courage, justice and self-control. I once read, you know, that some North American Indians held a belief rather like this. I do not remember the exact words attributed to them, but the saying was something of this sort: 'The truly brave man knows neither pain nor pleasure, fear nor joy, agony nor self-indulgence.' This sounds very like the famous Stoic apatheia, and reminds me, in fact, of Epictetus' aphorism 'Those whose bodies are in good condition can endure heat and cold; so also those whose souls are in

*an excellent condition can endure anger, and grief, and great joy,
and every other emotion."⁹ The early Stoics aimed at indifference to
the accidents of life – to health, possessions and public reputation –
but their successors come to accept that, while these goods should not
be essential for inner peace and public service, nevertheless they
were advantages in life.*

*What, though I think you will find most significant and
imitable in the Stoic doctrine is their belief in the brotherhood of
persons – their belief that, whatever race or creed a person has,
whether foreigner or slave or co-religionist or atheist, the divine
spark unites everybody; that the moral law is the way in which the
divine nature shows itself in human concerns; and that this provides
a common moral structure for everyone in the world. Stoic duty, in
other words is the duty of a citizen of the world, not of one
particular country; it is a duty to promote the well-being of all those
you can affect. You may like to think about some of these ideas, and
in the meantime I will write to you soon about the theories of
Spinoza, which are not so far removed from these ancient doctrines.*

Yours,
Sophia

It was only a few days later that I received a further letter from
Sophia – as it turned out, the last she was to send.

Seventeenth Letter from Sophia

Dear Q,
*It seemed to me that both the life and ideas of Spinoza might
interest you. Spinoza was opposed to the religious dogmatism of his
day, and I know that you, too, have set your face against dogmatism, belief, that is, that does not permit of questioning. Spinoza's
own family had fled from persecution, first from the Spain of the
Inquisition, then from Portugal. It seems an irony, then, that the
Jewish community in Amsterdam, where Spinoza spent his life,*

rejected and indeed excommunicated him. He believed, you see, in the spirit of Judaism, but not its narrow legalism and orthodoxy.

His is essentially an ethical *philosophy. Like ancient Stoicism, it provides a way of life – or perhaps I should say an* approach *to life: a way of finding an attitude and response to the eventualities and contingencies of living.*

You could say that the love of God underlay the whole system that he worked out, but this would be paradoxical, for the fact is that during his life-time and after his death Spinoza was regarded by many as an atheist. Indeed, his Tractatus Theologico-politicus *was published anonymously (in Amsterdam, 1670), and his* Ethics *only after his death. He lived according to his principles: he refused the chair of philosophy at Heidelberg which was offered to him, preferring to retain his philosophical independence by earning his living as a grinder of optical lenses, although in the end this probably contributed to his early death from consumption.*

Spinoza took his starting-point from Descartes. His first philosophical work was an account of Descartes' philosophy.[10] *But where Descartes had depended in the end on a personal God to justify his claims to knowledge, Spinoza maintained an austerely impersonal conception of God, based on a geometrical and logical method of reasoning, stripped of all colour or imaginative embellishment. His central theories are set out in his* Ethics. *There he deals with the most ultimate categories of metaphysics: substance and attribute: causation, freedom and necessity. The deepest metaphysical questions – those concerning God and creation, the freedom of the human will and the freedom of God, human immortality, mind and matter – are all dealt with here. Descartes, in his system of philosophy, had seen reality as divided into two irreducible categories, two ultimately disparate kinds of substance, thought and extension – the mental and the physical. But Spinoza argued that logic compels us to the belief that there can be only one ultimate substance, which is self-sufficient and uncaused.*

The reasons for this are complicated; what I can say briefly, though, is that Spinoza held that to understand or to explain anything, you must know what it essentially is, not what it just happens to be. But he argued that nothing 'just happens to be'. If you can't find an explanation in the nature of the thing itself, then you will find it in something else. In the end, though, only one thing (which must therefore be everything*) could be both a complete explanation (cause) of itself, (the Latin phrase that Spinoza used was* causa sui*) and also the cause, in the more usual sense, of everything else (*causa omnium rerum*).*

For this reason, Spinoza believed it did not make sense to suppose that there might be two *self-contained systems in the universe; the hypothesis that there might be, led to insoluble problems about the interaction between the two. For how could mind affect matter? Or matter affect mind? (I believe you mentioned that you had reached a conclusion rather like this yourself.) For Spinoza, then, thought and extension are not two different things, but two ways of thinking about the same thing. This single substance must be infinite – it cannot be bounded, since it is itself everything. It follows, then, that if God is defined, as orthodox theology did define him, as infinite being, then the single substance identified with Nature must also be identified with God.*

It is, of course an important aspect of Jewish and Christian religious thought that the creator is to be distinguished from his creation. But this notion of a separate and separable God has engendered many of the problems that beset theological orthodoxy, in particular the problem of evil. Not that it is only a problem for the religious. As I told you in my previous letter, the Stoics had already recognized the need for some kind of explanation of pain and suffering. But there is a special problem for those who believe in a benevolent and all-powerful creator. For religious believers, faith strains at certain questions: Is there any answer to a child's meningitis? Or a baby tossed up in the air and caught on a soldier's bayonet?

This problem of pain and evil is also the problem of freedom – ours and God's. Part of the world's evil is a product of our freedom – and that that should inevitably be so is a restraint on the freedom of God: God could not both make human beings free and also make the evil that results from human freedom impossible. For

Spinoza that was no problem: he believed that everything is necessary, pain as well as evil. Everything must be as it is. This leaves no freedom either for ourselves or for God. So Spinoza's account neither demands nor allows for conventional free will, and the idea of a transcendent creator – a creator outside and apart from its creation – is a logical impossibility.

Spinoza offered an argument for this that a modern physicist might find understandable in other terms. Spinoza argued that changes and exchanges of matter can only take place within the system of nature – that the proportions of motion and rest must remain constant within the system of nature taken as a whole. The physicist might agree that the idea of the entire system being penetrated by energy from outside is incoherent. Spinoza's, though, was a logical rather than an empirical point: it does not make sense to speak of a totality, and then posit something affecting that totality from outside.

God, in the Judaeo-Christian tradition, is often conceived in this external role. But the idea of God simply creating, by fiat, an arbitrarily chosen world, which was only one of many possibilities, was, for other reasons as well, rationally repugnant to Spinoza. Much better conceive of a God constrained by necessity; better, too, to conceive of the world as rationally explicable, in the sense that everything in it is as it has to be a world of which it is true that understanding any part can, in principle lead to a complete understanding of the whole.

That God might simply have wanted to create the world would presuppose that he had a need or a lack – something which again is an absurd hypothesis. An imperfect, insufficient or inadequate being is not what any of the world's major religions mean by God. And both Jewish and Christian thought has hinted at the idea that God's creatures are not external objects to their creator, in those many suggestions that God has direct access to our minds and thoughts. Consider, for example, this passage from Psalm 139:

> *O Lord you have searched me*
> *and you know me*

You know when I sit and when I rise;
you perceive my thoughts from afar.
You discern my going out and my lying down;
you are familiar with all my ways.
Before a word is on my tongue
you know it completely, O Lord.

You hem me in – behind and before;
you have laid your hand upon me,
Such knowledge is too wonderful for me,
too lofty for me to attain.

Where can I go from your Spirit?
Where can I flee from your presence?
If I go up to the heavens, you are there;
if I make my bed in the depths, you are there.
If I rise on the wings of the dawn,
if I settle on the far side of the sea,
even there your hand will guide me,
your right hand will hold me fast.

If I say, 'Surely the darkness will hide me
and the light become night around me,'
even the darkness will not be dark to you,
the night will shine like the day,
for darkness is as light to you.

For you created my inmost being;
you knit me together in my mother's womb.[11]

But without a transcendent God, if there is religious truth, it can only be metaphorical – an illuminating picture or aid to understanding, rather than a literal explanation of the facts of change and existence. Faith and reason must, if Spinoza is right, be kept apart.

And yet, as I said, the path of Spinoza's reasoning could be called a route to God. There are two reasons why this is so. One is to be found in Spinoza's account of the human mind; the other in his account of truth.

The human mind, according to Spinoza, is a 'created, thinking substance', a thinking thing (ens cogitans). This characteristic is sufficient to give a permanency lacking to the body, which is a fleeting and perishing part of extension. The human mind, by contrast, is 'part of the infinite intellect of God'.[12] But it is not, as Descartes had claimed, something different and distinct from the body; indeed, it is a kind of mirror or reflection of the body – or, in a different metaphor, it is the form or shape of the body. As Spinoza himself put it: 'The mind and the body are one and the same thing, which is conceived now under the attribute of thought, now under the attribute of extension.'[13] He went on to say that: 'the decision of the mind, together with the appetite and determination of the body, are simultaneous in nature, or rather that they are one and the same thing, which, when it is considered under the attribute of thought and explained in terms of it, we call decision, and when considered under the attribute of extension, and deduced from the laws of motion and rest, we call determination.'[14]

This double aspect explanation of mind and body is easiest to grasp in the case of sense-perception, where the effect of something physical – an external object – on the body is to produce an idea in the mind – something which is neither solely physical nor solely mental – or, if you prefer, something which is both of these things at the same time. Spinoza rated the kind of knowledge generated by sense-perception as, after mere dreaming or imagining, the lowest, most uncertain kind – what Plato called 'opinion'. He held that scientific knowledge takes us to a higher level of understanding, and that the highest level of all is a single unified system of interlocking ideas.

So by understanding what a person is, and understanding man's place in nature as a thinking being, one can begin to approach those important questions of human happiness and freedom which are the goal of so much of this kind of reflection. If you follow Spinoza, then this is to come to understand yourself and others sub specie aeternitatis.

I know that you cling to the idea of individual self-determination, so the complete determinism of Spinoza's system may not appeal to you. If you were to accept it completely, then that personal *and individual perspective must ultimately vanish. But Spinoza himself provided a simile in a letter which he wrote, which might help to make his perspective more convincing: imagine, he said, a parasitic worm living in the bloodstream and trying to understand and interpret its surroundings. The worm would see each drop of blood as an independent entity; it would not be able to recognize the part played by individual drops in the bloodstream as a whole – nor could it understand that the more meaningful unit is the bloodstream as a whole, rather than the droplets of which it is constituted. But even the bloodstream taken as a whole is inadequately understood until it is seen in relation to all the other fluids in the body and to the body as a whole. If as a human being, you see your body and the bodies of others as isolated independent entities, you are like the worm in relation to the drops of blood. You have missed out on the wider understanding which is the key to real illumination.*

But I said there was another way in which Spinoza's theory could be seen as a route to God. This consists in the fact that Spinoza saw his theories about knowledge and truth as necessary for salvation and for happiness. In his system, the truth of an idea is a matter of its relationship to other ideas, a matter of fitting with the whole system. An illusion, for instance, would simply be an idea which does not cohere with everything else that is known. And a judgement of perception is false when it does not fit in with other judgements of perception. I said before that in our knowledge of things, in Spinoza's view, we can ascend from the commonsense level of knowledge which is characteristic of sense-perception, to the scientific knowledge which explains our perceptual observations, finally reaching a higher level of logic, science, or metaphysics which is capable of explaining the explanations of science itself.

Unlike Descartes, Spinoza thought that we could recognize clear ideas – if you remember, Descartes thought it made sense to conceive of the possibility of deception even where clear and distinct ideas were concerned, if there were a malignant demon with sufficient powers. Spinoza would not entertain such a hypothesis. For him, mathematics and logic provided the standard of indubitability.

This explains his philosophical method, which I dare say you may find surprising – a deductive system, imitating Euclidean geometry, in which propositions are derived from axioms, using a limited number of primitive terms. The nature of Spinoza's system is such that only one set of necessarily connected propositions can be true, and, since they all interlock and are interdependent, it would be possible to enter the system at any point and work out the rest from there.

The distinctive feature of Spinoza's view of truth, then, is this: that, for him, truth is something that is grasped by thinking clearly rather than by seeing, touching or otherwise observing by the senses. It is possible to know things independently of experience, for experience is only partial. While truth, as Spinoza has argued, is interlocking – parts, only, may be grasped, but ultimately every partial truth leads to every other. Potentially, knowledge is of a totality – and a grasp of that, or even of an aspect of it, is not a matter of sense-observation.

Some would say that this search for infallible knowledge is doomed to failure because it is misconceived. They would say that knowledge is only of the particular, and is only yielded by the senses. That is why I suggested that the appeal of Spinoza's system to you must be, for want of a better word, an intuitive appeal. It is an example of what a metaphysical system can offer, and I hope that you will be encouraged to explore further this and other systems. But I know that the cast of your mind is empirical. You have grown up in an age of technology and are accustomed to thinking that science is the only sound source of both questions and answers.

You are not, of course, alone in this, and indeed, as far as philosophy is concerned, metaphysics has been an unpopular study for most of the twentieth century. The only article of faith permitted to adherents of the positivist and empiricist philosophy prevailing in the English-speaking world was that metaphysics is meaningless.

But you may find more inspiration in some of the ideas I have mentioned than in that austere denunciation. I leave you to think about these things. For myself, I think this is a time for me to reflect

> on Spinoza's most famous statement: 'A free person thinks of
> nothing less than of death, and the wisdom of such a person is a
> meditation not of death but of life.'

Yours,
Sophia

I was touched and, I must admit. wryly amused, to notice the
way in which Sophia had adapted the usual translation of
Spinoza's dictum, which appears to relate to 'men' rather than
'persons.' But after a while, I began to reflect on what she had
written. I found myself impressed with the theories she had
described. But as she so astutely observed, I cannot alter the
temper of my mind. On the other hand, I have seen, too, the
limitations of empiricism. In sum, I feel that the unsophisticated
theories of the past, whether rationalist or empiricist, are unlikely
to offer me the complete understanding I seek. It is time, then,
to consider whether the illumination I am seeking lies in the
sophisticated developments of these positions to be found in
contemporary sources.

NOTES

1 See chapter 5, pp. 92–5.
2 Lucretius, *The Nature of the Universe.*
3 Condillac, *Traité des systèmes* (1749), quoted in R. J. White, *The
 Anti-Philosophers*, p. 44. The anti-philosophical tradition is marked
 by the presentation of ideas in terms which are comprehensible to
 the ordinary person, using the vernacular as opposed to formal
 academic language, or a foreign tongue understood only by an
 educated minority. 'Establishment' philosophers tend to reject such
 contributions as damaging to their professional mystique. Historically, however, the anti-philosophers have outlasted their critics: it
 is, after all, a tradition to which both Descartes and Voltaire belong.
4 Plato, *The Republic*, Book VII

5 Plato, *The Seventh Letter*, in Plato, *Phaedrus; and The Seventh and Eighth Letters*

6 L. Wittgenstein, *Tractatus Logico-Philosophicus*, 6.54 (see also the reference to Wittgenstein and the picture theory of meaning in chapter 6). Wittgenstein wrote his famous *Tractatus* whilst serving as an Austrian soldier during the First World War. He sent his manuscript to Bertrand Russell, whom he already knew from an earlier period of study in England, who immediately recognized its interest and importance. The sentence quoted indicates that, having seen his way in philosophy, as Wittgenstein then believed, he had no further use for it. Consistently with this, Wittgenstein worked in other occupations for the next twenty years, returning to philosophy only when he became dissatisfied with his earlier answers. There are thus an 'earlier' and a 'later' Wittgenstein, who approach philosophy in very different ways. For a full and comprehensive account of Wittgenstein's life and his philosophical ideas, see R. Monk, *Ludwig Wittgenstein: the duty of genius*. See also N. Malcolm, *Ludwig Wittgenstein: a memoir.*

7 Epictetus, *Discourses*, Book III, xxiv, 8–12. Passage specially translated for this volume by Christopher Strachan.

8 For an account of ancient Stoicism, see R. D. Hicks, *Stoic and Epicurean*; and for some readings in these philosophers, see J. L. Saunders (ed.), *Greek and Roman Philosophy after Aristotle*. The modern work referred to is *A Stoic Philosophy of Life* by Keith Campbell.

9 Epictetus, *Fragments*, 20. *Stobaeus*, III, 4.94 (Loeb, vol. II, p. 465).

10 Spinoza, *The Principles of Descartes' Philosophy*.

11 Psalm 139, i–xiii; translation taken from New International Version of *The Holy Bible*.

12 Spinoza, *Ethics*, Part II, Prop. XI Coroll.

13 Ibid. Part III, Prop. II, Note.

14 Ibid. Part IV, Prop. LXVII.

READING GUIDE

Stoic and Epicurean by R. D. Hicks provides a readable account of these ancient systems, and there is a selection of readings in J. S. Saunders (ed.), *Greek and Roman Philosophy after Aristotle*. The argument from design as developed by the Stoics is presented by Cicero in *On the Nature of the Gods*.

Spinoza's *Ethics*, originally published in Latin in 1677, shortly after his death, is best read in a modern translation. In particular, see that by E. M. Curley.

For a readable and clear account of Spinoza, see S. Hampshire, *Spinoza*, or see the chapter on Spinoza in R. Scruton's *A Short History of Modern Philosophy*. This also includes chapters on other metaphysical systems: those of Descartes, Leibniz, Kant and Hegel. The contemporary philosopher T. L. S. Sprigge (b. 1932) defends a modern Spinozist point of view in *The Vindication of Absolute Idealism*, and, more briefly, in ch. 8 of his *Theories of Existence*.

9

Moving On

Two things fill the mind with ever new and increasing admiration and awe, the oftener and the more speedily we reflect on them: the starry heavens above and the moral law within.

Immanuel Kant, *Critique of Practical Reason*

The glimpse I have just had of Spinoza's system has shown me the connection between two of the great dualisms of philosophy: the dualism of mind and matter – the mental and the physical – on the one hand, and the contrast between free will and determinism on the other.

The free will issue connects with my first concerns – what to do; what *we* as members of communities and citizens of the world should do – because some kind of 'mental' or spiritual freedom seems to be a condition of morality. This might not be so if I had accepted the possibility of translating the moral into other terms as, for instance, the utilitarians do, but I recall that my reflections left me with an intact notion of irreducible good and evil, right and wrong, and for this I need, in some way or other, to see myself as free to choose.

But this suggests another dichotomy – another dominating contrast – which underlies both the moral questions and the questions which, in philosophical terms might be called ontological, linguistic and epistemological: questions, that is, about what there really *is*; about how I may talk about it; and how I may know it. *This* dichotomy can be described as the contrast between objectivity and subjectivity... between realism and anti-realism . . . between belief in some external ground of knowledge – some fact of the matter – and relativism.

I may think of this contrast first in relation to morality: does value attach to actions or situations lying outside myself in the world of other people, their doings and circumstances? Or is the attaching of value strictly a response of mine to the way things strike me?

This problem of objectivity is also, however, a problem about the world of science and the senses. It can be presented in terms of a story. Suppose, in some science fiction world, a scientist had been able to remove my brain and place it in a vat of fluid. Suppose it could be kept alive and computer-programmed to have all the experiences I now have. (This hypothesis does no more, of course, than place me in the same position as Descartes deceived by his 'malignant demon' – the hypothesis I encountered at the start of my quest – but it has a more convincing science-fiction 'feel' about it.) Suppose furthermore that all memory of a previous life had been technologically eliminated, would there be any way that I could distinguish my Brain-in-a-Vat existence from 'normal' human existence?

Already in my opening reflections I encountered problems of knowledge and of truth that are sharpened and pointed up by entertaining such fanciful sceptical hypotheses. There, too, I was obliged to consider questions of objectivity and subjectivity in relation to morals or principles for social living. Subsequently, I saw a similar debate opening up again in relation to science, this time as the contrast between rationalism and irrationalism. And then, later, thinking about language revealed to me important questions about reference and representation which I can now see also involved this problem of objectivity – a problem which is itself at bottom *the* problem of truth and knowledge of truth.

I have just used the world 'realism' to describe what I might see as a commitment to truth in the sense of a belief that there is some kind of correspondence between true assertions and the way the world is – a belief that there is, in other words, a fact of the matter. Accepting this, as I have so far done at each stage of

my quest, provides one half of an answer to many of my initial
questions as well as to others that I have encountered subsequently – an approach to an answer which involves the repudi-
ation of scepticism, irrationalism and subjectivism. There is
another half to my answer, though, that explains some of the
recurring dichotomies my quest has exposed, and explains, too,
why realism is not, after all, a terminus to philosophical discussion. This is that, nevertheless, my perceptions of that reality, that
world, are conditioned by my own experience.

Bishop Berkeley, the eighteenth-century British philosopher,
understood this well, pointing out that if we even *try* to imagine
something unperceived-by-us, the very act of imagining places us
in the picture whether we like it or not. We can imagine only in
terms of our own ways of perceiving. As the contemporary
American philosopher, Hilary Putnam, has put this: 'There is a
real world *but* we can only describe it in terms of our own
conceptual system.'[1] The 'God's-eye' view, then, which the notion
of objectivity might suggest, is not available to me. My perspective must be affected by the fact that it is *my* perspective.

I can now see that these problems of realism, reference,
language and knowledge are inseperably linked together. I can
see, also, that they may involve questions of value or morality, if
that is sufficiently widely construed, since choosing a position
here – deciding what rationality *is* – itself involves evaluation. It
is in effect a moral stance. Since this is Putnam's view, too, I note
that Putnam's own realist intuitions are set within a theory which
he describes as a 'demythologized Kantianism'.

From Kant, Putnam believes, we can draw the lesson that
'*everything* we say about an object is of the form: it is such as to
affect *us* in such-and-such a way. *Nothing at all* we say about any
object describes the object as it is "in itself." '[2] Kant distinguished
noumena – things as they really are – from *phenomena* – things as
they appear to us. He pointed out that we are cut off from access
to the former, and confined to access to the latter. Putnam's
'mind-independent reality' is Kant's noumena or 'things-in-them-
selves'. But for Putnam, the noumenal world is simply what a

rational being with our sense organs would construct – the way in which, not arbitrarily but inevitably, creatures like us *must* interpret our surroundings.

Putnam's neo-Kantianism, then, is essentially the view that at one level, within the empirical realm, truth can be viewed as correspondence with the facts, but that, nevertheless, at another level all truth is in the end mind-dependent. Putnam's appeal to Kant is direct: 'It is not that the thinking mind *makes up* the world on Kant's view; but it doesn't just mirror it either',[3] or, more epigrammatically, 'the mind and the world jointly make up the mind and the world'.[4]

This is not, though, another restatement of relativism – of the view, that is, that truth is simply a matter of one's point of view. *That*, Putnam believes, is ultimately self-refuting. Relativism is essentially incoherent in that it is inconsistent both to *hold* a point of view and at the same time argue that *no* point of view is more justified or right than any other. It is self-defeating, too, in making it impossible to maintain a distinction between *being* right and *thinking* one is right – for no argument can be conducted on that basis.

Against this, the case for some kind of realism – for a claim that there *is* a fact of the matter – is strong. The strength of realism consists initially in the practical success of realist assumptions, even if later these may need some qualification, whether this is success in the field of science or success in terms of commonsense communication about material objects.

But a more sophisticated view of science and the physical world may lay stress on the way even the meaning of the words science uses to describe the world may change. And in the case of Kuhn and Feyerabend, for example, as I have already seen, this observation may be seen as anti-realist in its implications. To defend a realist perspective, then, it is necessary to deny this total fluidity of language and concepts and insist that change takes place only within certain parameters. Putnam, then, in maintaining a qualified realism, insists that there must be *some* convergence or constancy of meaning in scientific concepts, and that although our understanding of things may change, the scope for change is not totally unlimited. So, for example, 'electron' can't mean something now that has *nothing at all* in common with what it meant in the 1900s. It must either still refer to the same thing, or at least retain some of the same meaning – it must have either a shared reference, or a shared sense, in order to provide some kind of anchor-point for understanding, outside ourselves and our own thinking.

Finally, against relativist claims that what is accepted as true changes in step with changing human needs and interests, it is nevertheless possible to point to important factors in common between human beings, some universal aspects of human nature, which survive the test of time and which help to guarantee what Putnam calls the 'universal intercommunicability of human cultures'. As he says, 'human *interests*, human *saliencies*, human cognitive processes, must have a *structure* which is heavily determined by innate or constitutional factors. Human nature isn't all *that* plastic'.[5]

But this is not orthodox realism. It takes account of the reciprocity of internal and external factors, the dialectic between mind and the world. Putnam's aim is to break the traditional dichotomy – to find a middle ground between objectivism and relativism, to see the strength of the anti-realist case, but not to lose all purchase on the notion of reality. Indeed, he is prepared to sum up the entire programme for analytic philosophy in the twentieth century as 'the problem of how words "hook onto" the world'.[6]

The Commitment to Truth

At this point, I may now be in a position to look back and see some of the debates I have encountered as ways of dealing with that particular question and also as providing some insight into the kind of problems that provided the starting-point for my quest. I started with an initial commitment to two things only:

truth and virtue. How, I may now ask, has that double commitment survived my inquiry? What, first, of the notion of truth?

Descartes, I can now see, set the problem for subsequent
generations, although, as I have noted, the terms of the argument
had already been sketched out in ancient times. He might not
have recognized the problem under Putnam's brief idiomatic
description – the problem of how words 'hook onto the world –
although he would surely have been in sympathy with the elegant
economy and understandability of the phrase. After all, it was
Descartes who initiated the modern breakthrough from esoteric
language confined to the learned, to the ideal of describing
philosophical problems in everyday language, and in terms that
the ordinary person can understand.

The problem, then, concerns the gulf between what there is to
know and our knowledge of it. That gulf exists when I think of
ordinary everyday statements of observation: when I think of
truths of logic or arithmetic; when I reason scientifically about
what lies beyond my present experience; and even more when I
consider moral, religious or aesthetic truth. It strikes me acutely
when I consider the grounds on which I claim knowledge of the
past or of other people's feelings; of the feelings, too, of animals;
and even when I reflect on my knowledge of myself as a continuing being. In the past, the different ways of answering these
questions might seem to have been summed up in the contrast
between finding the answer through the exercise simply of reason
itself – Descartes own solution – or, as empiricist philosophers
from Bacon onwards favoured, seeking for the primitive sense-
observations which would provide the rock-bottom data from
which to construct the edifice of knowledge.

In the first case, reason might provide an answer, as it did for
Spinoza, in terms of a whole system of thought, in which it is
impossible to answer a question about one aspect without, at least
implicity, describing the whole. In the second case, arriving at
truth is a piecemeal process of observation and consolidation.
Surprisingly, since I might have supposed that by now some
agreement would have been reached on these issues, it is at a

crossroads like this that I find philosophy at the present time – though now with scepticism on the part of some philosophers as to the validity even of the questions.

The view that it is reason rather than observation that provides an integrated answer, an interlocking system of truth, is the essential characteristic of a metaphysical system. I know that much of this century's philosophy has been a reaction *against* metaphysics. Indeed, it was from the hegemony of such metaphysical systems as those of F. H. Bradley (1856–1924) and J. McTaggart (1866–1925) that G. E. Moore (1873–1958) and Russell broke free at the turn of the century. As Russell described this in his intellectual autobiography:

He [G. E. Moore] took the lead in rebellion, and I followed, with a sense of emancipation. Bradley argued that everything common sense believes in is mere appearance; we reverted to the opposite extreme, and thought that *everything* is real that common sense, uninfluenced by philosophy or theology, supposes real. With a sense of escaping from prison, we allowed ourselves to think that the grass is green, that the sun and stars would exist if no one was aware of them, and also that there is a pluralistic timeless world of Platonic ideas. The world, which had been thin and logical, suddenly became rich and varied and solid.[7]

Moore and Russell, I know, were both unable to hold to this simple perception of our knowledge of the world, but the attempt was symbolic of the twentieth-century preoccupations of philosophy: philosophy under the dominance of science. 'Scientism' consists, essentially, in the view that there are appropriate criteria for the solution of well-defined problems and that rationality is a matter of applying them. It epitomizes the desire for objectivity. Its quintessential expression was the logical positivism of the thirties, which was dominated by the two dogmas of (a) the analytic-synthetic distinction and (b) the idea that empirical knowledge is constructed from simple, incontrovertible foundations. Its basic assumption is that there is just one truth. This is the notion of convergence, of the possibility of a consensus of all reasonable – or all rational – people.

But I have seen how this notion of convergence, and hence of the inter-translatability of systems of thought and ideas – of different 'language' or conceptual systems – is under challenge today. The attack on the idea of convergence, the metaphor of inquiry, the belief in the possibility of a unified science and a common conception of truth is well summed up in the American philosopher Richard Rorty's dismissal of such aims as old-fashioned religion – the kind of 'motives which once led us to posit gods'.[8] It displays a tendency, Rorty believes, to claim a broad human perspective for what is in reality no more than a 'lonely provincialism'. We should see ourselves, therefore – and 'we' are 'the liberal Rawlsian searchers for consensus, the heirs of Socrates, the people who wish to link their days dialectically each to each'[9] – as representing just one of many possible movements in human society, not as typifying a tradition open to, and common to, all human beings in virtue simply of their reason and common humanity.

But it was Quine who first opened the Pandora's box which dealt the death-blow to the 'scientistic' assumptions of analytic philosophy. Although himself a representative of the analytic tradition, Quine has supplied a holistic turn which has led to a new favouring of coherence over correspondence in theories about what truth consists in – a turn which fits well with the pragmatist traditions of American philosophy. Holism is the view that partial truths cannot stand alone – every partial truth implies the whole of which it is part. But Quine's holism is not sceptical – it consists in the idea that science is essentially a two-tier network of sentences: a central core of sentences which are only with reluctance relinquished, and other, peripheral ones which can more readily be revised in the light of experience. In Quine's view, it is a network of sentences like these that, when adopted by a particular community, constitutes a conceptual scheme.

Davidson's challenge to the 'very idea of conceptual scheme' is therefore yet more radical and iconoclastic in its implications. For in suggesting that it is impossible to conceive of *alternative* conceptual schemes, Davidson is saying that the idea of a conceptual scheme is in itself incoherent. He attacks the 'dogma of the dualism of scheme and reality', claiming that concepts do not depend on an uninterpreted reality. It is believing in this *dualism* – believing that there are two things: a conceptual scheme *and* reality – that leads, on his view, to conceptual relativism, and to the notion that *truth* is relative to a conceptual scheme. He says:

In giving up the dualism of scheme and world, we do not give up the world, but re-establish unmediated touch with the familiar objects whose antics make our sentences and opinions true or false.[10]

Davidson's holism is therefore of a different order from Quine's. Nevertheless, both are agreed in taking the step that is the distinctive hallmark of holism: this is to say that the basic units of significance are not isolated sentences but rather whole systems of sentences. Truth can therefore only be a quality of the whole, not of any individual element. This, which was the distinguishing characteristic of the great metaphysical systems constructed on rationalist foundations, is essentially the standpoint I now find in common between those contemporary heirs to the analytic tradition, Quine, Davidson and, indeed, Putnam, too, in spite of his realist aspirations.

But this means that the question of truth can no longer be seen, as the positivists saw it, in terms of the analytic/synthetic distinction. In place of that distinction, which carefully separated truths of meaning (analytic truths), to be arrived at by reflective reasoning, from truths of substance (synthetic truths), there is a new unified approach, a 'methodological monism' which rejects the empiricist's clear line of demarcation. And since different or alternative 'true' pictures of the world become possible on this understanding of things, the move from correspondence to coherence as a test for truth is also a step in the direction of pragmatism – usually understood as the theory that a statement is true if believing that it is so works in practice. From such a perspective, which is indeed that of Rorty, the belief that observations are theory-laden leads to the view that ideas, words and language are not mirrors which copy the 'real' or 'objective' world, but rather tools people use to cope with their environment.

As I have seen, Putnam is willing to concede this to some extent. He says: 'The idea that truth is a passive copy of what is "really" (mind-independently, discourse-independently) "there" has collapsed under the critiques of Kant, Wittgenstein and other philosophers even if it continues to have a deep hold on our thinking.'[11]

So Putnam agrees with these philosophers in rejecting the idea that there is just one true and complete description of the way the world is — he calls this the 'externalist' or 'God's-eye' view. Indeed, his answer to the Brains-in-a-Vat problem is that it can be rejected simply because there *is* no God's-eye view from which to tell the story. As he puts it: 'If we are Brains in a Vat, we cannot think that we are.' It follows, then, that it is not *possible* that we are.[12]

Nevertheless, words cannot *simply* be tools to cope with our environment — both the notion of 'ourselves' and the notion of 'environment' smuggle back the realist conceptions that are being attacked in such arguments.

But Putnam, unlike Rorty, seeks to retain the essence of realism. He does this through the notion of rational acceptability: the criterion for a fact, he suggests, is what it is rational to accept. This is a concept of rationality not restricted to science. To assume that restriction would be yet another hangover from positivism. Many current views of truth, Putnam claims, are alienated views: 'They cause one to lose one part of one's self and the world, to see the world as simply consisting of elementary particles swerving in the void (the "physicalist" view . . .) or to see the world as simply consisting of "actual and possible sense-data" (the older empiricist view), or to deny that there is a world at all.'[13]

In place of the 'God's-eye' view, then, Putnam puts what he calls an 'internalist' perspective. By this he means, to begin with, that the question 'What objects does the world consist of?' admits of more than one true answer. It also means that the question itself can only be asked *within* a theory or description. Putnam insists that truth is 'ideal coherence of our beliefs with each other and with our experience *as these experiences are themselves represented in our belief system*'.[14] It is this that Putnam means by the notion of rational acceptability, and unlike the straightforwardly objective notion of truth, it is not fixed by some immutable book of rules. It is a flexible notion: what it is rational to accept depends on who you are and where you are.

However, Putnam does not see this as a break with objectivity. On the contrary, it provides, he believes, as much as we can aspire to: that is, 'objectivity for us'. To achieve this it may be necessary to follow a Kantian procedure of transcendental investigation – the kind of investigation, that is, that explores the 'preconditions of reference and hence of thought – preconditions built into the nature of our minds themselves'.[15]

So Putnam's 'internalism' is not a facile relativism that says 'Anything goes'. As he says, I *could* adopt a conceptual scheme in which I could fly, but I would soon find something wrong with that scheme if I tried to jump out of the window. Internal coherence, in other words, is not the *only* constraint on what I may think. The rules are not immutable, but it would be irrational to try to construct and reconstruct them according to the arbitrary whim of the moment. Our notions of coherence and acceptability are 'deeply interwoven with our psychology. They depend upon our biology and our culture'; 'Objectivity and rationality humanly speaking are what we have; they are better than nothing.'[16]

Our experience is limited, however, and our biology fallible. This is what sets limits to our ability to build up an unchallengeable picture of the world. So 'We use our criteria of rational acceptability to build up a theoretical picture of the "empirical world" and then as that picture develops we revise our very criteria of rational acceptability in the light of that picture and so on and so on forever.'[17]

The Commitment to Virtue

So Putnam's 'objectivity for us' is not a final destination, even if it is a claim to a more substantial reality than some overtly relativistic and irrationalist alternatives. It connects, too, with the second commitment which I acknowledged at the beginning of my inquiry: the commitment to virtue.

The connection is a double one. First, what it is rational for me to believe is essentially connected with the sort of creature that I am. So a theory of human nature is presupposed in the answers I give to these deep epistemological questions. And the question of what human nature is is itself an issue which is partly empirical, partly evaluative. Biology, history, psychology sociology all contribute to a view of human nature. But so, too, does our judgement of what is ideal, as opposed to what merely happens to be the case. Social arrangements, economics, the interference or malevolence of other people, may all contribute to making what human nature currently *is* different from what ideally it might be.

But secondly, both Putnam and Rorty, different though their views may be, come close to accepting something like the American pragmatist William James's (1842–1909) view of truth as 'the name for whatever proves itself to be *good* in the way of belief'.[18]

This linking of truth and goodness at the heart of a philosophical theory shatters the remaining dichotomy to which philosophy has clung in its positivistic phase – the gulf Hume claimed to detect between facts and values.[19] This explains why 'objectivity for us' is, as a matter of fact, a concept which is as applicable in the realm of values as it is in the realm of facts. My earlier conclusions about the need for a common world-order committed to basic human rights; my subsequent observations about a range of positive values common to human beings for personal and domestic living; these are aspirations connected, as is

Putnam's notion of rationality, with some notion of human flourishing.

'Objectivity for us' in the realm of morals involves renouncing the claim that values are external entities – 'out there' to be discovered. But it also involves renouncing the suggestion that in morals and politics 'anything goes'. Again, by careful garnering of the facts about human beings, by drawing a picture of human nature as it is, but also by using this factual information to form a conception of what it *might* be, it is possible to answer some of the questions about values, too, with which I began my quest.

On the very widest front, I can see how a total conception of such a moral ideal would involve an awareness of human beings within the context of their physical – geographical, biological and social – existence. Hence the widest political and moral values must be dictated by environmental concern. Learning to live in harmony with nature may be the first priority for securing a setting within which human nature itself can flourish.

But if I take 'environment' to mean more than fresh air, living forests, clean lakes and an unbroken chain of animal life; if I interpret it positively as 'making the place that we are good' then that apparently apolitical environmentalist goal becomes immediately political in a narrower sense. For the 'setting' within which human beings may hope to flourish must include the way people treat each other, as well as the way they treat the planet.

Again I am confronted with large questions, and large strategies seem to be dictated to me by my reflections on both facts and values. I can now see the point of Plato's parable of the shackled prisoners in the Cave, which I considered earlier. There is a time for reflection on the widest and most abstract of truths – indeed, on the question of truth itself – and this is the traditional concern of philosophy. But there is a pressing need for action, as well as for philosophical reflection. Even the limited aim of creating a world in which the practice of philosophy, with the leisure and freedom that this involves, is a practical possibility presents a challenge of enormous dimensions. Perhaps this is why

Kant so emphatically linked contemplation of the physical world – the 'starry heavens above' – to attention to 'the moral law within'. Perhaps, too, it is the reason why Russell, writing in the twentieth century, found his own contemplation of philosophy deflected earthwards by the 'echoes of cries of pain' that tore him from his private pursuit of love and knowledge.

For me, no less than these, philosophical reflection must give place to action, or at least to a programme of commitment to the values I would wish to see embodied in social and personal living. Perhaps this can only express itself in a negative way – that I will not add to the pain which I detect around me, that if I cannot build, then at least I will not destroy. And in so far as pain and death are unavoidable aspects of human existence, perhaps I will try to cultivate that acceptance of the whole of which these are parts recommended by Spinoza and the Stoics.

Last Thoughts

My initial commitment, then, was to truth and virtue. I have followed this commitment through, and find that it has, in effect, brought me full circle. I passed from personal decision-making to social and political action, finally touching on the most abstract and detached questions of language, logic, realism and representation. From there I found myself faced with the task of forming a conception of human nature, which itself in turn now compels me to form a view of the kind of social and political setting within which human nature can reach its ideal fulfilment.

But as an individual, there may be little I can do to affect these grand questions of global strategy. It may be that I will be obliged to retreat closer to what most directly concerns me: those intimate domestic and workplace situations where indeed I can make a difference to the potential of others for 'flourishing' – for *their* personal happiness and fulfilment.

Even here, though, my power to affect others must be limited. So that, in the end, I may find that it is only my own moral character that is ultimately within my control. And here it is the notion of personal integrity, of choosing the kind of life I would like to have led, the kind of person I would like to have been, that will be the ultimate test of the validity of both my inquiry and my conclusions.

But this is far from being a counsel of despair. As Putnam says: 'If we are doomed to have neither a computer's-eye view nor a God's-eye view of ourselves and each other, is that such a terrible fate? We are men and women; and men and women we may be lucky enough to remain. Let us try to preserve our humanity by, among other things, taking a human view of ourselves and our self-knowledge.'[20]

Perhaps, though, I still have some hankerings after those grand notions of God, immortality and the soul which I hoped philosophy might supply for me. If so, I may reflect on some words written to me a long time ago by Sophia:

> • *You didn't think, because there is nothing separate that was mind, there is no mind. So you should not think that, if there is nothing separate which is God, there is no God; or if nothing separate which is soul, that there is no soul. It is not absurd, or ultimately incomprehensible, to say that the world is God, mind, soul; that this is the only path to immortality; and that understanding this is the only peace of mind.*
>
> *Some people turn to the East for this sort of insight – Buddhist and Hindu religion are not antipathetic to these ideas; fatalism and integration with nature are two common strands in those systems of belief. But you chose me as your guru, and I represent a more austere, but enormously fruitful, tradition. You will have to be mentally and emotionally stronger to take your sustenance from me. But Western religious traditions are strong, too, and nothing I have said is incompatible with an open and compassionate religious faith. After all, in ethical stance, Socrates and Jesus have striking elements in common with each other and against the traditions of careless, evil or unthinking people.*
>
> *But create for yourself your own notion of deity or of God, and then look for it in the people and the traditions you find around you. Do not neglect nature either, as a source of useful instruction, and do not ignore the lessons of birth and death, termination and renewal that nature silently teaches.*

And if you can share with others what you know, or the values that this compels you to hold, then this knowledge and these values can themselves become part of the common mind – the common store of wisdom – which has the power to outlast the individual. For that, really, is what philosophy is: not an esoteric discipline, but the common endeavour of the human race to understand and come to terms with its own perilous, fragile and ultimately ephemeral existence.

NOTES

1 H. Putnam, *Meaning and the Moral Sciences*, p. 32.
2 H. Putnam, *Reason, Truth and History*, pp. 60–1.
3 H. Putnam, *Meaning and the Moral Sciences*, p. 1.
4 H. Putnam, *Reason, Truth and History*, p. xi.
5 H. Putnam, *Meaning and the Moral Sciences*, p. 56.
6 H. Putnam, 'After Empiricism' in *Post-analytic Philosophy*, ed. J. Rajchman and C. West.
7 B. Russell, 'My mental development' in P. A. Schilpp (ed.), *The Philosophy of Bertrand Russell*, p. 12.
8 R. Rorty, 'Solidarity or Objectivity?' in J. Rajchman and C. West, *Post-analytic Philosophy*, p. 10.
9 *Ibid.*, p. 12.
10 D. Davidson, 'On the very idea of a conceptual scheme' in D. Davidson, *Enquiries into Truth and Interpretation*, p. 198.
11 H. Putnam, *Reason, Truth and History*, p. 128.
12 Ibid. pp. xi–xii.
13 Ibid. pp. 50–1.
14 Ibid. p. 50.
15 Ibid. p. 16.
16 Ibid. p. 55.
17 Ibid. p. 184.
18 W. James, *Pragmatism*, p. 42.
19 In a famous passage in his *Treatise of Human Nature*, III, 1, 1 (first published 1739–40), Hume drew attention to the problem of passing from reasoning about what *is* to what *ought* to be. For an account of Hume's argument in its historical setting, see A.

MacIntyre, *A Short History of Ethics*, ch. 12.
20 H. Putnam, *Meaning and the Moral Sciences*, p. 77.

READING GUIDE

The postmodernist preoccupations of this chapter are of interest from
the point of view of literary theory, the arts and sociology as well as
philosophy. A book which supplies some of the background for these
developments is Q. Skinner (ed.), *The Return of Grand Theory in Philosophy*. There is also an influential feminist critique of foundationalist
epistemology, which takes much of its inspiration from the work of
Rorty and Lyotard and is well represented in *Feminism and
Postmodernism*, a collection of essays edited by Linda Nicholson.

John Passmore's *Recent Philosophers* provides an excellent guide to the
work of a number of more orthodox professional philosophers on these
issues. See in particular ch. 5, 'Realism and Relativism', for discussion of
some of the topics touched on in this chapter, and for an account of
their context and relationship to other aspects of contemporary philosophy not touched on here. Passmore's book includes, on these issues and
others mentioned in this volume, detailed and descriptive guides to
further reading of an advanced nature in current academic philosophy.

Putnam's own work is best approached through *Reason, Truth and
History* and *Meaning and the Moral Sciences*. There is also a three-volume
collection of his papers, of which the second, *Mind, Language and
Reality*, is of most relevance to issues discussed earlier in this book, while
vol. 3, *Realism and Reason*, is particularly concerned with the issue of
realism. See also his *Renewing Philosophy* and *Realism with a Human Face*.
For other perspectives on subjectivity, see W. Sellars, *Science and Metaphysics* and T. Nagel, *The View from Nowhere*.

Richard Rorty's views are to be found in his *Philosophy and the Mirror
of Nature*, in *Consequences of Pragmatism* and in *Contingency, Irony and
Necessity*. H. Morick's (ed.), *Challenges to Empiricism* provides an important collection of critical essays exploring new directions. Authors include Quine, Carnap, Popper, Feyerabend and Chomsky.

A variety of views on what philosophy is by well-known philosophers, including, among others, J. J. C. Smart, Karl Popper, Brand
Blanshard and Sidney Hook, may be found in *The Owl of Minerva*, edited

by C. J. Bontempo and S. J. Odell. Another variety of opinion more representative of British and European thinking is to be found in *The Impulse to Philosophise*, ed. A. P. Phillips Griffiths, while Genevieve Lloyd surveys the Western philosophical tradition from the point of view of philosophical feminism in *The Man of Reason*.

Appendix:
The Kant Mottoes

The quotations from Kant at the beginning of each chapter are from the following sources:

Chapter 1: See T. K. Abbott, 'Memoir of Kant', in *Immanuel Kant's Critique of Practial Reason and other works on the theory of ethics*, trans. T. K. Abbott, London: Longmans (1st edn 1879) 6th edn 1909, photoreprinted, 1954, p. xxxiii.

Chapter 2: *Immanuel Kant's Critique of Pure Reason*, trans. N. K. Smith, London: Macmillan, 1963, A 805; B 833; NK635.

Chapter 3: *Perpetual Peace*, AA 380 in *Kant's Political Writings*. Edited with an introduction and notes by Hans Reiss, trans. H. B. Nisbet, Cambridge: Cambridge University Press, 1970.

Chapter 4: Immanuel Kant, *The Metaphysics of Morals*, AA 332.

Chapter 5: *Immanuel Kant's Critique of Pure Reason*, trans. N. K. Smith, London: Macmillan, 1963, A 305; B 362; NK305.

Chapter 6: *Immanuel Kant's Critique of Pure Reason*, trans. N. K. Smith, London: Macmillan, 1963f, A 51; B 75; NKS93.

Chapter 7: *The Moral Law, Kant's Groundwork of the Metaphysic of Morals*, trans. H. Paton, London: Hutchinson (1st edn 1948), AA 448.

Chapter 8: Immanuel Kant, *Prolegomena*, trans. P. Lucas, Manchester: Manchester University Press, 1953, AA 274 PL 28.

Chapter 9: Immanuel Kant's *Critique of Practical Reason and other works on the theory of ethics*, trans. T. K. Abbott, London: Longmans, p. 260.

Bibliography

CHAPTER 1

Appiah, A., *Necessary Questions*, Englewood Cliffs, NJ: Prentice-Hall, 1989.

Augustine, *Confessions*, trans. H. Chadwick, Oxford: Oxford University Press, 1992.

Bunnin, N. and E. James (eds), *A Companion to Philosophy*, Oxford: Blackwell, 1994.

Copleston, F. C., *A History of Philosophy*, rev. edn, New York: Doubleday 'Image Books', 1962–66; 3 vol. edn 1985.

Davies, N., *God's Playground*, Oxford: Clarendon Press, 1981.

Descartes, R., *Meditations*, in *The Philosophical Writings of Descartes*. Vol. 2, trans. J. Cottingham, R. Stoothoff, and D. Murdoch, Cambridge: Cambridge University Press, 1985.

Hollis, M., *An Invitation to Philosophy*, Oxford: Blackwell, 1985.

Montefiore, A., Review of H. G. Skilling's *Charter 77 and Human Rights in Czechoslovakia*, *Journal of Applied Philosophy* 1, 1984.

Murdoch, Iris, *Metaphysics as a Guide to Morals*, London: Penguin 1993.

Nagel, T. *Mortal Questions*, Cambridge: Cambridge University Press, 1979.

O'Connor, D. J. (ed.), *A Critical History of Western Philosophy*, London: Macmillan 1985. First published 1964.

O'Hear, A., *What Philosophy Is*, London: Penguin 1985.

Passmore, J., *A Hundred Years of Philosophy*, Harmondsworth: Penguin 1968.

——, *Recent Philosophers*, London: Duckworth 1985.

Plato, *The Last Days of Socrates*, trans. H. Tredennick, Harmondsworth: Penguin, 1968. Contains *Euthyphro, Apology, Crito, Phaedo*. Or see *The Collected Dialogues*, ed. E. Hamilton and H. Cairns, Princeton, New Jersey: Princeton University Press, 1961.

Russell, B., *The Problems of Philosophy*, London: Oxford University Press, 1986. First published 1912.

——, *A History of Western Philosophy*, London: Allen & Unwin, 1984.

Scruton, R., *A Short History of Modern Philosophy*, London: Routledge & Kegan Paul, 1984.

Skilling, H. G., *Charter 77 and Human Rights in Czechoslovakia*, London: Allen & Unwin, 1984.

Urmson, J. O. and J. Rée, *The Concise Encyclopedia of Western Philosophy and Philosophers*, London: Unwin Hyman, 1989.

Wittgenstein, L., *Philosophical Investigations*, 3rd edn. trans. G. E. M. Anscombe, Oxford: Blackwell, 1968.

CHAPTER 2

Almond, B. and D. Hill, *Applied Philosophy: morals and metaphysics in contemporary debate*, London: Routledge, 1992.

Almond, B., *Moral Concerns*, Atlantic Highlands, NJ: The Humanities Press, 1987.

Anscombe, E., 'Modern Moral Philosophy' *Collected Philosophical Papers*, vol. 3, *Ethics, Religion and Politics*, Oxford: Blackwell, 1981. First published in *Philosophy* 33 (1958).

Aristotle, *Ethics*, trans. J. A. K. Thomson, rev. edn H. Tredennick, Harmondsworth: Penguin 1976.

——, *Politics*, trans. T. A. Sinclair, rev. edn T. J. Saunders, Harmondsworth: Penguin 1981.

Beauchamp, T. and N. Bowie (eds), *Ethical Theory and Business*, 4th edn, New York: Simon & Schuster 1992.

Bentham, J., *An Introduction to the Principles of Morals and Legislation*, London: Athlone Press 1970. First published 1789.

Bok, S., *Lying*, New York: Random House, 1979.

——, *Secrets*, New York: RAndom House, 1984.

Butler, J., *Fifteen Sermons*, in *The Works of Joseph Butler*, ed. W. E.

Gladstone, Oxford: Clarendon Press, 1896. Also published in Butler's *Fifteen Sermons*, ed. T. A. Roberts, London: SPCK, 1970.

Dworkin, R., *Law's Dominion*, London: Harper Collins, 1993.

Epictetus, *Moral Discourses*, 2 vols, trans. W. A. Oldfather, London: Heinemann, 1925, 1928, or *The Discourses*, trans. N. White, Hackett, 1988.

Ezorsky, G. (ed.), *Moral Rights in the Workplace*, New York: SUNY Press, 1986.

Fisher, M., *Personal Love*, London: Duckworth, 1990.

Foot, P., *Virtues and Vices*, Oxford: Oxford University Press, 1978.

Frankena, W., *Ethics*, 2nd edn, Englewood Cliffs, NJ: Prentice-Hall, 1973.

Gaita, R., *Good and Evil: An absolute conception*, London: Macmillan 1991.

Gilbert, P. *Human Relationships*, Cambridge: Cambridge University Press, 1992.

Gilligan, C., *In a Different Voice: psychology and women's development*, 2nd edn, Cambridge, Mass.: Harvard University Press, 1993.

——, 'In a Different Voice: women's conceptions of self and morality', *Harvard Educational Review* 47, 1977.

Graham, G., *Living the Good Life: An introduction to moral philosophy*, New York: Paragon House 1990.

Hare, R. M., 'Principles', Proceedings of the Aristotelian Society 73, 1972–73.

——, *Freedom and Reason*, Oxford: Clarendon Press, 1963.

——, *Moral Thinking*, London: Clarendon Press, 1981.

Hobbes, T., *Leviathan*, ed. C. P. Macpherson, Harmondsworth: Penguin, 1981; or ed. R. Tuck, Cambridge: Cambridge University Press 1991. First published 1651.

Hume, D., *Enquiries Concerning Human Understanding and Concerning the Principles of Morals*, ed. L. A. Selby-Bigge, rev. edn P. Nidditch, London: Oxford University Press 1975. First published 1748 and 1751.

Hursthouse, R., *Beginning Lives*, Oxford: Blackwell, 1988.

Kant, I., *Groundwork of the Metaphysics of Morals* trans. H. Paton (also published under the title *The Moral Law*), London: Hutchinson 1948. Another translation is by L. W. Beck, *Foundations of the Metaphysics of Morals*, New York: Macmillan 1990.

MacIntyre, A., *A Short History of Ethics*, London: Routledge, 1967.

——, *After Virtue*, London: Duckworth 1981.

——, *Whose Justice? Which Rationality?* London: Duckworth, 1988.

Mackie, J., 'Can there be a right-based moral theory?' in Waldron, J. (ed.).

Midgley, M., *Wickedness*, London: Routledge, 1984.

Mill, J. S., *Utilitarianism*, London: Dent, 1954. First published 1861.

Nagel, T., *Mortal Questions*, Cambridge: Cambridge University Press, 1979.

Norman, R., *The Moral Philosophers*, Oxford: Oxford University Press, 1984.

Plato, *The Collected Dialogues*, ed. E. Hamilton and H. Cairns, Princeton, NJ: Princeton University Press, 1961; or see separately: *The Republic*, 2nd edn. trans. D. Lee, Harmondsworth: Penguin, 1974; *The Last Days of Socrates*, trans. H. Tredennick, Harmondsworth: Penguin, 1968; *Gorgias*, trans. W. Hamilton, Harmondsworth: Penguin, 1960; *Protagoras and Meno*, trans. W. K. C. Guthrie, Harmondsworth: Penguin, 1956.

Rachels, J., *The Elements of Moral Philosophy*, 2nd edn, New York: McGraw-Hill 1993.

Rawls, J., *A Theory of Justice*, Cambridge, Mass.: Harvard University Press, 1971.

Ryle, G., *Dilemmas*, Cambridge: Cambridge University Press, 1954.

Scruton, R., *Sexual Desire*, London: Weidenfeld & Nicolson, 1986.

Singer, P. (ed.), *A Companion to Ethics*, Oxford, Blackwell, 1991.

Smart, J. J. C. and B. Williams, *Utilitarianism: for and against*, Cambridge: Cambridge University Press, 1973.

Waldron, J. (ed.), *Theories of Rights*, Oxford: Oxford University Press, 1984.

Williams, B. *Ethics and the Limits of Philosophy*, London: Fontana, 1985.

CHAPTER 3

Arendt, H., *The Origins of Totalitarianism*, New York: World Books, 1958.

Arblaster, A., *The Rise and Decline of Western Liberalism*, Oxford: Blackwell 1984.

Austin, J., *The Province of Jurisprudence Determined*, ed. H. L. A. Hart, London: Weidenfeld & Nicolson 1954. First pub. 1832.

Aristotle, *Politics*, trans. T. A. Sinclair, rev. edn T. J. Saunders, Harmondsworth: Penguin 1981.

Avineri, S. and de-Shalit, A. (eds), *Communitarianism and Individualism*, Oxford: Oxford University Press, 1992.

Bentham, J., *An Introduction to the Principles of Morals and Legislation*, London: Athlone Press, 1970. First published 1789.

Berlin, I., 'Two Concepts of Liberty' in *Four Essays on Liberty*, London: Oxford University Press, 1969.

Burke, E., *Reflections on the Revolution in France*, Oxford: Oxford University Press, 1993 or Harmondsworth: Penguin, 1982, First published 1790.

Devlin, P., *The Enforcement of Morals*, Oxford: Oxford University Press, 1978.

Dworkin, R., *The Philosophy of Law*, Oxford: Oxford University Press, 1977.

Gramsci, A., *Prison Notebooks*, vol. 1, New York: Columbian University Press, 1992. There is an earlier edition: by Q. Hoare and G. Nowell-Smith, London: Lawrence & Wishart, 1973.

Gray, J., *Liberalism*, Milton Keynes: Open University Press, 1986.

Hampshire, S., *Public and Private Morality*, Cambridge: Cambridge University Press, 1978.

Hart, H. L. A., *Law, Liberty and Morality*, London: Oxford University Press, 1971.

——, *The Concept of Law*, Oxford: Clarendon Press, 1961.

Hayek, F. A., *The Road to Serfdom*, London: Routledge, 1976. First published 1944.

Hobbes, T., *Leviathan*, ed. C. B. MacPherson, Harmondsworth: Penguin 1981 or ed. R. Tuck, Cambridge: Cambridge University Press 1991. First published 1651.

Jaggar, A., *Feminist Politics and Human Nature*, Totowa, NJ: Rowman & Allanheld, 1983.

Kamen, H., *The Rise of Toleration*, London: Weidenfeld & Nicolson, 1967.

Kelsen, H., *The Pure Theory of Law* (trans. M. Knight), Berkeley & Los Angeles: University of California Press, 1967; Magnolia, MA: Peter Smith, 1990.

Kymlicka, W., *Contemporary Political Philosophy*, Oxford: Oxford University Press, 1991.

Marx, K. and F. Engels, *The Communist Manifesto*, Harmondsworth: Penguin 1967. Also in E. Kamenka (ed.), *The Portable Karl Marx*, Harmondsworth: Penguin 1983, or see *Marx and Engels: Basic Writings on Politics and Philosophy*, ed. L. S. Feuer, London: Fontana, 1969, or D. McLellan (ed.), *Karl Marx: Selected Writings*, Oxford: Oxford University Press, 1977.

Malthus, T. R., *An Essay on the Principle of Population*, ed. D. Winch, Cambridge: Cambridge University Press, 1992. First published 1798.

Mill, J. S., *On Liberty*, Harmondsworth: Penguin, 1982. Also in *Utilitarianism, Liberty and Representative Government*, London: Dent, 1910 and subsequent reprints, and in *On Liberty, The Subjection of Women and Chapters on Socialism* (ed. S. Collini), Cambridge: Cambridge University Press, 1989.

Mulhall, S. and Swift, A., *Liberals and Communitarians*, Oxford: Blackwell, 1992.

Nozick, R., *Anarchy, State and Utopia*, Oxford: Blackwell, 1974.

Okin, Susan Moller, *Women in Western Political Thought*, rev. edn, Princeton, NJ: Princeton University Press 1992. First published 1979.

Pettit, P., and Goodin, R. (eds), *A Companion to Political Philosophy*, Oxford: Blackwell, 1993.

Plato, *The Republic*, ed., trans. D. Lee, Harmondsworth: Penguin, 1974. *Crito*, in *The Last Days of Socrates*, trans. H. Tredennick, Harmondsworth: Penguin, 1968. Both also available in *The Collected Dialogues*, ed. E. Hamilton and H. Cairns, Princeton, NJ: Princeton University Press, 1961.

Popper, K., *The Poverty of Historicism*, 2nd edn, London: Routledge & Kegan Paul, 1960.

Rawls, J., *A Theory of Justice*, Cambridge, Mass., Harvard University Press, 1971.

Raz, J., *The Morality of Freedom*, Oxford: Oxford University Press, 1986.

Rousseau, J.-J., *The Social Contract and the Discourses*, trans. G. D. H. Cole, rev. by J. H. Bromfit and J. C. Hall, London: Dent, 1973, or *The Social Contract*, trans. M. Cranston, Harmondsworth: Penguin, 1968 and *Discourse on Inequality*, trans. M. Cranston, Harmondsworth: Penguin, 1984.

Sassoon, A., *Gramsci's Politics*, 2nd edn, Minneapolis and London: University of Minnesota/UCL Press, 1988.

Singer, P., *Practical Ethics*, 2nd edn, Cambridge: Cambridge University Press, 1993.

Singer, P., 'Famine, Affluence and Morality', *Philosophy and Public Affairs* 7 (1972) pp. 229–43.

Talmon, J., *The Origins of Totalitarian Democracy*, London: Secker & Warburg 1952.

Waldron, J. (ed.), *Theories of Rights*, Oxford: Oxford University Press, 1984.

CHAPTER 4

Almond, B. (ed.), *Introducing Applied Ethics*, Oxford: Blackwell, 1995.

Almond, B. and D. Hill (eds), *Applied Philosophy: morals and metaphysics in contemporary debate*, London: Routledge, 1991.

Aristotle, *Ethics*, trans. J. A. K. Thomson, rev. edn H. Tredennick, Harmondsworth: Penguin 1976.

——, *Politics*, trans. T. A. Sinclair, rev. edn T. J. Saunders, Harmondsworth: Penguin 1981.

Attfield, R. and Wilkins, B., *International Justice and the Third World*, London: Routledge, 1992.

Attfield, R., *The Ethics of Environmental Concern*, 2nd edn, Athens, GA and London: University of Georgia Press, 1991.

Belsey, A. and Chadwick, R. (eds), *Ethical Issues in Journalism and the Media*, London: Routledge, 1993.

Benn, S., 'Deterrence or Appeasement? or, On trying to be rational about nuclear war' *Journal of Applied Philosophy* 1, 1984.

Brown, A., *Modern Political Philosophy*, London: Penguin, 1986.

Clark, S., *The Moral Status of Animals*, Oxford: Oxford University Press, 1984.

Cooper, D. and J. Palmer (eds), *Just Environment*, London: Routledge, 1994.

Dworkin, R., *Taking Rights Seriously*, 2nd edn, Cambridge, Mass.: Harvard University Press, 1978.

Elliot, R. and A. Gare (eds), *Environmental Philosophy*, Milton Keynes: Open University Press, 1983.

Flew, A., 'The Concept and Conceptions of Justice' in Almond and Hill, (eds), pp. 196–201

Finnis, J., *Natural Law and Natural Rights*, Oxford: Clarendon Press, 1980.

Goodin, R., *Protecting the Vulnerable*, Chicago and London: University of Chicago Press, 1985.

Gray, J., *The Moral Foundations of Market Institutions*, London: Institute for Economic Affairs, 1992.

Green, D., *Reinventing Civil Society*, London: Institute of Economic Affairs, 1993.

Gutmann, A., *Liberal Equality*, Cambridge: Cambridge University Press, 1989.

Hardin, G., 'Lifeboat Ethics: the case against helping the poor' in Rachels J. (ed.), pp. 279–91.

Kant, I., *Groundwork of the Metaphysics of Morals* trans. H. Paton (also published under the title *The Moral Law*), London: Hutchinson 1948. Another translation is by L. W. Beck, *Foundations of the Metaphysics of Morals*, New York: Macmillan 1990.

Hobbes, T., *Leviathan*, ed. C. B. McPherson, Harmondsworth: Penguin, 1968.

Hume, D., *A Treatise of Human Nature*, ed. L. A. Selby-Bigge and P. Nidditch, Oxford: Oxford University Press 1978 (first published 1739–1740); and *Enquiry Concerning the Principles of Morals*, ed. L. A. Selby-Bigge and P. Nidditch, Oxford: Oxford University Press, 1975 (first published 1751).

Lackey, D., *The Ethics of War and Peace*, Englewood Cliffs, NJ: Prentice-Hall, 1989.

Leopold, A., *A Sand County Almanac*, Oxford: Oxford University Press 1993. First published 1949.

Nielsen, K., 'Global Justice and the Third World', *Journal of Applied Philosophy* 1, 1984.

Nozick, R. *Anarchy, State and Utopia*, New York: Basic Books, 1974.

O'Neill, O. *Faces of Hunger*, London: Allen & Unwin, 1986.

Passmore, J. *Man's Responsibility for Nature*, London: Duckworth, 1980.

Plato, *The Republic*, 2nd edn, trans. D. Lee, Harmondsworth: Penguin, 1974, or in *The Collected Dialogues*, ed. E. Hamilton and H. Cairns, NJ: Princeton Unviersity Press, 1961.

Rachels, J. (ed.), *Today's Moral Problems*, 3rd edn, New York: Harper & Row, 1979.

Rawls, J., *A Theory of Justice*, Oxford: Oxford University Press, 1971.

Regan, T., *The Case for Animal Rights*, Berkeley: University of California Press, 1983.

Sandel, M., *Liberalism and the Limits of Justice*, Cambridge: Cambridge University Press, 1982.

Scherer, D. and T. Attig (eds), *Ethics and the Environment*, Englewood Cliffs, NJ: Prentice-Hall, 1983.

Singer, P., *Practical Ethics*, 2nd edn, Cambridge: Cambridge University Press, 1993.

——, *Animal Liberation*, 2nd edn, New York: Random House, 1990. First published 1975.

Smith, Adam, *The Theory of Moral Sentiments*, Oxford: Clarendon Press 1976.

Sumner, L. W., *The Moral Foundation of Rights*, Oxford: Oxford University Press, 1987.

Walzer, M., *Just and Unjust Wars*, Harmondsworth: Penguin, 1987. First published 1977.

——, *Spheres of Justice: a defence of pluralism and equality*, Oxford: Blackwell, 1983.

Wasserstrom, R., *War and Morality*, Belmont, CA: Wadsworth, 1970. *Today's Moral Problems*, 3rd edn, New York: Macmillan, 1985.

CHAPTER 5

Aristotle, *Organon*, trans. H. Cooke and H. Tredennick, London: Heinemann, 1938.

Ayer, A. J. *Language, Truth and Logic*, Harmondsworth: Penguin, 1971. First published 1936.

Ayer, A. J. et al., *The Revolution in Philosophy*, London: Macmillan, 1956.

Barnes, J., *The Presocratic Philosophers*, London: Routledge, 1982.

——, *Early Greek Philosophy*, Harmondsworth: Penguin, 1987.

Chalmers, A. F., *What is this Thing called Science?* 2nd edn, Milton Keynes: Open University Press, 1982.

Davis, P. J. and R. Hersh, *The Mathematical Experience*, Hassocks, Sussex: Harvester, 1981.

Feyerabend, R., *Against Method*, New Left Books, 1975.

Fisher, A., *The Logic of Real Arguments*, Cambridge: Cambridge University Press, 1988.

Flew, A., *Thinking about Thinking*, Fontana, 1985.

Goodman, N., *Fact, Fiction and Forecast*, 4th edn, Cambridge Mass.: Harvard University Press, 1978.

Grünbaum, A., *Modern Science and Zeno's Paradoxes*, London: Allen and Unwin, 1968.

Haack, S. *Deviant Logic*, Cambridge: Cambridge University Press, 1975.

——, *Philosophy of Logics*, Cambridge: Cambridge University Press, 1978.

Hacking, I., *Representing and Intervening*, Cambridge: Cambridge University Press, 1983.

Hanfling, O., *Logical Positivism*, Oxford: Blackwell, 1981.

——, (ed.), *Essential Readings in Logical Positivism*, Oxford: Blackwell, 1981.

Hodges, W., *Logic*, Harmondsworth: Penguin, 1977.

Hughes, G. E. and M. Cresswell, *An Introduction to Modal Logic*, London: Methuen, 1972.

Hume, D., *Enquiries Concerning Human Understanding and Concerning the Principles of Morals*, ed. L. A. Selby-Bigge and P. Nidditch, London: Oxford University Press 1975. First published 1748 and 1751.

Jeffrey, R. C., *Formal Logic: its scope and limits*, New York: McGraw-Hill, 1967.

Kirk, G. S. and J. E. Raven, *The Presocratic Philosophers*, Cambridge: Cambridge University Press, 1957.

Kant, I., *Critique of Pure Reason*, trans. N. K. Smith, London: Macmillan, 1963. First published 1791; 2nd edn 1787.

Kuhn, T. S. *The Structure of Scientific Revolutions*, 2nd edn, Chicago: University of Chicago Press, 1970.

Lakatos, I. and A. E. Musgrave (eds), *Criticism and the Growth of Knowledge*, Cambridge: Cambridge University Press, 1970.

Leibniz, G. W., *Monadology*, in *Leibniz: Philosophical Writings*, ed. G. H. R. Parkinson, London: Dent, 1973.

Lemmon, E. J., *Beginning Logic*, London: Nelson, 1981.

Lewis, D., *Counterfactuals*, Oxford: Blackwell, 1973.

——, *On the Plurality of Worlds*, Oxford: Blackwell, 1986.

Mill, J. S., *A System of Logic*, London: Longmans, 1949. First published 1843.

Newton-Smith, W., *The Rationality of Science*, London: Routledge and Kegan Paul, 1981.

Plato, *The Collected Dialogues*, ed. E. Hamilton and H. Gairns, Princeton, NJ: Princeton University Press, 1961.

Popper, K., *Conjectures and Refutations*, 3rd edn, London: Routledge, 1969.

——, *Objective Knowledge*, London: Oxford University Press, 1973.

——, *The Logic of Scientific Discovery*, London: Hutchinson, 1974.

Quine, W. v. O. *The Ways of Paradox*, New York: Random House, 1966.

Read, S., *Relevant Logic*, Oxford: Blackwell 1988.

Rist, J. M., *The Stoics*, Berkeley: University of California Press, 1978.

Routley, R. and V. Routley, 'Rehabilitating Meinong's Theory of Objects' *Revue Internationale de Philosophie* 27, 1973.

Routley, R. et al., *Relevant Logics and their Rivals*, Atadascero, CA: Ridgeview, 1982.

Russell, B., *The Problems of Philosophy*, London: Oxford University Press, 1986. First published 1912.

Sainsbury, R. M., *Paradoxes*, Cambridge: Cambridge: University Press, 1988.

Salmon, W. C., *Space, Time and Motion*, 2nd edn, Minneapolis: University of Minnesota Press, 1981.

Skyrms, B., *Choice and Chance: an introduction to logic*, Belmont, CA: Wadworth, 1986.

Smullyan, A., *What is the Name of this Book?* Harmondsworth: Penguin, 1981.

Voltaire, *Candide*, trans. J. Butt, Harmondsworth: Penguin, or trans. D. Frame, New American Library.

CHAPTER 6

Austin J., *How to do Things with Words*, Oxford: Oxford University Press, 1962.

Ayer, A. J., *Philosophical Essays*, London: Greenwood Press, 1980.

——, *The Concept of a Person*, London: Macmillan, 1963.

Bennett, J., *Locke, Berkeley, Hume: Central Themes*, Oxford: Oxford University Press, 1971.

Berkeley, G., *Three Dialogues*, available in *Philosophical Works*, ed. M. R. Ayers, London: Dent, 1975.

Blackburn, S., *Spreading the Word: groundings in the philosophy of language*, Oxford: Clarendon Press, 1984.

Chomsky, N., 'A Review of B. F. Skinner's "Verbal Behavior"' in J. A. Fodor and J. J. Katz (eds).

——, *Cartesian Linguistics*, New York: Harper & Row, 1966.

——, *Aspects of the Theory of Syntax*, Cambridge, Mass.: MIT Press, 1965.

——, *Problems of Knowledge and Freedom*, New York: Random House, 1972.

——, *Language and Mind*, New York: Harcourt, Brace & World, rev. edn 1972.

——, *Rules and Representations*, New York: Columbia University Press, 1980.

——, *Reflections on Language*, London: Fontana, 1976.

——, *Knowledge of Language*, London: Prism, 1975.

Davidson, D. and G. Harman (eds), *Semantics of Natural Language*. Dordrecht, Reidel, 1972.

Derrida, J., *On Grammatology*, trans. G. Spivak, Baltimore, Maryland: Johns Hopkins University Press, 1976.

——, *Speech and Phenomena*, trans. D. Allison, Evanston, Illinois: Northwestern University Press, 1973.

Dummett, M., *Frege: philosophy of language*, London: Duckworth, 2nd edn 1981.

——, *Truth and Other Enigmas*, London: Duckworth, 1981.

Evans, G., *The Varieties of Reference*, Oxford: Oxford University Press, 1982.

Feigl, H. and W. Sellars (eds), *Readings in Philosophical Analysis*, New York: Appleton-Century-Crofts, 1949.

Feyerabend, P. K., *Against Method*, London: New Left Books, 1975.

Fodor, J. A. and J. J. Katz (eds), *The Structure of Language*, Englewood Cliffs, NJ: Prentice-Hall, 1964.

Frege, G., *Philosophical Writings*, trans. P. T. Geach and M. Black, Oxford: Blackwell, 1962.

Guttenplan, S. (ed.), *Mind and Language*, Oxford: Clarendon Press, 1975.

Hacking, I., *Why Does Language Matter to Philosophy?*, Cambridge: Cambridge University Press, 1975.

Katz, J. J., *The Philosophy of Language*, London, Harper & Row, 1966.

Kripke, S., *Naming and Necessity*, Oxford: Blackwell, 1981.

——, 'Identity and Necessity', in S. Schwartz (ed.).

Locke, J., *An Essay Concerning Human Understanding*, ed. P. Nidditch, Oxford: Clarendon Press, 1975. First Published 1690.

Lyons, J., *Chomsky*, London: Fontana, 1970.

Monk, R., *Ludwig Wittgenstein: the duty of genius*, Oxford: Blackwell, 1991.

Piaget, J., *The Language and Thought of the Child*, 3rd edn, London: Routledge, 1978.

——, *Structuralism*, trans. and ed. C. Maschler, London: Routledge, 1971.

Putnam, H., *Mind, Language and Reality, Philosophical Papers: vol. 2*, Cambridge: Cambridge University Press, 1975.

——, *Meaning and the Moral Sciences*, London: Routledge, 1978.

Quine, W.v.O., 'Mind and Verbal Dispositions', in S. Guttenplan (ed.), *From a Logical Point of View*, New York: Harper & Row, 2nd rev. edn, 1961.

——, *Word and Object*, Cambridge, Mass.: MIT Press, 1960.

Rhees, R., *Discussions of Wittgenstein*, London: Routledge, 1970.

Rorty, R., *Philosophy and the Mirror of Nature*, Princeton, NJ: Princeton University Press, 1979.

Russell, B., *The Problems of Philosophy*, London: Oxford University Press, 1986. First published 1912.

——, *Introduction to Mathematical Philosophy*, London: Allen & Unwin, 1919.

——, *Logic and Knowledge*, ed. R. Marsh, London: Allen & Unwin, 1977.

——, 'On Denoting', *Mind* 1905. Reprinted in Feigl and Sellars (eds).

Sampson, G., *Schools of Linguistics*, London: Hutchinson, 1980.

Sapir, E., 'The Status of Lingistics as a Science' in *Culture, Language and Personality*, Berkeley: University of California Press, 1957.

——, *Language: an introduction to the study of speech*, New York: Harcourt 1949. First published 1921.

Schwartz, S. (ed.), *Naming, Necessity, and Natural Kinds*, Ithaca, NY: Cornell University Press, 1977.

Searle, J., *Speech Acts*, Cambridge: Cambridge University Press, 1969.

Skinner, B. F., *Beyond Freedom and Dignity*, rev. edn, Harmondsworth: Penguin, 1973.

Sturrock, J. (ed.), *Structuralism and Since*, London: Routledge & Kegan Paul, 1979.

Wiggins, D., *Sameness and Substance*, Oxford: Blackwell, 1980.

Winch, P., *The Idea of a Social Science*, London: Routledge & Kegan Paul, 1958.

Wittgenstein, L., *Tractatus Logico-Philosophicus*, trans. D. F. Pears and B. F. McGuiness, London: Routledge & Kegan Paul, 1974.

——, *Philosophical Investigations*, 3rd edn, trans. G. E. M. Anscombe, Oxford: Blackwell, 1968.

CHAPTER 7

Anderson, A. Ross (ed.), *Minds and Machines*, Englewood Cliffs, NJ: Prentice-Hall, 1964.

Block, N. (ed.), *Readings in Philosophy of Psychology*, vols 1–2, Cambridge, Mass.: Harvard University Press, 1980, 1985.

Carroll, Lewis, *The Annotated Alice: Alice's Adventures in Wonderland and Through the Looking Glass* with an introduction and notes by Martin Gardner, New York: Bramhall House, 1960; also Harmondsworth: Penguin, 1970.

Chappell, V. C. (ed.), *The Philosophy of Mind*, Englewood Cliffs, NJ: Prentice-Hall 1962. Also available in Dover, 1982.

Churchland, P. M., *Matter and Consciousness*, rev. edn, Cambridge, Mass.: MIT Press, 1988.

Davidson, D., 'Thought and Talk' in S. Guttenplan (ed.), *Inquiries into Truth and Interpretation*, Oxford: Oxford University Press, 1984.

——, *Essays on Actions and Events*, London: Oxford University Press, 1980.

Dennett, D., *Brainstorms*, Hassocks: Harvester Press, 1978.

——, *Consciousness Explained*, London: Penguin, 1993.

Derrida, J., *Of Grammatology*, trans. G. Spivak, Baltimore, MD: John Hopkins University Press, 1976.

Foucault, M., *The Order of Things*, London: Routledge, 1990.

Greenwood, J. D. (ed.), *The Future of Folk Psychology: intentionality and cognitive science*, Cambridge: Cambridge University Press, 1991.

Guttenplan, S. (ed.), *Mind and Language*, Oxford: Clarendon Press, 1975.

Hume, D., *A Treatise of Human Nature*, ed. L. A. Selby-Bigge and P. Nidditch, Oxford: Oxfod University Press 1978. First published 1739–1740.

La Mettrie, J. O. de, *Man a Machine*, trans. G. Bussey, Chicago: Open Court, 1977.

Lycan, W. G. (ed.), *Mind and Cognition: a reader*, Oxford: Blackwell, 1990.

Malcolm, N., *Problems of Mind*, London: Allen & Unwin, 1971.

Nagel, T., 'What is it like to be a bat?' in *Mortal Questions*, Cambridge: Cambridge University Press, 1979.

O'Connor, D. J., *Free Will*, London, Macmillan, 1972.

Parfit, D., *Reasons and Persons*, Oxford: Oxford University Press, 1984.

Penrose, R., *The Emperor's New Mind: Concerning Computers, Minds and the Laws of Physics*, Oxford: Oxford University Press, 1989, and London: Vintage, 1990.

Place, U. T. 'Is Consciousness a Brain Process?' in V. C. Chappell (ed.). Also in W. Lycan (ed.). First published in *British Journal of Psychology*, 1956, pp. 44–50.

Putnam, H., *Mind, Language and Reality: Philosophical Papers*, vol. 2, Cambridge: Cambridge University Press, 1975.

Quine, W.v.O., 'Mind and Verbal Dispositions' in S. Guttenplan (ed.), *Philosophy of Logic*, Englewood Cliffs, NJ: Prentice-Hall, 1970.

Russell, B. *The Problems of Philosophy*, London: Oxford University Press, 1986. First published 1912.

——, *The Analysis of Mind*, London: Allen & Unwin, 1921.

Ryle, G., *The Concept of Mind*, Harmondsworth: Penguin, 1963. First published 1949.

Searle, J., *The Rediscovery of the Mind*, Cambridge, Mass.: MIT Press, 1992.

Skinner, B. F., *About Behaviorism*, London: Cape, 1975.

——, *Beyond Freedom and Dignity*, rev. edn, Harmondsworth: Penguin, 1973.

——, *Walden Two*, New York: Macmillan, 1976. First published 1948.

Smart, J. J. C., 'Sensations and Brain Processes' in V. C. Chappell (ed.). First published in *Philosophical Review* 68, 1959, pp. 141–56.

Stich, S. P., *From Folk Psychology to Cognitive Science: the case against belief*, Cambridge, Mass.: MIT Press, 1983.

Strawson, P. F., 'Persons' in V. C. Chappell (ed.).

——, *Individuals*, London: Methuen, 1964.

Tarski, A. 'The Semantic Conception of Truth' *Philosophy and Phenomenological Research* 5, 1943–4, reprinted in Feigl and Sellars (eds).

Turing, A., 'Computing Machinery and Intelligence' in A. Ross Anderson (ed.).

Watson, G. (ed.), *Free Will*, Oxford: Oxford University Press, 1983.

Williams, B., *Problems of the Self*, Cambridge: Cambridge University Press, 1973.

Wittgenstein, L., *Philosophical Investigations*, 3rd edn, trans G. E. M. Anscombe, Oxford: Blackwell, 1968.

Van Inwagen, P., *An Essay on Free Will*, Oxford: Clarendon, 1983.

CHAPTER 8

Campbell, K., *A Stoic Philosophy of Life*, Lanham: University Press of America, 1986.

Cicero, *On the Nature of the Gods*, trans. McGregor, Harmondsworth: Penguin, 1972.

Epictetus, *Moral Discourses*, 2 vols, trans. W. A. Oldfather, London Heinemann, 1925, 1928, or *The Discourses*, trans. N. White, Hackett, 1988.

Hampshire, S., *Spinoza*, Harmondsworth: Penguin, 1951.

Hicks, R. D., *Stoic and Epicurean*, New York: Russell, 1962 (reprint of 1910 edn).

Lucretius, *The Nature of the Universe*, trans. R. Latham, Harmondswroth: Penguin, 1970; or *The Way Things Are*, trans. R. Humphries, Indiana University Press, 1970.

Malcolm, N., *Ludwig Wittgenstein: a memoir*, 2nd edn, Oxford: Oxford University Press, 1984.

Monk, R., *Ludwig Wittgenstein: the duty of genius*, Oxford: Blackwell, 1991.

Plato, *The Republic*, trans. D. Lee, rev. edn. Harmondsworth: Penguin, 1987.

——, *Phaedrus; and The Seventh and Eighth Letters*, ed. W. Hamilton, Harmondsworth: Penguin, 1973.

Saunders, J. L. (ed.), *Greek and Roman Philosophy after Aristotle*, New York: The Free Press/Collier-Macmillan, 1966.

Scruton, R., *A Short History of Modern Philosophy*, London: Routledge & Kegan Paul, 1984.

Spinoza, B., *The Collected Works of Spinoza*, vol. 1, ed. and trans. E. Curley, Princeton, NJ: Princeton University Press, 1985. Contains *Ethics, Principles of Descartes' Philosophy*, etc.

——, *The Ethics and Other Works*, Princeton: Princeton University Press, 1994.

——, *The Ethics and Selected Letters*, trans. S. Shirley, ed. S. Feldman, Indianapolis: Hackett, 1982.

Sprigge, T. L. S., *The Vindication of Absolute Idealism*, Edinburgh: Edinburgh University Press, 1983.

——, *Theories of Existence*, Harmondsworth: Penguin, 1984.

White, R. J., *The Anti-Philosophers*, London: Macmillan, 1970.

Wittgenstein, L., *Tractatus Logico-Philosophicus*, trans. D. F. Pears and B. F. McGuiness, London: Routledge & Kegan Paul, 1961. First published 1921.

CHAPTER 9

Bontempo, C. J., and S. J. Odell (eds), *The Owl of Minerva: Philosophers on Philosophy*, New York: McGraw-Hill, 1975.

Davidson, D., On the very idea of a conceptual scheme', in *Inquiries into Truth and Interpretation*, Oxford: Oxford University Press, 1984.

Hume, D., *A Treatise of Human Nature*, ed. L. A. Selby-Bigge and P. Nidditch, Oxford: Oxford University Press, 1978. First published 1739–1740.

James, W., *Pragmatism*, Cambridge, Mass.: Harvard University Press, 1975. First published 1907.

Lloyd, G. *The Man of Reason*, 2nd edn, London: Routledge, 1993.

MacIntyre, A., *A Short History of Ethics*, London: Routledge & Kegan Paul, 1967.

Morick, H. (ed.), *Challenges to Empiricism*, London, Methuen, 1980.

Nagel, T., *The View from Nowhere*, New York: Oxford University Press, 1986.

Nicholson, L., *Feminism and Postmodernism*, London: Routledge, 1991.

Norris, C., *The Truth about Postmodernism*, Oxford: Blackwell, 1993.

Passmore, J., *Recent Philosophers*, London: Duckworth, 1985.

Phillips Griffiths, A. P. (ed.), *The Impulse to Philosophise*, Cambridge: Cambridge University Press, 1992.

Putnam, H., *Meaning and the Moral Sciences*, London: Routledge & Kegan Paul, 1978.

——, *Philosophical Papers*, vols 2 and 3, Cambridge: Cambridge University Press, 1983.

——, *Reason, Truth and History*, Cambridge: Cambridge University Press, 1981.

——, *Realism with a Human Face*, Cambridge, Mass.: Harvard University Press, 1992.

Rajchman, J. and C. West (eds), *Post-analytic Philosophy*, New York: Columbia University Press, 1985.

Rorty, R., *Philosophy and the Mirror of Nature,* Princeton, NJ: Princeton University Press, 1979.

——, *Contingency, Irony and Solidarity,* Cambridge: Cambridge University Press, 1989.

——, 'After Empiricism', in J. Rajchman, and C. West (eds).

——, 'Solidarity or Objectivity?' in J. Rajchman and C. West (eds).

Russell, B., 'My mental development', in Schilpp, P. A. (ed.).

Schilpp, P. A. (ed.), *The Philosophy of Bertrand Russell,* New York: Harper & Row, 1963.

Sellars, W., *Science and Metaphysics,* Atadascero, CA: Ridgeview, 1993. First published 1968.

Skinner, Q. (ed.), *The Return of Grand Theory in the Human Sciences,* Cambridge: Cambridge University Press, 1985.

Index